More Praise for
The Best Service Is No Service

"It makes a lot of sense to embrace the notion of 'best service.' Not only can companies learn how to listen better to their customers, they can also increase customer satisfaction by figuring out which customer interactions they and their customers want handled by a live person, and which should simply go away or be handled via self-service."

—Marc Singer, director, McKinsey & Company

"The Best Service Is No Service gives the inside scoop on how to create a 'no service needed' company. Companies large and small need to make sure that their products work right in the first place, and that their self-service functions answer what customers want, while listening to the signals constantly streaming in from their customers."

—Jeff Bussgang, general partner, IDG Ventures; co-founder and former president and COO of Upromise

"Customer service experiences for customers are inconsistent at best. The key, as authors Price and Jaffe point out, is to eliminate the reason and situations that prompt customers to contact you! Follow their advice and focus your efforts here to make life easier for your customers, your customer service reps, and your bottom line."

—Jeanne Bliss, author, chief customer officer, president, CustomerBLISS

"David and Bill have brought some insightful but common-sense approaches to the area of customer service. Their book will be an invaluable guide to any company that has a significant volume of service interactions."

—Jane S. Hemstritch, non-executive director, Commonwealth Bank of Australia; retired managing director, Accenture, Asia Pacific

"The 'best service' ideas and principles on how customer service should work are valuable for any business. They challenge the way that many companies have dealt with customers in the past and show that there is a better way by eliminating defects or mistakes that constantly frustrate customers."

—John Egan, vice president, Lenovo Group, Shanghai

"Almost every corporate mission statement promises to 'delight' customers and 'exceed their expectations.' Yet most companies continue to frustrate their customers with shoddy service and dash their expectations with broken promises. This book is the cure for all that. It's a blend of smart strategies and best practices for leaders who want to make it easy, quick, even fun, for customers to interact with their companies—and even more, to learn from those interactions to make their companies better. Read this book—your customers will be delighted that you did!"

—William C. Taylor, founding editor, Fast Company; coauthor,
Mavericks at Work

THE BEST SERVICE IS NO SERVICE

THE BEST SERVICE IS NO SERVICE

How to Liberate Your Customers from Customer Service, Keep Them Happy, and Control Costs

Bill Price

David Jaffe

JOSSEY-BASS
A Wiley Imprint
www.josseybass.com

Published by Jossey-Bass
A Wiley Imprint
989 Market Street, San Francisco, CA 94103-1741—www.josseybass.com

Jossey-Bass books and products are available through most bookstores. To contact Jossey-Bass directly
call our Customer Care Department within the U.S. at 800-956-7739, outside the U.S. at 317-572-3986,
or fax 317-572-4002.

Jossey-Bass also publishes its books in a variety of electronic formats. Some content that appears in
print may not be available in electronic books.

Library of Congress Cataloging-in-Publication Data
Price, Bill, 1950-
    The best service is no service : how to liberate your customers from customer service, keep them
happy, and control costs / Bill Price, David Jaffe.
        p. cm.
Includes bibliographical references and index.
ISBN 978-0-470-18908-5 (cloth)
        1. Consumer satisfaction.   2. Customer services—Management.   3. Service industries—
Customer services.   4. Service industries—Management.   I. Jaffe, David, 1963-   II. Title.
III. Title: Liberate your customers from customer service, keep them happy, and control costs.
    HF5415.335.P75 2008
    658.8'12—dc22

                                                                                    2007038037

Printed in the United States of America

FIRST EDITION
HB Printing 10 9 8 7 6 5 4 3 2 1

CONTENTS

Introduction: Why We Wrote This Book   xi

1   Challenge Customer Demand for Service:
Instead of Coping with Demand   1

2   Eliminate Dumb Contacts: Instead of
Handling Them Again and Again   29

3   Create Engaging Self-Service: Instead
of Preventing Contact   65

4   Be Proactive: Instead of Waiting to Respond   99

5   Make It Really Easy to Contact Your Company:
Instead of Dodging the Bullet   125

6   Own the Actions Across the Organization:
Instead of Blaming Customer Service   165

7   Listen and Act: Instead of Letting Customer
Insights Slip Away   203

8   Deliver Great Service Experiences:
How to Delight Customers with
Awesome Support When They Need It   241

Appendix A: Best Service Survey   277

Appendix B: Glossary   287

Appendix C: Bibliography   293

Notes   299

Acknowledgments   301

About the Authors   305

Index   307

*To Erika, Rachel, Rebecca, and
Patrick, our children*

INTRODUCTION: WHY WE WROTE THIS BOOK

Providing awesome customer experiences shouldn't be hard. Companies produce cool new products and services for their customers, meeting their expressed demand and often providing a little bit more than the customers wanted. Customers want to use these products and services to enrich their daily lives or achieve their own personal or business success. That's why they purchase the product or service: to use or exploit it. They don't buy goods and services in order to contact the customer care or service department.

We call this the "wake up in the morning test": Do customers wake up in the morning wanting to contact your company for help, or do they wake up simply wanting to use your goods and services? Do we really need to answer this question?

Unfortunately, a whole industry, customer relationship management (CRM), has grown up claiming that customers want "relationships" with companies. We agree that customers want and need to work with companies to obtain goods and services that let them achieve their goals. If the products and services work well, as customers have the right to expect, customers will start to feel some sense of loyalty to that company; they'll return for more and recommend the company to others.[1] However, this is not the same as customers wanting to have a relationship with the company's customer service department. The best customers, for most companies, are those who never call or visit but who get what they want from the product or service and then come back for more. In other words, companies might seek a relationship (as CRM espouses), but customers don't want a relationship—they would rather not know the service arm at all.

When something doesn't make sense or work correctly, the customer calls the company, sends an e-mail message, launches a chat session, sends a text message, writes a letter, or walks into a branch office—and if the service or care processes work, the company responds and clears up the confusion or solves the problem. Good outcome? Not for us—this is a necessary but not sufficient short-term response, or what we will define as Basic Service. We ask, "Why did the customer need to make this contact at all?" rather than focus on how well the contact was handled.

Although some companies have invested heavily in new processes and technologies for customer service, unfortunately both companies and customers wind up getting into an endless "do" loop: companies add more customer support resources as they grow the business, and customers become frustrated when they encounter the same broken situations. As the demand for service grows, companies add more resources to handle it or try to find smarter or more efficient ways to do so. Some companies have tried to "push" customers to self-service, resorting to such tactics as charging for staffed service or expecting customers to wait for responses by phone or e-mail. It is no wonder that customers have become frustrated and annoyed by the poor service they receive. Customers have every right to be frustrated because companies do not seem to be concerned about why customers needed to interact with them in the first place.

Today these customers can express their upset in damning blogs and by exercising their right as consumers to shop elsewhere. Many authors have described the rising tides of customer frustration. A 2006 survey found that poor customer service caused nearly half of U.S. consumers to switch at least one service provider over the year.[2] Some surveys have spotted satisfied customers, but in most cases companies are continuing to use tired practices and old metrics, failing to provide awesome levels of service (or even what we will describe as Better Service). A recent study of U.K. consumers found that 77 percent of them had experienced a problem with their goods and services.[3] That is not good enough in anyone's book.

Fortunately, there is a better way, one that we feel compelled to describe in this book as a manifesto:

———————————

Stop coping with customer demand for service, which simply increases customers' frustration; instead, challenge customer demand for service so that, ideally, everything works perfectly, eliminating defects and confusion so that there is no need at all for customers, or even prospective customers, to contact the company for information or for help.

———————————

While challenging demand for service and eliminating what we call dumb contacts, companies will need to put into place self-service that works and to become more proactive to prevent contacts from hitting their customer service centers. This is what we call the Best Service Is No Service. To achieve Best Service will take a sea change in behaviors, processes, and metrics, but the returns are well worth it: more satisfied customers, reduced operating costs leading to higher profits, and happier employees.

We have been building the seven Principles ideas of *Best Service Is No Service* for many years, frustrated both as consumers and as customer service practitioners. To paraphrase TV network anchorman Howard Beale, played by Peter Finch in the movie *Network*, we're "mad as hell and don't want to take it anymore!" Our goal is to raise the bar for customer service while reducing the need for customer service, no less. After painting the overall picture in Chapter One, "Challenge Customer Demand for Service," we will introduce six Best Service Principles in Chapters Two through Seven, pulling them together in Chapter Eight with new metrics and frameworks for delivering great customer service experiences (the seventh Principle).

Throughout the book we will reference the following at-a-glance Best Service flow diagram that summarizes the main ideas for creating the proactive, listening, ownership culture that delivers great service experiences:

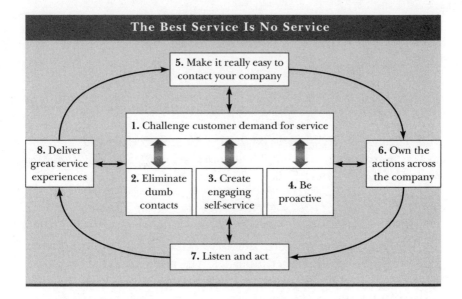

Each chapter covers a new Principle for moving from Basic Service to Best Service:

- **Principle 1: Eliminate dumb contacts.** Apply root-cause improvements that prevent the need for many contacts, once and for all. (Chapter Two)
- **Principle 2: Create engaging self-service.** Because you cannot eliminate all contacts, the next best thing is to enable contact mechanisms like Web, kiosk, short message service (SMS, or text message), or interactive voice response (IVR) self-service. These mechanisms need to enable customers to service their needs and complete their objectives successfully. (Chapter Three)
- **Principle 3: Be proactive.** Alert customers before they need to contact you, practicing preventive maintenance. (Chapter Four)
- **Principle 4: Make it really easy to contact your company.** At first glance this might seem strange for a No Service book, but we will argue that it's far better to open the floodgates to the needs of customers than to dodge the bullet. In doing so, you can ferret through what your customers need, and construct more comprehensive change strategies. (Chapter Five)
- **Principle 5: Own the actions across the company.** It is time to stop blaming the customer service department, which, in

the vast majority of the cases, is the messenger and not the cause of customer contacts. (Chapter Six)

- **Principle 6: Listen and act.** Not all contacts will go away or, as we will demonstrate, should go away; customers are terrific sources of new feature and product requests, competitive information, and lots more. (Chapter Seven)
- **Principle 7: Deliver great service experiences.** In addition to listening to and acting on the contacts that will still occur, you need to revamp your performance metrics and implement other new programs in order to deliver great service experiences. (Chapter Eight)

To introduce and describe these critical ideas, we will use a similar structure in Chapters Two through Seven; in each of them, we

- Define the Principle (the core theme or "the idea") of each chapter.
- Introduce examples outside the world of customer service that demonstrate this Principle.
- Share "bad cases" (disguising the names of the companies) so that you'll know how *not* to apply the Principle.
- Highlight "good cases" (identifying the companies' names) and their results so that you can see that it really is possible to achieve Best Service.
- Propose a framework by which your company can achieve the Principle.
- Wrap up with a short summary.
- Pose multiple-choice questions so that you can test your own company (or those you know).

The assessment in Appendix A will enable you to determine if your company is providing Basic Service, Better Service, or, ultimately, Best Service. We will use this three-category typology to show the difference that companies can make to their customers by fundamentally rethinking how to assess customer contacts and challenge customer demand for support. In Appendix B we present a glossary of customer service terms used in the book.

WHERE DID THESE PRINCIPLES COME FROM?

We have been building these Best Service concepts for a long time, influenced by observing firsthand mistakes being made across a wide range of organizations, coping with demand instead of challenging demand, and listening to frustrations with the sorry state of customer support. We are also cautiously optimistic, for we have seen elements begin to take shape that we will present as the seven Best Service Principles in Chapters Two through Eight.

Briefly, we have spliced stories and our experiences to create Best Service from these and other sources:

- How Tom Peters and Bob Waterman's *In Search of Excellence* has continued to remind us to be "close to the customer"

- How Toyota has empowered its factory assembly workers to be able to slow or stop the production line if they believe that the vehicle has any quality defects
- How MCI has reduced the size of its Sacramento, California, contact center by issuing invoices in Asian languages and Spanish instead of devoting precious time in the center to translating customers' bills into their native language
- How Amazon has cut its contacts per order year after year by obsessing over *why* its customers have bothered themselves to contact the company, pursuing its mission to "Be Earth's most customer-centric company"
- How customer blogs have increased customer "voice," with companies such as Dell sitting up and taking notice to change processes and create new products

Along the way, we started to explain how Best Service works, in white papers, articles, and industry conference presentations around the world, with such headlines as

"Best Service Means Fewer Painful Calls" (Simon Canning, *The Australian*)
"Don't Improve Contacts, Eliminate Them" (LimeBridge Australia)
"Businesses Should Fix, Not Hide, Problems" (Bill Virgin, *Seattle Post-Intelligencer*)
"Listen and You Will Be Prosperous" (Mark Lawson, *Australian Financial Review*)
"The Best Service Is None at All" (Julian Lee, *Australasian Business Intelligence*)

These observations and experiences have influenced our approach to Best Service and inspired us to write this book and accelerate the momentum behind this new and exciting approach. There is still much work to do, however: many companies experience flat or lower levels of customer satisfaction, but continue simply to cope with customer demand. It's time for Best Service!

THE BEST SERVICE IS NO SERVICE

CHAPTER ONE

CHALLENGE CUSTOMER DEMAND FOR SERVICE

Instead of Coping with Demand

Insanity: doing the same thing over and over again and expecting different results.
—ALBERT EINSTEIN

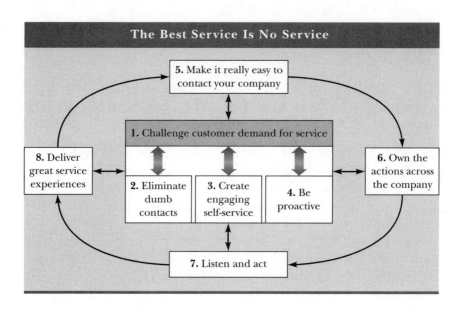

THE PROBLEM WITH CUSTOMER SERVICE TODAY

Over the past twenty years, we have enjoyed unprecedented innovation in product design, technologies, and services to make our life easier, but, sadly, we have not often seen customer service improve at the same rate. Although some companies have embraced new technologies and business practices to create what we call Best Service, in many industries customer service is stuck, in others it's broken, and unfortunately it's getting worse. The Best Service companies are raising customer expectations of what is possible, widening the gap.

Before we begin our exploration of the seven Best Practice Principles, in this chapter we will first ask, "Why is service broken?" We'll examine the ways in which companies and government bodies have largely forgotten what the customer wants and needs, how to service those requirements quickly and completely, and how to challenge the demand in the first place. One of the reasons for this situation is that CEOs and other senior executives are often detached from the day-to-day support operations that touch their customers. Many treat customer service as a necessary evil or as a cost center to be run with interchangeable parts rather than as the heartbeat of the company. Very few treat it as the canary in the coal mine that can provide invaluable feedback about the company's competition, current product faults, future requirements, and much more.

We will then explore how service can be fixed using the seven Best Service Principles to overcome service challenges, and lay out the agenda for the rest of the book. We will provide examples of companies that are getting it right and the benefits they are obtaining.

For those readers who are still unconvinced, we will profile three possible objections to the Best Service Principles and explain why these objections are misplaced. We will then wrap up with reasons why service matters to the company and to the customer.

Why Is Service Broken?

With all the advances in management theory, processes, and technology, customer service should be getting better. However, we find overwhelming evidence that companies continue to subject their customers to more and more "dumb things," experiences and interactions that make no sense to the customer and almost always prompt multiple contacts and perhaps a blog entry as well. Let's look at some examples:

- A leading IT company calculated that it took customers on average five minutes to navigate its interactive voice response (IVR) menus before being put on hold to speak to someone, and it still had trouble routing the customer to the right person.
- A major telecommunications provider forced customers to use a speech recognition IVR system, knowing that 89 percent of their requests would fail.
- An online retailer refused to publish phone numbers on its Web sites.

- A utility forces customers with temporary age or disability concessions to call in and claim them for every bill they receive, even though the concessions have a known expiration date.
- Many companies will not allow someone who is not the official account holder to interact with an account, even when all the person wants to do is pay money into that account for the account holder.
- A large mobile phone company calls its customers to advise them about their account usage, but then forces these customers to identify themselves. "Didn't you just call me?" the customers ask.
- Many companies send bills for zero amounts or amounts so small that their automated payment systems will not accept the payment (for example, less than $5.00). The cost of sending the bill and processing the payment using a person-to-person interaction is greater than the revenue received!

We could go on, but you get the idea; you will find many more examples of these dumb things throughout the book.

A news story emerged recently about one company's poor service, and within twenty-four hours, seven hundred people had recorded their similar bitter experiences on two related Web sites. Customers can now express their frustration publicly in blogs and Internet feedback sites, and they are strident when they encounter poor service. Here's a small sampling of some of the headlines on just a few of the many sites where customers are ranting:

"What Is the Value of Customer Service? (meaty question)"
"The Customer Service Hall of Shame"
"Tales from seething souls in phone hell"
The "Get Human 500 Database"

Customers are showing their frustration in other ways. A study by the U.K. National Consumer Council found that across all industries, switching levels had increased 52 percent, and people who had switched were happier with the result. The impacts of service failure are significant.[1]

Some consumers yearn for the "good old days" when their local branch manager or the owner of their corner store recognized them by name, knew their preferences, and anticipated their needs when they walked in. Maybe they're right—as companies have become larger and more diverse, senior management has become separated from those interacting with customers. There is increased geographical separation from those who "manage" service and those who deliver it. Contact centers are already farther from the customer than the branch or local office used to be. Headquarters may be at yet another location, and trends such as outsourcing have added another layer of remoteness, separating customer experiences from those who own and manage them.

There is evidence that service is declining, only recently returning to earlier levels, or at best is stuck in the industries that have high "service intensity"—those where service plays a key part of the total solution for customers, such as airlines, telecommunication companies, online retailers, and financial services (see Figure 1.1). The American Customer Satisfaction Index (ACSI) tracks satisfaction with businesses and brands (not just service).

FIGURE 1.1: ACSI Scores by Industry, 1995–2006

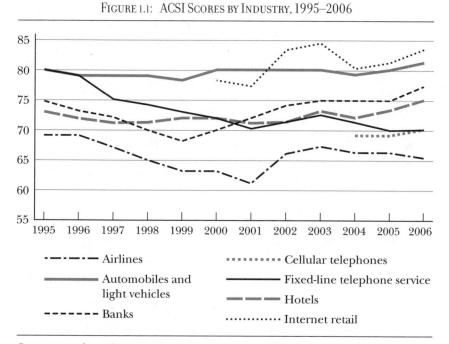

Source: www.theacsi.org

Only the Internet retail industry has improved by 5 percentage points over the past six-plus years; four other service-intensive industries have lost ground. What have the Internet retail industries been doing that others have not? Why can't other service-intensive industries match this improvement? We will explore the lessons that the service leaders, such as Amazon and eBay, have learned and the mechanisms they are applying to get service right and to strive for what we term Best Service. This problem isn't confined to the United States. In the United Kingdom, consumers are equally unhappy. A study by Accenture found that two-thirds of customers believed that service had not improved in the last five years.[2]

Articles over the past several years have captured the mood and some of the symptoms of poor customer service and experiences. Some eye-catching headlines tell much of the story:

"You Call This Service?"
"Customers Find Service Put on Hold; Filing Complaints Isn't Easy, Getting Action Even Tougher"
"Cases of 'Customer Rage' Mount as Bad Service Prompts Venting"
"37 Fruitless Calls"
"Bruising the Customers Costs Companies Dear"
"Luxury Goods Without the Luxury Service"
"Companies Find They Can't Buy Love with Bargains"
"Whatever Happened to Customer Service?"
"Press '0' If You've Had Enough"
"1-800-USELESS"
"Does Customer Service Still Exist?"

At the heart of the issue, there are stark data on the amount of contacts customers have to make to get things done. As we pointed out earlier, none of us wakes up the morning wanting to call our utility company to find out why our latest invoice balance doesn't make sense, nor do we want to contact our bank—no matter how "friendly" it is—to complain that our last check didn't make it in time to the loan company. Instead, we expect everything to work perfectly and do not want to bother ourselves to call or send an e-mail or text message. Yet companies invest huge amounts of time and money to handle or "cope" with the demand that they have created. Too few companies ask why their customers need to spend their precious time to ask for help, clear up their confusion, or find out how something is supposed to work.

Let's consider how often some organizations force us to make contact with them:

- A leading cable TV company requires three contacts for each new connection—why not just one contact?
- Some mobile phone companies handle as many as ten to twelve contacts per subscriber per year, whereas others have only three to four. Why do we need to call mobile providers so often? Shouldn't we just be making calls and paying bills, preferably online?
- A water utility was averaging two contacts for each fault call. The first call should have been enough to fix the problem. The subsequent calls asked "Why isn't it fixed yet?" or "When are you coming to fix it?" Not good enough.
- A leading self-service bank averaged one contact per customer per year and nearly two for each new customer. Don't we sign up for self-service applications like Internet banking so that we don't have to call? Other banks have half this contact rate, so clearly something is broken.
- A leading insurance company was averaging more than two contacts per claim. The first contact makes sense, setting the claim in motion, but why were subsequent contacts needed?
- "Customers reported making an average of 3.5 contacts in an attempt to resolve their most serious customer-service problem in the past year."[3] Why isn't this 1.0 contact or, perish the thought, zero contacts because nothing needs to be resolved in the first place?

We should make it clear that we are not talking about such interactions as placing orders, making payments, or using self-service solutions, such as checking balances, that the customers chose to use. Instead, we are talking about having to call or take the time to write or visit a branch to get something done or to get something fixed. In some industries, these contact rates are much worse: every contact with a technical support area of an Internet provider or computer manufacturer is a sign that something is broken. Ideally, customers should never need to make these contacts.

This book is about questioning why those contacts are necessary, in essence challenging the need for customers to use customer care or technical support lines. The reasons we argue that the Best Service Is No Service is that we know that customers would prefer not to contact companies in the way they are forced to do to get answers or solutions. They would either prefer not to make contact at all or, in many situations, prefer the flexibility and convenience of well-designed self-service that they can use whenever they have the time, or of proactive alerts to them before an issue becomes serious.

HOW DO WE FIX SERVICE?

Let's look at the issues that have prevented significant improvements in service. Here we identify seven reasons that service isn't getting better and seven responses, the Best Service Principles, to address these reasons:

1. Companies keep handling issues that are not adding value for them or for customers, so instead we need to eliminate dumb contacts.
2. Self-service is insufficient or broken, so we need to create engaging self-service that customers want and will use.
3. Service is reactive, so instead we need to exploit opportunities for proactive service with alerts.
4. Companies have made themselves hard to contact, so instead we need to make it easy to obtain service.
5. The customer service department gets blamed for others' mistakes, so instead we need to assign ownership across the whole company.
6. Companies can't listen properly, so instead we need to learn to listen and act on what customers are telling us.
7. The customer service industry is stuck with outdated practices and metrics that produce poor experiences, so instead we need to design and deliver great experiences for customers.

PRINCIPLE 1: ELIMINATE DUMB CONTACTS

Customer demand for service equals the volume of requests that customers make of companies when they need help, are confused, or have to change something. In most companies, demand is a given—lots of time and effort go into forecasting demand based on past demand, measured in thirty-minute increments across a range of contact channels. Then companies work hard at matching their resources to this demand: putting people on the right shifts at the right time, finding partners if needed, and so forth. These companies are so busy trying to manage the demand and their "service supply" that few, if any, question why the demand is there in the first place. For example, how many companies report that they have made themselves easier to deal with by reducing the demand for contact? How many boards of directors monitor their rate of contact as well as the speed and cost? Very few companies think this way (although Amazon comes close by proclaiming year-by-year reductions in contacts per order). There is an unfortunate obsession with how quickly phones and e-mails are answered. The standard across most service operations is to report and track how quickly things were done, not how well they were done or how often, or why they needed to be done at all.

This issue of demand for contact is fundamental to our thinking. If companies want to rethink service radically, they need to rethink the *need* for service. This book is titled *The Best Service Is No Service* because too many service interactions aren't necessary; they reflect, instead, as we've begun to show, the dumb things that companies have done to their customers: processes that customers don't understand, bewildering statements, incorrect letters, badly applied fees and charges, or services not working as the customer expects. Fundamental changes in service require companies to question what has driven the demand for service. In Chapter Two, we will explore how companies can follow this Principle and eliminate dumb contacts.

PRINCIPLE 2: CREATE ENGAGING SELF-SERVICE

How often have you given up on a Web site or gotten lost in one? Have you ever listened to a set of toll-free menus and been overwhelmed by the choices, and tried desperately to find the option that lets you talk to an operator? How often have you filled out an application form online and then been told that you don't meet the criteria for an online application? How often have you searched for an online service and found that it is no longer available? How often have you been flummoxed by the operating manual for a new electronic device or for your new car? These are just some of the examples of the dumb things that organizations do or don't do in self-service.

When self-service works well, customers love it. Companies like Amazon and first direct couldn't have grown the way they have if customers didn't like well-designed self-service. ATMs took off because they were much more convenient than queuing in a branch. Internet banking is so convenient that it has increased the volume of transactions and inquiries that customers perform.

Why do so many companies get it wrong? Our perspective is that they understand neither the need for self-service nor how to create self-service solutions that their customers will embrace. In Chapter Three, we will explore how to follow this Principle and create self-service that customers will want to use.

PRINCIPLE 3: BE PROACTIVE

The reason why companies have to invest so much time trying to predict demand and then supplying appropriate resources is that the modus operandi is one of reactive service: if the customer calls, the company is there to deal with it. But in many cases the company knows that there is a problem yet still waits for the customer to contact the company to fix it.

Take product recalls, for example. Recently a leading company that had no idea which of its customers had the affected product needed to wait for customers to try to figure it out and then call the company, sometimes in panic mode. In Chapter Four, we will explore how companies can reverse this trend by actively approaching and dealing with the customer whenever necessary by exploiting opportunities for proactive service.

PRINCIPLE 4: MAKE IT REALLY EASY TO CONTACT YOUR COMPANY

Do you ever get the impression that some companies would rather not hear from you? Have you ever been on a Web site and searched in vain for a phone number to call? Have you ever found that companies expect you to get service only when they want to give it to you? If any of these situations seems familiar, it's another example of a company making itself hard to contact.

In Chapter Five, we will explore how companies need to open the taps, making it really easy for customers to reach them.

PRINCIPLE 5: OWN THE ACTIONS ACROSS THE COMPANY

A bizarre myth has grown up in many companies that the head of customer service is responsible for customer service. Although we recognize that someone needs to be held accountable and be dedicated to service, we do not believe that the service operations can fix service without the help of all the other company departments and, increasingly, outside partners in the supply chain or in other functions. Although the head of service does need to forecast the demand for service, and handle those contacts well, many other areas of a business cause the customer contacts that drive the demand—for example, billing, IT, marketing, credit, and finance. IT and process and product areas can also influence how well the customer service area can service the demand. The norm is for the head of customer service to be held accountable for the standard and methods of service. Our perspective is that responsibility for service must be spread across the whole organization, so in Chapter Six, we explore how companies need to change accountability for service and follow Principle 5, putting ownership in the right place.

PRINCIPLE 6: LISTEN AND ACT

Some companies have millions of contacts per year with their customers, yet they still spend considerable money and time researching their customers. In fact, head-office functions as marketing, product design, and IT have gotten further and further from frontline delivery, the information gap has increased between the head office's understanding of the customer and the behaviors and wants of customers as expressed at the front line. The interactions that companies have with customers today offer an amazing amount of insight about customers, the company's products and services, and even competitors—if companies can tap into what their customers are telling them. Unfortunately, most companies have not even thought to "listen" to their customers in this way when these interactions occur.

This disconnect is illustrated by the gap between the perceptions of CEOs and those of customers in general, as shown in the following graph. Over 70 percent of CEOs believe that their companies provide "above average" customer care, but nearly 60 percent of these companies' customers stated that they are somewhat or extremely upset with their most recent customer service experience.

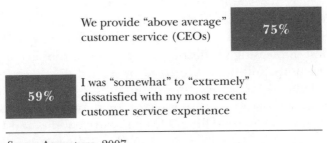

We provide "above average"
customer service (CEOs)   75%

59%   I was "somewhat" to "extremely"
dissatisfied with my most recent
customer service experience

Source: Accenture, 2007

Unfortunately, CEOs and board members are cosseted—they often fly first class, have "personal" or "relationship" bankers, get queued faster, and rarely set foot in a branch or pay their own bills. Because they have become disconnected with what their own customers experience, they will have to listen even harder.

Managers in larger companies who control market and customer research or set the budget for service rarely, if ever, spend time with the frontline staff who are dealing directly with customers. In small businesses this isn't the case—an owner who runs a restaurant or cafe doesn't need to conduct research into what his customers like or dislike. He hears it directly from customers: if customers are asking for cake or health food or gluten-free products or soy milk, the restaurant owner can respond quickly, or quickly be out of business. It's too bad that many companies have forgotten how to listen in this way. In Chapter Seven, we will describe how some companies haven't forgotten these lessons: they've become closer to the customer and thus more effective by following Principle 6, learning to listen and apply what they learn.

PRINCIPLE 7: DELIVER GREAT SERVICE EXPERIENCES

Companies have created large centralized contact centers or service functions, separated service from sales or production, added lots of new technology, deluged themselves with meaningless or misleading metrics, and built walls around the customer service functions. They have then become stuck delivering service experiences that have forgotten the customer; stuck obsessing about speed, not quality; and stuck thinking that faster is more efficient. It is hardly a surprise that many customer experiences disappoint customers.

Companies Are Stuck with Service Experiences That Have Forgotten Who the Customer Is

Customers are often expected to navigate the organization and repeat account information and what happened ad nauseam, from agent to agent. The processes simply haven't been designed from the customers' perspective, and it shows. For example, as illustrated by the cartoon at the end of the Introduction, customers are justifiably miffed when companies (still!!) ask them to repeat their credit card number, frequent flyer account number, or order identification number after just having done so in an IVR or with another agent or, as is increasingly the case, after doing so online. "Don't you know me?!?" they might say. Then companies add in complexity for customers, such as by asking them to repeat data the company already knows or to provide information to comply with a procedure that someone in the legal department dreamed up. These are just two illustrations of experiences that haven't been designed with the customer in mind. In Chapter Eight, we will describe how to design and deliver superior customer experiences that are also simpler.

Companies Are Stuck Obsessing About Speed, Not Quality, as an Overall Measure of Service

Quality, like beauty, is in the eye of the beholder, in this case the customer. Unfortunately, measuring speed seems to be the only way that most companies measure quality. Although to some customers, "one-ring pickup" or "twenty-four-hour e-mail response" might connote a well-run outfit, such insular metrics as speed of answer or average handle time (AHT) simply cannot be equated with quality. Unfortunately, there are still benchmark studies galore supporting this misplaced theory, missing the mark entirely. Instead, quality is a complex weave (customer specific and changing like the sands on the beach) of such elements such as first contact resolution (FCR, aka "one and done"), educational and informative responses (giving more than the right answer by being proactive), and ideally doing away with the need to have to ask the question in the first place. No one likes standing in lines or waiting for phone queues, but quality starts after pickup or once the e-mail response is launched or during the chat, because that is when the customer starts taking note of "service" performance. In Chapter Eight, we will describe how to measure the right things and report on them across and up and down the organization.

Companies Are Stuck Thinking That Faster Is More Efficient

Some companies slavishly hold to an old operational-productivity shibboleth that shorter "customer handle time" is better, both overall and per staff member. Rubbish! What if your technical support representative is still in the middle of a complex solution call with a brand-new customer or one who has bought her fifth consecutive printer for her home office and the clock hits twelve minutes, the amount of time his supervisor told him is "ideal" and "the target"? Do you want him to hustle up the call and underserve? Of course not. The duration of service contacts is a complex issue, one that you need to understand very closely in order to determine overall service center staffing effectively and to link with corporate budgets and plans. However, the concept of duration falls apart when applied to any specific contact or customer service person. In Chapter Eight, we will present measures that balance speed and effectiveness, and show how to design and deliver great experiences.

EXAMPLES OF GETTING IT RIGHT

We have presented evidence of the malaise that has caused service to be stuck, but don't despair! The good news is that there are many shining lights—companies that are getting service right, with benefits for the companies and their customers. Each chapter will describe examples of companies that are demonstrating Better Service or Best Service behaviors. Here we will briefly introduce one example company as a preview to each Principle.

ELIMINATE DUMB CONTACTS—BRITISH TELECOM

In 2001, British Telecom (BT) was receiving 2.4 million customer contacts each day; over 35 percent were repeats, and many were unnecessary. BT set about reducing these and other forms of unwanted contacts systematically, and by 2004 had reduced the contact volume to only one million per day, a 60 percent reduction; at the same time, customers were more satisfied, the BT staff was happier, and the cost savings proved that Better Service was also cheaper.

CREATE ENGAGING SELF-SERVICE—EBAY

eBay represents one of the finest cases of customers' desire and willingness to use self-service. Not only do customers willingly buy directly from vendors, but the sellers themselves learn through various forms of self-service how to set up their stores on eBay, how to use eBay's payment and other services, and even what software is available to help them run their sales businesses. eBay also opens the communication channels between buyers and sellers through their seller and buyer ratings systems. If customers were unwilling to use self-service, eBay and the thousands of businesses that it supports would not be in existence today.

BE PROACTIVE—NOVADENTAL CLINIC

Dentistry is not an industry most would associate with great service. The Novadental clinic in Australia is run by one of Melbourne's leading dentists, whose consultancy firm advises other dental practices in how to run their businesses. The clinic demonstrates how to be proactive at every level: (1) promoting dental hygiene services to patients as a form of preventive dentistry; (2) monitoring that customers are getting checkups and hygiene services at regular intervals; (3) calling each customer more than twenty-four hours in advance of each appointment to ensure that he or she will be coming; and (4) maintaining a waiting list of other customers willing to "backfill" anyone who cannot keep his or her appointment. This is not only good service for the clinic's customers, ensuring that they remember their appointments, but also prevents costly no-shows for the dental practice.

MAKE IT REALLY EASY TO CONTACT YOUR COMPANY— USAA INSURANCE

One of the more successful U.S.-based property and casualty insurance companies is USAA; it also has the highest loyalty rate in the industry. (The biggest reason that USAA loses "members" is death, not switching to the many other choices that members have.) USAA has always made it really easy for members to contact it for service, change their address, and learn about new products. The company publishes different toll-free numbers prominently on its Web site, in monthly magazines, on invoices and other notices, and in many other media. USAA will transfer its members to other services, but it always tells the member what that number is so that the member can call directly the next time he might need help.

OWN THE ACTIONS ACROSS THE ORGANIZATION—YARRA VALLEY WATER

Award-winning utility Yarra Valley Water was determined to reduce the number and cost of complaints. To do this, the company established a "complaints council" that met each month to review the ownership and cause of any complaints that had reached the regulatory body (the industry ombudsman). After the council assigned ownership of each complaint to a particular department, it charged the new owners not just with ensuring resolution of that complaint but also with reporting back to the complaints council about underlying causes that led to the complaint in the first place, and how they could be addressed. This systematic process meant that all of Yarra Valley Water's departments were drawn in to tackle service issues and forced to acknowledge and act on their impact on service contacts. The company has recognized the value of taking a strategic perspective on complaints, and the process has resulted in a significant reduction in complaints, according to the industry ombudsman, Fiona McLeod. Pat McCafferty, the general manager who established the process at Yarra Valley Water, says, "What made this process powerful was that it drew together the key players across the business into the issues that impacted customers. We recognized that we couldn't solve these problems without ensuring all those that impacted service had a seat at the table."

LISTEN AND ACT—AMAZON

All contact centers hold team meetings, usually weekly one-hour sessions that bore the agents with the latest policy changes, next work-shift details, and perhaps new company product releases. Amazon decided to inject life into these weekly sessions by asking the agents, "What have our customers been saying to you this past week?" which quickly became known as WOCAS (what our customers are saying). The company produced a weekly WOCAS report that quickly became popular reading for departments outside customer service.

In one of these weekly sessions, a customer service representative mentioned that in the middle of a call about a lost password, the customer told her that she really liked Amazon's 1-Click™ service (which enables customers to click only once with a preset shipping address, shipping method, and credit card to speed the order on its way); however, she said that she often shipped to different addresses and had two credit cards, so for any shipments other than her 1-Click settings, she had to navigate through the additional checkout process, easy to do but still time consuming. Another agent remarked that he too had occasionally heard customers talk about how cool it would be to have multiple 1-Click combinations, so the first agent asked if she could lead a task force to study how this could be done. (This was a frequent process at Amazon—engaging and encouraging Amazon agents and supervisors to launch or participate in cross-company task forces.)

After a couple of months, Amazon quietly launched drop-down 1-Click, "quietly" being another of Amazon's methods. Instead of announcing that customers could register additional shipping addresses, shipping methods, and credit cards beside their current

1-Click setting, Amazon (1) researched all previous multiple combinations, (2) preloaded them into this new feature, and (3) let customers discover it, allowing the "serendipity" for which Costco is also well known in its warehouse stores. The result? Increased customer orders and more convenience for customers.

Amazon CEO and founder Jeff Bezos likes to send e-mail messages to all Amazon customers whenever the company launches a new store. One day he decided to add this line to his message: "Please write and tell me what you think about this new store!" As he often said, Amazon's customers were the company's best focus group, and once again they didn't disappoint. With his intentional invitation for responses, Bezos and the rest of Amazon collected hundreds of thousands of e-mail replies in the next week, divided into three categories: (1) "I love your other stores so don't lose focus," (2) "Thanks for letting me buy this new stuff online," and (3) "When can I also buy other products from you guys?" In that third category, Amazon mined many requests that prompted "We didn't know it was so popular!" responses across the marketing and supply chain departments, such as considerable interest in buying kitchenware and small appliances online from the company. As a result, Amazon advanced timing to launch what is now called Kitchen & Dining inside the Home & Garden store and the Apparel & Accessories store.

DELIVER GREAT SERVICE EXPERIENCES—UNION SQUARE CAFE

Successful NYC-based restaurateur Danny Meyer has had hit after hit, the earliest and best known being Union Square Cafe. In his recent memoir, *Setting the Table: The Transforming Power of Hospitality in Business,* Meyer echoes Best Service when he defines "enlightened hospitality" that "stands some more traditional business approaches on their head." Among the elements that Meyer carefully plants and then allows to flourish in his restaurants and catering businesses, all completely applicable to the broader topic of customer service in our book, are (1) creating a dialogue with guests and ensuring that they feel that you are doing something *for* them and not *to* them; (2) choosing to look for new ideas and "tuning in to the feedback"; (3) hiring and nurturing "agents" instead of "gatekeepers" who share optimistic warmth, intelligence, work ethic, empathy, and self-awareness; and (4) embracing mistakes with awareness, acknowledgment, apology, action, and additional generosity. Pursuing these guest-centric processes means taking time, not hurrying the guest or the meal because they blend to become one—the experience.

POSSIBLE OBJECTIONS TO THE PRINCIPLES

We think the seven Best Service Principles are common sense and, as the examples we have just discussed illustrate, the Principles work and deliver benefits. There are many more examples throughout the book. However, we have encountered companies and individuals who take issue with our philosophy, so let's deal with those possible objections before we move on in our discussion of Best Service. We will cover three of the more common objections to our thesis: the recovery theory, the cross-sell theory, and the warm body theory.

RECOVERY THEORY

Past studies have claimed that "recovery from failure" is the best way to deliver customer loyalty and satisfaction. One famous paper in the 1990s argued that customer recovery produces more loyal customers than situations when nothing breaks. We are not saying that customer recovery is wrong (in Chapter Two we will address how to conduct recovery operations through management of repeat contacts), but we believe that the idea of focusing efforts on recovery rather than prevention is a flawed strategy. First, it's expensive—recovery costs money in time and effort. Second, it adds risk—what if the company doesn't catch all the failures? Won't that leave some customers in a deeply unsatisfied state? We are not saying that companies don't need to be great at recovery; of course they do, because even in the best company things will go wrong. However, we advocate that an even stronger strategy is to be great at avoiding the need for recovery or, in other words, preventing issues and failures in the first place rather than being really good at fixing them.

CROSS-SELL THEORY

A second objection occurs in industries where the perception is that every contact is good because the company can use those contacts to sell additional products or services to those customers, also called cross-selling or up-selling. There are two counters to that argument. First, if a customer is calling when she didn't want to contact you, sales efforts are likely to be wasted, producing very low success rates, stressed agents trying to make the sale, and upset customers. What can you sell when the customer is trying to track her claim for something she needed to get yesterday? What can you sell when a customer wants to return a defective item or wants his broadband connection that keeps dropping service to work? Until the company demonstrates that its claim process works, a customer is hardly likely to want more insurance; until a customer receives her first item, she will probably not want to place another order. Second, if companies can get rid of all this wasted and unneeded contact, they can reinvest all that time and effort in sales at a more appropriate time. We will illustrate this further in Chapter Four, where we describe examples of companies reaching out to customers proactively to build their relationship.

WARM BODY THEORY

Many executives still like to say, "Our customers want to speak to a real person and not to a machine," but nothing could be farther from the truth. This objection goes on to claim that only customer service agents (or tellers or other customer-facing employees) can provide the warmth and understanding needed to deal with customer complaints or frustration. We will argue that it is far better, cheaper, and more desirable from the customer's perspective, and for the company, to eliminate the defects or errors in the first place, design engaging self-service in as many places as possible, and be proactive. Today we're used to pumping our own gas (at least in North America), scanning items at the supermarket self-serve, and using ATMs to withdraw cash quickly. Do we miss the human touch? Maybe, but mostly we chuckle at movies like *Back to the Future* that show the gas station attendants flocking to wash windows, check oil, and pump gas—besides, we know that we're getting less expensive products or services if we can do some of the work for ourselves. Moreover, as such recent articles as "Expanding Banks Bemoan Lack of Qualified Tellers" describe, it is getting harder to find and hold on to talent.[4]

WHY SERVICE MATTERS

We have explained that service is stuck at best and sometimes broken in many service-intensive industries. Why is the fact that service is stuck or broken so important to companies? Customers who encounter bad service tell their friends, find other companies with which they want to do business, and cost companies dearly; those who encounter good service also tell their friends, stick around longer, and cost companies less. Two recent surveys punctuate these important findings. In the first, executive MBA students described what they do when they encounter poor service or great service, choosing from five possible actions (as shown in Figure 1.2). Over 40 percent of those encountering poor service said that they switch companies, as opposed to

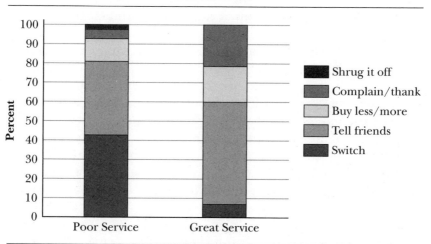

FIGURE 1.2: "WHAT DO YOU DO WHEN YOU ENCOUNTER POOR SERVICE? GREAT SERVICE?"

Source: University of Washington executive MBA class, Bill Price, 2004

only 5 percent of those encountering great service (meaning that great service didn't save the companies from the consequences of poor products or prices); and a whopping 40 percent in each situation say that they tell their friends, spreading both the good news and the bad news to others. Intriguingly, fewer than 10 percent of those encountering poor service say that they register a complaint, confirming that complaints represent only the tip of the iceberg, and reinforcing our points in Chapter Five regarding making it really easy to contact your company so that these voices can be heard and understood.

In another, wider survey conducted by Customer Think, formerly known as CRM Guru.com, consumers with positive memorable experiences ("promoters") expressed a significantly higher propensity for recommending the products or services to friends than did those with negative memorable experiences ("detractors"). The promoters also purchased more products and services, and complained far less. The survey results appear in Figure 1.3.

As these and other studies indicate, there are multiple "costs" or impacts of not getting service right. We will look at the revenue, cost, and brand implications in turn.

LOST REVENUE

The first impact of poor service is loss of revenue. Faced with poor service experiences, in many industries customers will switch to other providers—perhaps not as a result of a single experience, so the switch might not happen immediately, but with some customers it will happen sooner or later. Sometimes companies do not pick up on the implications of service failure as they research customer switching. Customer exit surveys usually ask why the customer switched, and many customers cite such reasons as "I got a better offer" or that their new choice was "cheaper." However, the customers may have been open to the offer only because they have had service experiences that did not satisfy them. The fact that poor service experiences weakened loyalty or made customers look for alternatives is often not picked up by these types of exit research.

This is equally true in a business-to-business environment; the *Journal of Service Research* investigated the relationship between

FIGURE 1.3: PROMOTERS' AND DETRACTORS' REACTIONS TO SERVICE

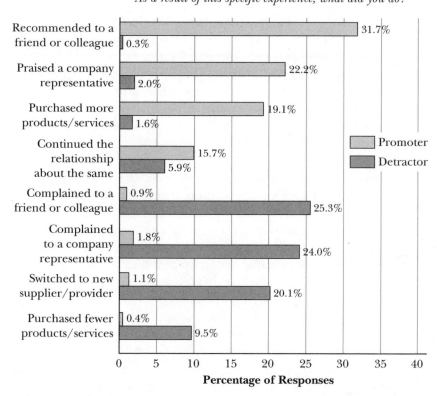

Actions After Memorable Experience
As a result of this specific experience, what did you do?

Source: Thompson, 2006, p. 6. Used with permission of the author.

service received and the amount of business or share of wallet that customers would give to a given company and found that "The relationship between satisfaction and actual share-of-wallet in a business-to-business environment is not only a positive relationship but the relationship is non-linear, with the greatest positive impact occurring at the upper extreme of satisfaction levels."[5] Tom Peters reported similar issues in *The Pursuit of Wow!* citing a Forum Corporation of America report that 15 percent of customers migrated because of quality issues, and another 15 percent changed supplier because of price issues.[6] The remaining 70 percent moved because "they didn't like the human side of doing business with the prior provider of the product or service"—getting service wrong hurts the bottom line, too.

INCREASED COST

We will discuss in depth the additional costs of poor service and dissatisfied customers, the largest being the cost of handling unnecessary contacts and overall demand for service, as we will describe in Chapter Two. The costs, of repeat contacts are clearly an unnecessary overhead, but these are often a fraction of the costs, of other "first time" contacts that customers would have preferred not to have made. There are further costs of handling complaints, some of which incur legal and other statutory costs. We calculated that for one utility the costs of repeat contacts and complaint handling alone represented 30 percent of its operating budget (see Figure 1.4).

Moreover, there are other, less obvious costs of poor service. Operations that deliver poor service typically have staff who are more dissatisfied, which produces high turnover and associated replacement costs. These companies may also suffer higher write-off costs, such as waived fees or charges, and incur other additional costs, such as increased mail charges. All in all, poor service produces much higher operating costs.

There is a perception that some companies reduce the level of customer service in order to cut costs. We will prove later in the book that this is a false economy—at best it defers costs or creates a service operation that can deal only with a smaller customer base, and at worst it alienates customers who will leave in droves (and tell many others in blogs). There are few companies that are "overservicing" their customers to such an extent that they can afford to cut service without having other business impacts. The short-term strategy of cutting service to cut costs is the opposite of our recommendations in this book. We will demonstrate how to improve service and cut costs at the same time.

IMPACT ON BRAND AND REPUTATION

The third major impact of poor service is damage to brand and reputation. Once a company has a reputation for poor service, it

FIGURE 1.4: COMPARISON OF CUSTOMER CONTACTS AND COSTS, UTILITY COMPANY

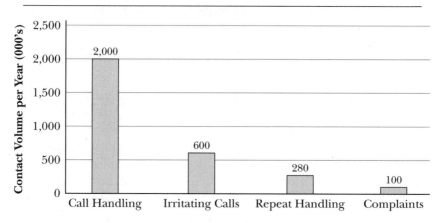

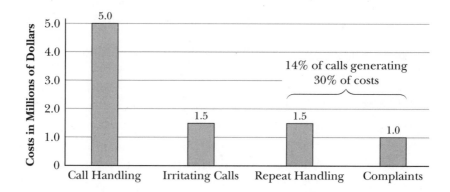

will have great difficulty recovering. Research studies have shown that customers who have a poor service experience tell many more people than those with a good one, as shown in Figure 1.3. This is understandable behavior—as customers we expect service to be satisfactory, and when things work as they are designed, we don't feel a need to tell anyone. When we encounter poor service, our emotional response makes it far more likely that we will tell others. Companies that deliver poor service destroy their brand value.

The same week in February 2007 that *BusinessWeek* declared JetBlue Airways to be one of the top twenty-five companies in customer satisfaction in the United States, the company suffered a huge black eye when it stranded thousands of passengers during ice storms, unable to handle the crush of calls into its contact center. Although the CEO apologized profusely, the company's stock took a beating, and later the CEO stepped aside from running the company that he founded.

The combined negative impact of poor service on revenue, costs, and the brand makes it clear that delivering better service delivers improved returns for any business. The researchers at the University of Michigan who track the ACSI have been able to quantify the impact of customer satisfaction on the value of businesses over the past six years, and the results are strikingly clear: companies that satisfy their customers outperform the market and deliver superior returns (see Figure 1.5). Delivering Best Service is a strategy with great financial returns. It reduces costs, boosts revenue, and increases brand value; further examples throughout the book will illustrate the success that companies are achieving.

BEST SERVICE

This book presents a new canvas, a new approach for companies to take: that the Best Service companies can provide to their customers (and to their prospects) is to ensure that everything works so well and is so clearly laid out that customers do not need to bother themselves to contact customer service. Or as we've been saying, the Best Service Is No Service. We will present and dissect dumb contacts that companies force their customers to make and their customer service agents to handle, and we highlight the difference between good and bad customer service.

This Web posting sums up the disconnect that exists between frontline staff and management and highlights the gulf that needs to be breached, a key part of this book:

> I work for a utility company. A few years back I was having lunch with the Director [of Customer Service] and relayed a normal event in our customer service dept. where I spent 15 minutes on a customer call after which the customer mentioned that she's never been informed as well during my call and wished that she

FIGURE 1.5:   SHARE PERFORMANCE OF TOP-PERFORMING ACSI COMPANIES COMPARED TO MARKET PERFORMANCE

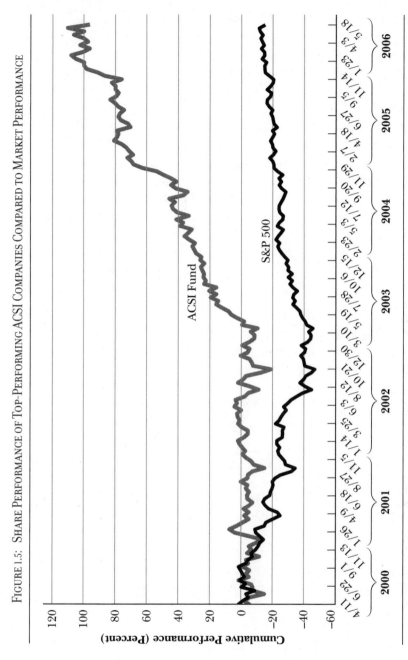

Source: S&P 500 data from msn.com; ACSI data from www.theacsi.org

had been much sooner as she's called multiple times over the past couple years. To this my Director said that he's not so sure he wants 15 minutes spent on one customer. I was stunned and have never forgotten this. I believe wholeheartedly that spending that extra 10 minutes with this woman avoids repeat calls from her AND she'll tell two friends and they'll tell two friends, etc. So, I'm not surprised that CEO's are not aware about true customer service levels. They're still not walking the walk.[7]

We believe that a new approach, a sea change, is sorely required to prevent companies from repeating past mistakes and to help customers do without the need to seek customer service—all by challenging customer demand for support instead of simply coping with that demand, yet all the while ensuring that customers who do contact the company get awesome levels of assistance when they really need it. This quotation from an article otherwise slamming the state of U.S. customer service sums up our argument:

> I've never had to contact Amazon about any matter. I have had, in essence, no customer service from Amazon. Put another way, I have had such perfect customer service, the service itself has been transparent. That is exactly what Amazon wants. The goal is perfect customer service through no customer service.[8]

CHAPTER TWO

ELIMINATE DUMB CONTACTS
Instead of Handling Them Again and Again

Customers are totally out of patience. They won't tolerate an organization making mistakes over and over again.
—ART HALL, NETBANK US, *1TO1 MAGAZINE*, APRIL 2007

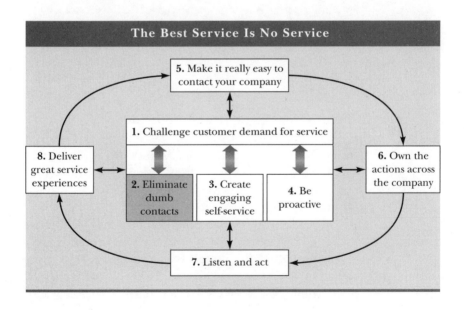

THE PRINCIPLE

As we introduced in Chapter One, companies have learned how to cope with demand from their customers for service instead of challenging demand. In this chapter we will describe how roadblocks are still in place to increase these coping mechanisms; we share emerging success stories and specific tools to use to challenge demand.

Most companies continue to assume that as they sell more products or services, they need to add support costs roughly on a pro rata basis, meaning that they need to recruit and train more agents and managers, invest in new contact centers and technologies, and expand their customer care operations. In some cases, customer service managers measure their success by the number of agents they have or the total customer care budget they control.

Many companies have shuffled the customer to the "most available agent" or maybe moved offshore to reduce costs, instead of finding better ways to handle the issues in the first place.

When faced with too much demand and when supply (agents) cannot scale fast enough, companies typically reach into three bags for solutions, none of them successful in the medium to longer term: (1) applying classic triage techniques to handle the most important issues and customers faster, which is very hard to do, especially on the fly; (2) busying out phone lines or stretching e-mail response times, restricting the number of phone lines so that customers get a busy signal (also known as "busying out") deluge (see our bad cases in Chapter Five); or (3) pushing agents to work faster, which leads to burnout (and remember that attrition is already high), mistakes, and upset customers.

There is another way. In most service operations there is a significant volume of unnecessary contacts, or demand, of three different types. The first is "dumb contacts," caused by the company due to confusion, delays, poor processes, or defective products. Customers ask "where is my X?" or "why haven't you done Y?" or "why did you send me Z?" In this chapter we'll show how companies can challenge the demand for this type of contact.

The second type of unnecessary contacts is "repeat contacts," caused by the service operations' mishandling the first time. Here, customers remark, "I'm calling again about this" or "your e-mail didn't tell me X". In this chapter we will show how companies can reduce these repeat contacts drastically. The third unnecessary contact type is simple and straightforward questions such as "what's my balance?" or "when is my payment due?" We will describe how to identify this type and later in Chapter 3 show how to build engaging self-service to deflect them from the service center.

As we will show later in this chapter with a series of bad cases, there are many situations where companies are not challenging demand but appear to be encouraging contacts for no logical reason. These two blog postings describe two different customers' frustrations with the same U.S. mobile services provider:[1]

"Their hold times are ridiculous, no matter what time you call them. . . . I also have to call at least twice to get a change made and then call again when the bill arrives to have it adjusted. Then I have to explain for the 500th time why I need such-and-such credited which usually leads to needing to speak with a manager who finally gives me the small credit I am due."

"And like the others have posted, I've now come to EXPECT each change made to my account to require at least 2–3 more follow-ups on my part just to make sure things were done accordingly. The amount of effort required to supervise the health of my own . . . account is ridiculous. This is why I have not bothered to upgrade my account . . . in the past 3 years."

We want to see companies adopt better metrics (such as reducing the customer contacts per order or per product) and manage using these metrics. If they do, they will be able to cut customer support budgets and resources year by year and at the same time, be able to see an increase in customer satisfaction and loyalty. Fortunately, not all companies have slavishly hewn to the cope-with-demand rut; some have begun to scratch their heads to ask, "Isn't there a better way to help our customers?" and "How can we make it faster and simpler for our customers to do business with us?"

Challenging demand is a process that will involve the entire enterprise and key supplier partners, requiring the following four key steps that we will describe in detail later in this chapter:

1. Get a grip on the reasons your customers need to contact you today.
2. Establish a closed-loop system to challenge demand.
3. Work out what you can eliminate, automate, simplify or improve, and leverage.
4. Teach the contact channels to eliminate repeats by "melting snowballs."

Every company must attend to the customer issues when they arise at the "moment of truth," as SAS Airways CEO Jan Carlson first described it, but, as we will show, challenging customer demand in the first place, instead of coping with it, produces even more powerful benefits, including the following:

- Improved customer satisfaction; customers will know a lot more about your operations and processes, help themselves when they need automated support, and feel better about spending more with you (loyalty, at its core)

- Happier customer support staff; agents will no longer have to handle dumb contacts, but instead focus on more complex and challenging issues
- Greater collaboration across the enterprise and with key supplier partners
- Reduced customer service costs, on the order of 20 percent per year measured on a CPX basis (contacts per driver X, such as orders, transactions, or claims processed)
- Slowing, if not reversing, offshoring customer service because demand has ebbed (we see pros and cons to taking customer support operations offshore, but that's the subject of another book that we could write)

EXAMPLES OUTSIDE CUSTOMER SERVICE

Let's first examine situations where challenging demand has worked outside the realm of customer service. Challenging customer demand builds on core principles in Lean, preventive equipment maintenance, and disease and accident prevention—all aimed at identifying defects or risks, finding alternative solutions, and making sure that everything works well and is in synch. We will briefly describe five examples: Lean and the Toyota Production System, preventive equipment maintenance, hardware manufacturing, health care, and driving safety.

TOYOTA, LEAN, AND DEMING

During the 1950s and 1960s, Japanese manufacturers closely studied the writings of American statisticians Edward Deming and J. M. Juran, which emphasized eliminating defects in order to produce consistently higher-quality products, combining this with Kaoru Ishikawa's Quality Circles' quality improvement teams and other collaborative improvement programs. By the 1970s and early 1980s, the Deming Prize became one of the most highly sought awards in Japanese industry, reflecting the country's amazing rise to become an economic power. Later, ironically, Japan also exported to the United States these quality-as-process concepts, influencing the Malcolm Baldrige award (also for quality performance), J.D. Power and other quality indexes, and many of the elements in today's Six Sigma initiatives (for example, using the now famous Ishikawa "fishbone" technique to break down processes) and in Lean.

Toyota was one of the early winners of the Deming Prize, and its assembly-line operations provide an excellent insight into what has made the company the most profitable and largest vehicle manufacturer, and also helps describe how the Best Service Is No Service.

Toyota's final assembly plant in Toyoda City, outside Nagoya, connected each supplier with covered conveyor belts radiating from the plant as far as two kilometers. Inside the plant, each worker had three buttons next to his station—green, yellow, or red. If the worker noticed something wrong and wanted to take a closer look, he simply pressed the yellow button, and the entire assembly line slowed 50 percent, all the way back to each of the feeder suppliers' facilities; if the worker spotted a serious problem, he pressed the red button and the entire line stopped. When this happened, bells sounded, and an overhead light board (called *andon*) started flashing to indicate which station was experiencing the problem. The worker's colleagues and managers flocked to his station to help figure out what was wrong and how to fix the problem then and there, preventing the cars from proceeding down the assembly line or, worse, ending up being sold with defects. No recriminations, no finger-pointing—only team spirit to support the worker to fix the problems.

Toyota then created its now famous Toyota Production System (TPS) to ensure that lessons learned on the floor could be built into the design and production process to reduce defects before they left the factories, and continues to engage its workers to ferret out defects before they affect consumers. General Electric (GE), Motorola, and many other global companies have applied Six Sigma, an adaptation of these ideas, to eliminate variations and defects as well; Lean is probably the process most applicable to customer service.

The implications for Best Service are clear: if everything works perfectly, then customers don't have to complain or seek help. Employee and vendor-supplier engagement are critical for building in quality, eliminating defects, and delighting customers. Toyota defined this way of thinking with the phrase "Next process is customer." By this it meant treating all the downstream manufacturing processes as if they were the final customer, all the while emphasizing that the final customer deserves and demands perfection. The idea of challenging demand applies the same philosophy, asking all those outside customer service to understand their impact on the customer.

Preventive Equipment Maintenance

For many years, the U.S. Navy has enjoyed huge success with its preventive maintenance program system (PMP). PMP includes detailed attention to equipment maintenance, testing, and corrective actions so that the machinery never breaks down. With the Navy's ships patrolling off war-torn countries or "showing the flag" in South American goodwill cruises, it's often not possible to "cope with failures" (or, in our customer service parlance, cope with demand); rather, it is imperative to ensure that everything works perfectly (or, to challenge demand) while still in port, before the equipment is put to the test.

Among the advantages of preventive equipment maintenance is that it is "cost effective in many capital intensive processes and equipment" and that it "reduces equipment and/or process failures."[2]

There are other preventive maintenance examples that are closer to everyday life, also challenging demand for future service. One of the most popular TV ads in the United States in the 1970s and 1980s was for Fram oil filters. The grease monkey in the ad stands in front of a late-model car and says, "I just finished doin' a ring job on this car, and it cost 'em $1,000. But if they had only put in a new Fram [holding it in his hand] that woulda cost only five bucks, he wouldn't have needed the work. It's simple: you can pay me now [the Fram oil filter] or pay me later [the ring job]." Again, challenging demand is much cheaper and more effective than coping with demand.

Hardware Manufacturing

Hardware manufacturers provide excellent examples of how to challenge demand instead of coping with it later. Dick Hunter, former vice president of Dell's Americas manufacturing operations and, later, SVP of customer experience responsible for Dell consumer products support, has been passionate about eliminating defects in the Dell supply chain and throughout the company's customer care processes. According to Hunter, "In order to build any configuration at any time for any customer and do it quickly, we operate with a "lot size of one" mentality and couple that with Lean manufacturing techniques to eliminate waste in the process."[3] Further, he states that "I view our supply-chain efficiencies as one component of a perpetual success engine—it allows us to pass savings on to our customers which drives demand and market share and subsequently helps our suppliers drive their business. Rarely has such a seemingly disparate connection become so crystal clear." Dell's huge real-time manufacturing process isn't perfect, but the company has demonstrated rapid assessment of the underlying problems and corrective actions for long-term improvements, the essence of challenging demand at the root cause.

Another company deeply committed to eliminating defects early is U.S.-based Danaher, a $25 billion market cap company in mid-2007, whose Fluke Networks Division is located in Everett, Washington. Fluke Networks' director of sales operations, Harvey Trager, confirms how detecting hardware manufacturing defects early is much smarter, citing the basic tenets of the company's Danaher Business System (DBS) program. He says that a $0.10 resistor can cost ten times that amount to fix each step down the line from manufacturing to customer usage—not including incalculable ramifications if customers' equipment relying on that resistor malfunctions. Danaher infuses DBS into all its subsidiary operations, ensuring that quality is built into each process, significantly reducing downstream support costs and increasing customer satisfaction (just like "Pay me now or pay me later").

Health Care

We don't need to look very far to find numerous examples in personal health care (and animal health care) where attacking the causes of illness or injury is far cheaper than "handling" the situation later, and where treating symptoms today prevents the disease from spreading. Here is a small sampling:

- Applying UVA and UVB protection (sunscreens, protective clothing) to prevent skin cancer, avoid surgery, and save lives

- Reducing "bad" cholesterol (better diet, more exercise) to prevent heart attacks, avoid implanting stents or surgery, and also save lives
- Following occupational health and safety standards (time off, heavy lifting rules) to prevent injury and reduce downtime

There's still a lot of room for improvement. Susan Drink, coauthor of *A Change of Heart,* which described a seminal study that taught consumers and doctors about the risk factors that cause heart disease, more recently has shown that the United States has lagged behind most of the industrialized countries in preventing disease, focusing instead on dealing with the consequences. Noting certain pluses in the U.S. health care system in "Care in Need of a Cure," she says, "For starters, the American system doesn't measure up worldwide in controlling chronic diseases, such as diabetes or hypertension. Payment systems reward doctors for doing procedures, not for managing those chronic conditions."[4] We will come back to the pernicious effects of the wrong metrics and the wrong incentives as part of our discussion of the roadblocks to challenging customer demand.

DRIVING SAFETY

Our last example outside customer service is also related to safety: preventive programs in driving. The Victorian (Australia State) road and safety authority has invested millions of dollars for consumer education to reduce accidents by raising awareness in such famous campaigns as "If You Drink and Drive You're a Bloody Idiot" (featuring shock ads with horrific accident scenes) and "Wipe Off 5," showing the difference in stopping distance for each extra five kilometers per hour over the speed limit. Over the past ten years, the results have been dramatic: accidents and fatalities from accidents have been cut in half thanks to targeting four major strategic components: evaluation and research, engineering, education, and enforcement.[5] Similar results are found all over the industrialized world, reinforcing the benefits of prevention instead of cure.

Another driving and safety example in Japan clearly supports challenging instead of coping with demand. The speed limit for trucks is fifty miles per hour, and there is a federally mandated light box above the truck cab directly connected to the speedometer, which shows one of three colored lights: green if comfortably under the limit, yellow if just below, and red if exceeding the top limit. Truck drivers cannot tinker with the light box without incurring significant fines, and the system provides an easy warning for oncoming drivers (as well as the vigilant Japanese police).

BAD CASES

Now that we've spent some time looking at examples outside customer service that demonstrate that challenging demand is far better than coping with demand, it is time to examine this critical aspect of Best Service. We will first discuss "bad cases" in customer service, followed by "good cases" and our model for how companies can challenge demand.

The bad cases fall into one or more of the following buckets, which we've dubbed speed merchants, asleep at the wheel, carpetbaggers, department warriors, and bill maniacs.

SPEED MERCHANTS

Unfortunately, because it is so easy to measure and report contact center and branch operations speed of service, most customer service operations are led and driven by their executives as speed merchants. This has been reinforced by many so-called benchmarking studies that equated speed with quality. The typical speed standard relates to the speed of call answering (known as grade of service), supported by measurement of average handle time (AHT) and its flip side, contacts handled per hour (CPH); but both AHT and CPH are wrong, often dead wrong, in the pursuit of Best Service.

Some years ago, a U.S. computer manufacturer's VP of support complained to his team that AHT was trending up, over fourteen minutes on average for each call, so service levels (abandonment rates) were rising. He told his team that by his back-of-the-envelope calculations, if the agents on average hit twelve minutes AHT, they could restore service levels and, so the theory goes, increase customer satisfaction. His team shared this new target with the agents, and within a few weeks a miracle happened! The new AHT fell just below twelve minutes per call. Amazing . . . high fives all around, right? Wrong. Sensing (correctly) that their VP was going to punish agents with AHTs above twelve minutes, the customer support agents started to watch their case clocks closely, and if it looked as if the call would have to take longer than twelve minutes, they either (1) accelerated their solution, not listening to the customers' issues but applying whatever would get them off the phone; (2) simply said, "I'll have to do some research and call you back"; or, worst of all, (3) tell customers, "Well, go ahead and try *xyz* and call us back if you need any more help." Not magic, really, and not good for the customers, either. The agents knew that outbound calls to customers (alternative 2) didn't log against the original inbound call, so their "numbers" wouldn't be affected; all three alternatives achieved the VP's stated target of twelve minutes or less, but customers rebelled, satisfaction levels dropped, service levels got worse instead of better, and that VP was soon fired. Speed merchants usually crash and burn.

ASLEEP AT THE WHEEL

Other cases simply make you want to scratch your head and ask, "What were they thinking?" Unfortunately for the guilty, but fortunately for the rest of us, customers today can post their frustrations on blogs, and do they ever rant and provide great details. Here's a clear example of one U.S. mobile services provider asleep at the wheel, changing previous practices and ignoring the plight of customers:

> It all started this past Friday Night. I am finishing a call, and I notice that my phone's display started to fade out as I never saw it before, and the phone would just shut off. I turn it on, and make another call, and bam, it does it again. No biggie, I go to the [name withheld] store/service place in the morning to get it looked at . . . [where] I received not so very good service in the past. The service guy just appeared that everyone in [there] was on his nerves for one reason or another, and afterward wasn't even able to help me with my issue. . . . I am directed to another store 30 minutes away because they are no longer a service location . . . Whatever. . . . So I go to the other location, and the place was packed! You have to check in at the door to even see

anyone (regardless if you wanted to buy a simple product, or needed service). The place appeared as if there were enough service people in the store. However, I felt like I was at the worst Division of Motor Vehicles (DMV) of my entire life. Some employees were just talking amongst themselves, a group of 4 service people were just laughing and having a good ol' time amongst themselves when there is a line of about 8 people standing there for whatever they needed. There were a few service people assisting customers. The best is when I was asked my name and telephone number, and "So what is your Problem." Not what I thought would being appropriate "how can we help." It's the little things that make a big difference. Either way, I finally get a service consultant, who proceeded to ask for my phone number 5 different times rather than writing it down, and basically sent me away to come back 2 hours later after the tech could look at it. I was fine with that. I come back 2 hours later, went through the sign-in process again, waited another 20 minutes, and spoke with the same consultant who asked me my phone number 3 more times. Came out with my phone in pieces, and told me I will have to upgrade. Again. Whatever. He pointed me in the direction of the . . . phones. I requested information about switching between . . . and . . . for better phone options, and I was told I would have to make a separate call to [the company] to request these difficult changes and then come back and bla, bla, bla. Needless to say, I was already tired of this ordeal, so I reluctantly just went to find another [phone]. This is the best. The consultant tells me that I could pick any phone except for the 2 reasonable priced phones on display. I asked why not them, and he tells me that I would only have problems with them. So, of course I asked him, why even sell them then. No answer.[6]

Airlines often fall into this asleep at the wheel misstep, thankfully not when they're in the air. One of the larger U.S. airlines sent to its most loyal passengers an e-mail message proudly announcing a new frequent flyer benefit starting in new airports in the United States to get through security lines faster. The trouble is that the airline trumpeted the benefit in other cities as well, but one traveler had used one of those airports the week before, and the service wasn't working at all, delaying the experience instead of improving it. This manager had almost forgotten about that experience, but the promotional message reminded him, so he thought, "Gee, I'm sure that they'd like to get my feedback, so I'll just reply to their e-mail message and tell them." Simple, right? Wrong. Here's what the airline had buried in Pica font at the bottom of its e-mail message: "We cannot accept electronic replies to this e-mail address. Written inquiries may be sent to: . . ." In this day and age? Not wanting to send a letter, the traveler called the airline's reservations line, staffed by their most experienced (and expensive) agents, to complain about (1) the airport experience about which the airline's e-mail touted so many benefits, but also (2) the e-mail with the no-reply caveat. The agent was polite and said that she'd forward his comments, but when he asked her if she ever heard back from anyone after forwarding similar complaints and feedback, she paused and then said, "Well, no, our job is to send the complaints only." We'll cover the issues of accountability and listening to customers in more detail in Chapters Six and Seven.

In both of these bad cases, what could have been simple processes instead produced multiple contacts and frustrated customers. The clueless companies merely increase their workload instead of reducing it.

CARPETBAGGERS

Just like the notorious post–Civil War carpetbaggers who tried to capitalize on the misfortune of others, companies today have their own version, in this case, cross-sale-obsessed marketers erroneously trying to attach a new sale whenever the customer calls or e-mails the contact center. Often called up-selling and cross-selling, this tactic almost always upsets customers and makes the customer support agents uneasy too. A quick case illustrates this point.

Here's the idea: a customer calls for care or support; after fixing the customer's problem, the agent, following a sales script, sells something else to the unsuspecting customer. Recently, a respected online retailer decided to try this approach, instructing its agents to tell customers, "I hope that this solves your issue. Did you know that we also sell x and y? You really ought to try out these other products, and I can send you a coupon for 20 percent off your next purchase." When the agents started with "Did you know . . . ," customers either hung up in anger or told the agent,

"I don't want to hear about that." Care and support agents are not used to this kind of sales anger (their telemarketing peers are, and it's a tough job); customers usually object strongly to this carpetbaggery. Later we will make the case that companies should be using these and other energies to analyze root causes behind the care or support call—not trying to sell something else that might also be confusing or broken.

DEPARTMENT WARRIORS

Probably the most difficult set of bad cases of failing to challenge demand come about when the company's departments are not working together or, worse yet, are in fights with each other. As we've already mentioned, in very few cases does customer service "cause" the contacts that it is handling and fixing; the vast majority of the time, it is marketing or operations or IT or a partner company that caused the contact, due to a product defect or underlying confusion. Here is a quick example, with many more to come in Chapter Six. Satellite TV and digital video recording (DVR) companies are growing by leaps and bounds all over the world, and they try hard to make their services simple for customers to use. However, the average satellite TV provider gets three or four customer contacts to activate the service and make sure that it is working, and often more during the first year due to outages, error messages on the TV screen, service upgrades, or broken set-top boxes that need to be replaced. Clearly the sales, manufacturing, and marketing departments are at odds with the support department, demonstrating what we like to call the hidden costs of sales that most companies fail to recognize: the company might spend $50 to acquire a new customer or subscriber, but then spend another $100 or more to support him—instead of building easier instructions into the product or reducing defects in the set-top boxes.

BILL MANIACS

A telecommunications customer turned off his home service several years ago, but despite the fact that he no longer had the service, he continued to receive a monthly invoice for $12.50. Because he believed the bill to be in error, given that the service was terminated, he did not bother paying the bill. Next month, another arrived. Two months later, a third. Each bill arrived for $12.50 and was ignored. The customer expected the bills to stop after three months. However, over four years later, the bills continue to arrive each month and to be filed in the trash. The customer sees no need to contact the company to tell it about a problem of its own making. The bills alone have now cost the company well in excess of $50 to send and show no signs of abating.

Good Cases

Fortunately, there are a growing number of good examples of challenging demand and eliminating dumb contacts successfully in the customer service world, so let's take a close look at four of them, followed in the next section with the framework that ties them together and that other companies can use.

CPO at Amazon

Jeff Bezos, founder and CEO of Amazon, promoted Amazon as "Earth's most customer-centric company." Every Amazon manager lived by this mantra, defined as "listen to the customer but also invent for the customer." The customer pervaded all of Amazon's planning and discussions, and the company even created a new term for it, *customer XTC,* customer ecstasy.

From its early days, Amazon has obsessed over contacts per order (CPO), one of the core CPX metrics (others being contacts per unit shipped [CPU], contacts per transaction [CPT], and contacts per customer [CPC]), reckoning that more contacts per order represented mistakes that needed to be attacked and fixed and that fewer contacts per order suggested—but did not necessarily guarantee—greater levels of customer satisfaction that "everything was working." Bezos frequently reinforces this message in external communications: "First, we do continue to drive customer experience. The holiday season this year is an example. While delivering a record number of units to consumers, we also delivered our best-ever experience. Cycle time, the amount of time taken by our fulfillment centers to process an order, improved 17% compared with last year. *And our most sensitive measure of customer satisfaction, contacts per order, saw a 13% improvement*" (emphasis added).[7]

Inside the company, CPO was one of the few metrics well known to all managers and employees, so that in the quarterly "all-hands" meetings, when people heard that the CPO for the past week was x (sorry, still can't share the exact figure!), nearly everyone recognized that this was lower than previous reports and therefore a cause for celebration.

Two examples demonstrate Amazon's impressively low CPO and the company's emphasis on driving the figure even lower. In 2000, Amazon opened its Web site, distribution centers, and customer service for other online or offline retailers to take advantage of Amazon's scale and skills. Obviously every potential partner for these services was proud of the quality of its customer care and reticent to outsource its customer-facing support to another company. In one negotiating session, the potential partner's new head of customer service stopped the discussion and challenged Amazon to reveal its CPO. Amazon decided to comply, stating that the CPO was (shall we say) x for the previous holiday season (always a bellwether for online businesses). He stared, uncrossed his arms, and confessed that his company's CPO had been $10x$ during that same holiday period. That part of the negotiations ended immediately, and Amazon partnered successfully with this company.

Soon afterward Amazon's head of customer service met with his counterpart at one of the leading catalog retailers who had heard about Amazon's CPO and its downward positive trend. She asked how to define CPO, as her company tracked total contacts and not any CPX ratios. After factoring out contacts representing sales by agents (that is, she removed her company's sales orders from the numerator), her CPO was still four times that of Amazon's contact rate, on the one hand shocking her and on the other hand reinforcing that the Best Service Is No Service does indeed work.

Over the past years, Amazon has enjoyed a 90 percent reduction in its CPO, meaning that it could keep customer care costs (headcount and associated operational expenses) flat with a $9x$ increase in orders (revenues), a major contributor to the company's profitability beginning in 2002. In the following chapters, we will show how Amazon calculated its CPO, built an enterprise-wide following to find root causes and eliminate them or deflect them to highly successful online and IVR self-service, educated customers to learn how to work with Amazon, and was very proactive. Figure 2.1 shows the index of Amazon's CPO by year (1996–2006).

DELL'S CALL FACTORIES

Technology leader Dell has attacked dumb contacts on many fronts, starting with what the company measures, how it defines what to eliminate, and even how its support teams are organized. According to Dick Hunter, Dell's former SVP of customer experience for its global consumer business, Dell has been applying its hugely successful supply chain and manufacturing practices (which Hunter helped develop before moving over to the customer service side of the company), including Lean, to its customer care operations. Dell's just-in-time production system has used Lean to eliminate waste and unneeded steps that do not add value for the customer. "We are creating 'call factories' across our customer service network," says Hunter, "ensuring that they are highly disciplined, trained, and focused on executing with no variation." This means that Dell has rallied around "resolve in the first call" as one of its main metrics, arguing that any "second call" is clearly not adding any value, and providing tools

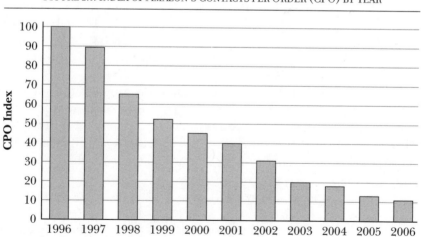

FIGURE 2.1: INDEX OF AMAZON'S CONTACTS PER ORDER (CPO) BY YEAR

(including Wiki-based knowledge sharing) and training to reward "the thirty-minute call as being far better than two twenty-minute calls," according to Hunter.

Moreover, Dell has determined that transferring the customer to experts (for example, agents with special knowledge of printers or operating systems) is not only frustrating for the customer but also costly for Dell. In response, Hunter has successfully piloted and is rolling out new cross-skilled teams that keep the customer in the same small group. Dell has enjoyed a win-win-win with this new approach: response rates are much higher, customer satisfaction (measured by asking the customer post-contact) is also much higher, and there has been a drastic reduction in agent attrition.

Hunter continues: "Our goal is two-fold: (1) prevent the call, in the future through auto diagnostics online, for example, and (2) improve all of our processes so that we only 'handle' with our agents the true value-added. To achieve this goal we have been mapping all of our processes from the customer's point of view, isolating two bad things in particular: (1) when we cannot effectively resolve the problem and (2) when we don't know what caused the problem." This is where Dell's Lean programs have spotlighted issues to address and fix, and customers are responding very positively.

Dell has always been "close to the customer" with the high percentage of its sales online, the rest with telesales agents, but Hunter has elevated this practice. "Instead of doing a bazillion surveys, we simply listen to the verbatim comments from the [post-contact] c-sat surveys," he says, "and this has led staff and program changes that otherwise we wouldn't have captured by other methods." This obsession over the customer can also be seen when Hunter blasts traditional customer service metrics with "average" in their heading (average speed of answer, average handle time, and so on). "I don't look at averages," notes Hunter, "I look at the 'tails,' even if it's coming from a single customer." This is another example of the canary in the coal mine, providing keen insights to achieve Best Service.

Dell has one challenge left in its "call factories" approach to eliminating dumb contacts: as is true with almost every other company, its customer and technical support partners need to fall in line with Lean, eliminating waste and only adding value for the customer. "Our OSPs [outsourcing service providers] are getting the message now!" states Hunter.

PROCESS MAPPING

CheckFree's customers rely on the company, the largest online billing transaction processor in the United States, for fast, accurate payments, so its customer service is also a critical part of the company's success. Soon after he took over customer service and other operating units, Jardon Bouska, now EVP and general manager of the electronic biller services division, realized that he needed to shake up the entire process to exceed demanding customer expectations. Bouska created an overarching program he called Right Care, whose first mission was "contact elimination" for unneeded customer interactions.

As Bouska puts it, "Right Care was all about process mapping—we had to figure out why customers were calling us, how we handled those contacts, and what alternatives were available to us, including totally eliminating the need." The results are clear: from 2002 through 2006, CheckFree's transactions increased by a factor of five and revenues by 250 percent, yet Bouska's customer service team shrank by 21 percent *and* customer satisfaction increased by 20 percent.

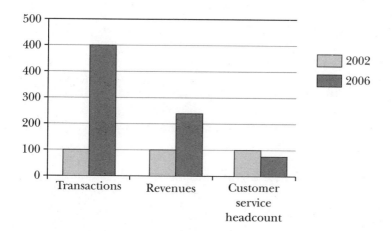

How did CheckFree accomplish this Best Service transformation?

First off, the company focused intensively on "fixing process first, then technology." One obvious area was to reduce repeat contacts, which went from 15 percent to under 1 percent once the company interpreted the underlying reasons for repeat contacts as (1) "We weren't fast enough" and (2) "We didn't do a good enough job the first time around."

Next, CheckFree moved to self-service a limited range of contact types that could achieve much higher success rates. Then, using the process mapping, CheckFree cut drastically the number of different areas and touch points that needed to research customer inquiries, in some cases from an average of 7 to only 1.1, partly by increasing the skills and permissions for agents, partly by working tightly with other departments, such as accounts payable (AP). Bouska notes that the real accelerator for these big changes was that "we charged back the costs of our operations to the product managers who helped us work with AP and other groups who were responsible for the contacts in the first place."

Last, as one of the key feedback devices, CheckFree implemented SHOUT (similar to WOCAS—see Chapter Seven): one person per contact center is assigned to collect from agents what needed to be fixed, address those changes with IT and other departments, and (this is critical) give feedback to the originator about what happened. All in all, from process mapping to ownership to SHOUT, CheckFree has exemplified how to eliminate dumb contacts while increasing customer satisfaction and reducing operating costs, another win-win-win.

DYSON U.K. RELIABILITY

Dyson, one of the leading vacuum cleaner manufacturers in the United Kingdom, demonstrates the value of tackling contacts at the root cause. In March 2006, the company issued the following press release:

> West vacuum cleaner firm Dyson announced another 42 job losses yesterday—because its products are getting so much better. The staff will mainly be lost in its call centre in Malmesbury, Wiltshire,

and the company says the main reason is that, despite rising sales, fewer people are calling in with problems with their vacuum cleaners and washing machines.

Other jobs included in the 42 announced yesterday will be lost from a team dispatching spare parts to customers. Dyson's last big product launch was the upright DC15 cleaner, which had a revolutionary ball design. That vacuum, along with advances in other products in the range, meant call centre staff were increasingly getting fewer calls from customers.

"This is due to increased reliability of our machines and excellent first time fix rate," said a spokesman. "The design of Dyson machines is becoming ever more durable and intuitive too. Our most popular machine has a reliability rating of 98 per cent. Such factors mean we simply have a lower volume of calls to our customer care line and as a consequence, we're looking to resize the customer care team."

This is a classic case of a company improving its products and services and reducing the need for service in the process. Dyson felt a need to "defend" its actions from press comment when in reality it demonstrated Best Service practices.

THE FRAMEWORK

How does a company begin to challenge demand? Earlier we introduced these four steps:

1. Get a grip on the reasons your customers need to contact you today.
2. Establish a closed-loop system to challenge demand.
3. Work out what you can eliminate, automate, simplify or improve, and leverage.
4. Teach the contact channels to eliminate repeats by "melting snowballs."

Now it's time to review each of these key steps in "challenging demand" in greater detail.

STEP ONE: GET A GRIP ON THE REASONS YOUR CUSTOMERS NEED TO CONTACT YOU TODAY

The first step is to understand "at a glance" the reasons your customers are taking time to call, send an e-mail, open a chat session, write a letter, or complain or comment in person. In this section we will describe why companies have struggled to understand reasons for contacts, and we'll also explain how to get the detail right and determine who is responsible in the company.

Drop-Down Frenzy

Over the past twenty years, the customer support industry has tried to produce ways to tackle customer contact reasons, including using customer relationship management (CRM) software. Unfortunately, the promise of CRM software has led companies down the wrong path, building complicated drop-down menus with such confusing terms as "disposition" and "driver," which tax the customer service agent to decide among a dizzying list of choices. The largest number of choices that we've seen is 2,148, and at the end of an often stressful phone call or research-filled e-mail response, the agent has to wade through hundreds and hundreds of options in one or two minutes, also collating "notes" that accompany the case in the CRM system. Accuracy suffers, yet analysts tend to pore over these data as valuable insights into customer behavior; and productivity suffers, further backing up customers on hold.

Why, Not What

Furthermore, most if not all of today's CRM reason code systems describe *what* the customer contacted the company to learn or complain about and not *why* she needed to call in the first place. For example, collecting ticks for "shipping issues" misses the boat completely; it would make much more sense to record "late by shipper" versus "warehouse delays," both easily discerned by the agent during the call, and more useful for the head of operations and fulfillment to begin to understand what's happening to frustrate customers. In addition, almost all CRM reason code systems offer "other" or "general," which almost always lead the pack for number one reason, yet provide no help at all in understanding why customers are contacting the company or what to do about it. As a result, companies lack data to make critical analysis and trade-off decisions, resorting to hunches to try to fix problems or start new initiatives.

No Reasons or Big Buckets

Whereas some companies have too many contact reasons or simply the wrong ones, others have too few, and many have none. We have worked in many companies that do not track or report on major contact drivers. They may know how many transactions are processed on their systems, but that isn't the same thing. It misses the inquiries, issues, and problems that do not produce transactions. Other companies simplify the problem to big-bucket reasons, such as billing, payments, credit, claims, and shipping. Those big buckets provide almost no insight at all. If the number of payment contacts goes up, are those good payment contacts or unnecessary ones? Capturing data at that level is an overhead, not a help.

Instead, to get a grip on the reasons customers contact them, companies need to follow the old McKinsey & Company maxim of MECE: explanations must be *mutually exclusive* and *collectively exhaustive*. Specifically, this means that each contact code can have one and only one "owner" whose department or group "caused" the contact in the first place (we will expand this in Chapter Six). For example:

- For reasons such as "Product missing in stock yet ordered anyway," the owner could be supply chain or procurement (one of them, not both, as we will soon cover).
- For reasons such as "Wrong balance," the owner is probably IT.
- For reasons such as "Do you have . . . ?" the owner could be Web design or marketing, whichever group is responsible for not making it clear what the company has to offer.

One of the easiest ways to challenge demand instead of coping with it is to take a "zero-based" approach to each and every contact, throwing out the old "what" metrics and creating new "why" reasons that explain simply, at a glance, the high-level explanations that can then be analyzed in greater detail using classic

Six Sigma, Lean, or other analytical techniques. Usually a cross-functional task force can develop the new reason codes to describe each customer-initiated contact type. We have found best practice to be between twenty and thirty codes, easy to remember yet distinct (MECE), each in the customer's language (not company-speak), such as "Where's my stuff?" "Lost password," "Runs slow," or "Missing statement."

Amazon once had 360 customer contact codes, 300 for e-mail contacts and 60 for phone calls, some created at the behest of a "store" marketing manager, IT, or the legal department. The company frequently added or removed codes, requiring ongoing training for the agents and even a metric to track "code use compliance." Few of these early codes attached to an owner, and the company fell into the trap of presenting weekly the "top ten"

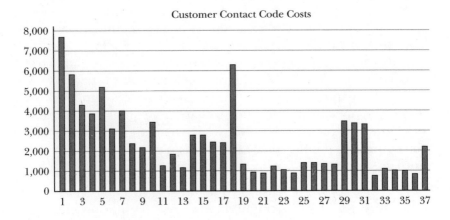

Customer Contact Code Costs

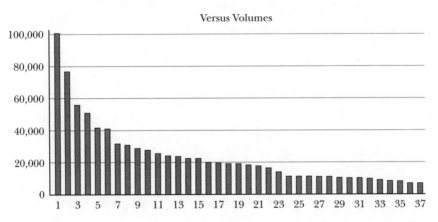

Versus Volumes

codes, which rarely moved up or down one position and which, by design, ignored the 350 reasons looming in the darkness below the top ten. The company decided to reengineer the contact coding system, led by a former tissue factory process manager, resulting in thirty codes that could be entered directly into the CRM system, each with an owner in the MECE tradition, codes that would never change . . . and they haven't, after all these years.

Next, companies need to apply activity-based costing to assign operating costs to each of the streamlined "why" reason codes. For example, whereas some contact codes might have a lot of calls that each average two or three minutes, others that last twenty or forty minutes reveal more fundamental costs that need to be examined and, one hopes, eliminated. In the example here, the bottom graph shows a declining number of contacts representing the company's top thirty-seven codes, but the top shows each code activity-costed, based on the time each takes to handle. Clearly, this company needs to focus on reasons 18 and 29–31, as they take so much time to resolve or answer in relation to the codes near them; 18 is almost as costly to handle as 1, in fact the second-highest code.

STEP TWO: ESTABLISH A CLOSED-LOOP SYSTEM TO CHALLENGE DEMAND

The second step is to create a process to connect the enterprise, and outside suppliers as needed, with the customer service department to challenge demand at its root and sustain the improvements over time. As with many closed-loop systems, you need the following five connected parts: clear reporting, designated owners, targets, exchanges, and rewards and consequences. Let's take a deeper look at each one of these parts required to establish the closed-loop system.

Clear Reporting

Many companies, if they track anything, report customer reasons or contact codes via a monthly or weekly top ten, separately showing phone calls, e-mails handled, and other channels supported. It is therefore very hard for executives to spot trends, compare with top-line revenue or units shipped, and see, at a glance, contacts across all channels. We have experimented with many different reporting devices, but come back to the Amazon model to accompany the new slimmed-down thirty codes and activity-based costing, called Skyline. Skyline clearly presents all the codes (thirty will take two pages) in a CPX format, combining all customer contact channels and showing the past six weeks so that recent trends are clear (four weeks at a glance are not enough to show monthly period effects from billing cycles, for example).

Designated Owners

We have found that on average, 10 percent of customer contacts are "caused" by customer service (examples being wrong answers generating repeat contacts, which we will cover later in step four, and cases when customer service invites callbacks). Who causes the vast majority of customer contacts? It is all the other departments whose process or output touches the customer. It is these other departments who need to become owners of the contact reasons. We recommend that when you are creating the new coding system, you ensure that only one owner is associated with each code, and here's why: that owner needs to roll up his or her sleeves with customer service to determine the root cause, lay out possible remedies, and invest in the most cost-effective improvements to reduce CPX. Ideally the code owner reports to the CEO and is therefore senior enough to direct his or her departments to figure out what is needed in their groups to fix the problem or clear up the confusion that led to the contacts. We should warn you now that many of those who need to be responsible will not want to assume that ownership; we will explore this in detail in Chapter 6.

Targets

The overarching metric when challenging demand is CPX, the contact rate index. By the same token, as noted earlier, each of the reduced set of contact codes needs to be expressed in terms of CPX, as the driver X might vary across codes—for example, transactions or units shipped, accounts, or subscribers. You need to find the X that best represents the volume of activity in the business with which contacts are associated. For example, in a company with one account per customer, contacts per customer may be effective. However, in a company where the number of accounts or orders or products is growing at a different rate than the customer base, then transactions may make a better denominator in the CPX calculation.

At this point it is essential that the company creates realistic and stretch targets to reduce CPX for unwanted codes and to increase CPX for those reasons that it wants. (See the discussion on the Value-Irritant Matrix in the next step.) It is entirely realistic to set 20 percent per year reductions in unwanted CPX. However, there is one immutable fact in this pursuit of Best Service, and it is just as important as targeting different levels of CPX by code—namely, over time, companies will "enjoy" longer AHTs per contact once shorter, simpler contacts are eliminated (this chapter), move to self-service (Chapter Three), or can be avoided thanks to proactive messaging (Chapter Four). Customer service resource planners often miss this important linkage, projecting the same average handle times (or faster, if they fall into the speed merchant trap described earlier), which simply creates higher levels of agent burnout and mistakes, worse service levels, and dissatisfied customers.

Almost every company pressures its agents to handle contacts faster (more contacts per hour, CPH, or shorter handle time, AHT), yet as the contacts get longer, these ancient rules must bend, or else one or more of the following will occur: (1) agents will simply transfer callers or forward e-mail to get it off of their metrics; (2) agents will tell customers that they will call them back, which often doesn't register in their call statistics yet creates an endless round of calls and messages, not resolution; (3) agents will offer a random answer so as to move on to the next caller; and (4) agents will simply hang up on the customer. None of these is maliciously performed; they are simply the result of too much pressure to "hit the numbers." Instead, customer service needs to relax call handle times *at each moment of truth,* continuing to use overall AHT to create work schedules and staffing plans, but implementing what we call *dynamic individual handle time* (DIHT) for each specific interaction. DIHT, in short, means that for each contact, in real time, companies must match the customer's importance and issue with the agent's skill and experience. Instead of tracking an average handle time for all customers and agents, companies need to think about appropriate measures for that type of contact, for that type of customer when handled by an agent with a certain level of experience. The intersection of those three valuables tells a company what an appropriate handle time might be. We will describe briefly in Chapter Eight how hard that is to do.

Exchanges

Now that we have clear reporting (such as Skyline) showing activity-based costing, designated owners (MECE, one per code), and targets (lower CPX for unwanted contacts, higher CPX for wanted ones, DIHT to deal with appropriate handle times), we need to create the best forums in which the entire enterprise can track results, share progress, and plan new solutions to challenge customer demand. In our experience, most companies barely cover customer experience or customer contact reasons in their monthly executive meetings; instead, companies spend huge amounts of time on the "front end" (attracting customers and selling more to them) or on the "engine" (operations or man- ufacturing). Perhaps one of the reasons that companies don't focus on customer issues is that the top ten reasons don't change or that they think they somehow "know" what's going on.

We beg to differ, and see it as Best Service practice to hold weekly operations meetings, led (as at Amazon) by the head of marketing, running through the classic speed metrics but spend- ing most of the customer service time on CPX reports. Owners of each code need to explain why their codes went up (bad news) or down (good news) each week; it's equally important to explain improvements to ensure that corrective actions are taking hold and can confidently be projected over time. Amazon held these meetings every Friday, but later the company advanced them much earlier in the week to get the fastest possible read on cus- tomer contact issues. In between meetings, the owners and their analysts would meet with customer service teams to listen to calls, review e-mail threads, compare notes to isolate root causes, and pilot possible solutions—all fodder for discussion in the weekly meetings. Maybe Amazon was lucky—the company held "Holiday War Room" meetings twice a day during the period between mid-November through Christmas, checking sales order status, Web site performance, shipping situations, customer service lev- els, and related critical matters; it was therefore a simple idea to keep the attention going after each holiday season with intensive weekly sessions.

Rewards and Consequences

We have saved the secret sauce of this closed-loop system for last: ensuring that the company creates consistent rewards and consequences in the pursuit of Best Service. Here we mean thinking outside the box to create and consistently apply appropriate rewards and penalties within the company and with key suppliers whose actions might be causing unwanted customer contacts. Some of these ideas include the following:

- Charge the owners the full operating cost for the customer contact codes that they "cause," including third-party organizations that are found to be at the root of the problem, such as the reluctant shipper or component supplier with faulty products. We have found that this final step brings most of the dividends—when owners get hit in the pocket, they pay more attention to the customer issues and help challenge demand.
- Arrange for the contact owners to present in all-hands and other company-wide meetings, as they do in the weekly operations meetings, why their codes have improved or worsened and what they are doing to improve on behalf of the customer and the company. (In other words, do not leave it to the head of customer service to carry this water.)
- Recognize "best agents" whose balanced performance is key to overall success (see brief discussion in Chapter Eight).
- Report "snowballs," introduced later in this chapter, noting which group is causing more repeat customer contacts and which group is "melting" more repeat contacts.
- Celebrate quick wins and sustained progress in internal memos and in external communications, including annual reports and the blogosphere.

Step Three: Work Out What You Can Eliminate, Automate, Simplify or Improve, and Leverage

With the foundation now set to challenge demand and move away from coping with customer demand for support, we can address how to determine the appropriate actions for each contact type. That means working out what to eliminate, migrate to self-service and other forms of automated support or to pro-active alerts, simplify or streamline, and leverage or exploit for lasting benefits. This is still an art and not a science, and reasonable managers disagree often about how important different customer contacts are. Having that debate is an important part of this process. For example, as noted earlier regarding carpet-baggers, most customer service professionals cringe when they hear their sales or marketing and product groups exhort them to cross-sell or up-sell each time a customer contacts them; they know that many contacts are complaints and need to be handled delicately, and are not good ones on which to "attach" new sales. This is not to say that inbound telesales or service can't pursue additional sales opportunities—it's just that the company needs to find the "best fit" across the four interlinked components: (1) the customer's temperament, (2) the offer, (3) the agent's skills, and (4) the original customer contact code. In fact, we can flip CPX to XPC, meaning "How can we increase sales per contact?" or increase sales conversion rates (the percentage of contacts on which sales are made), one of the hottest issues facing any sales or reservations operation. It turns out that many contacts arriving at sales centers have nothing to do with sales, so exhorting sales reps to "sell more" might not even be possible or advisable.

To work out the best disposition for each customer contact code, companies should follow these four actions:

1. Pull together a cross-functional team made up of the right people to debate the value to the company and customer of each contact type. This may involve product owners, channel owners, process owners, customer service, finance, and other company departments, but might also need to include other companies that provide components or carry the products to the customers (for example, the supply chain).

2. Debate with a simple yes-no to each question per code whether it is valuable to the company or an irritant and whether it is, at the same time, valuable to the customer or an irritant to the customer. We recommend avoiding a 1–7 Likert scale that could produce fence-sitters that score 4, or midway between

valuable and irritating; instead, force the debate around value-irritant only.

3. Add the activity-based costing covered earlier to assess the cost per code. (This might not be readily available, as few CRM systems routinely capture and report AHT per reason code, and agent costing is usually housed in yet another data repository; if so, we recommend estimating handle time and costs as high, medium, or low or skipping this step and editing the results later.)

4. Read from a plotted two-by-two matrix that we call the Value-Irritant Matrix (an example of which is shown in Figure 2.2) one of the four actions to take.

By using this Value-Irritant approach, companies can create a clear road map to challenge demand and to identify specific directions. The following are some examples of solutions that have been found once the contact reason was rated.

FIGURE 2.2: VALUE-IRRITANT MATRIX (EXAMPLE)

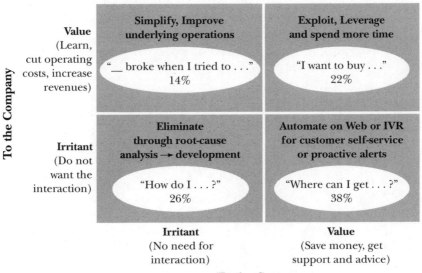

- For "Where's my stuff?" when the outbound shipper has missed deadlines for on-time delivery, rated an irritant for both the customer and the company (action: eliminate), the solution is to analyze why the outbound carrier isn't fulfilling its commitment, and work together to ensure 100 percent success; there should be zero tolerance for anything landing in the Irritant-Irritant quadrant.
- For "missing statement" when the company didn't include a printed statement with the invoice, rated as valuable for the customer but an irritant for the company (action: automate), the solution was to provide accounts and statements online for customers to view and print for their records, with the added benefit to the company of reducing expenses associated with mailings.
- For "customer praise" when the company does something noteworthy, valuable for the customer (or else he wouldn't have taken the time) and valuable for the company (it can figure out how to "wow" more customers) (action: exploit or leverage), the best approach is to dig into each positive feedback message or call and, if needed, go back to engage the customers for more details.
- For "employee ignored me," valuable information for the company but clearly an irritant to the customer (action: simplify or improve), the solution is to create new training programs, monitoring, and perhaps mystery shopping to turn around this deleterious behavior.

Figure 2.2 shows the composite percentages in each of the four quadrants of the Value-Irritant Matrix from customers with whom we have implemented contact optimization programs; only 22 percent of the total contacts are deemed valuable to the company and to the customer, so 78 percent of the contacts should be automated or eliminated, with the remainder changed after simplifying and improving the underlying operations.

It is important to recognize that a first-cut classification is just that, a first cut. You will need to dig deeper and look at the root causes that have led to contact rates, particularly for all the irritating contacts. When you start digging for those root causes, don't be surprised if you find multiple causes, some of which sit in different quadrants. In one company, for example, we found that what appeared to be a contact that could be automated turned out to have some root causes that could be eliminated and some where automation was the right answer. Getting the owners of contacts to think through the root causes helps them identify what the possible solutions might be and who are the true owners.

STEP FOUR: TEACH THE CONTACT CHANNELS TO ELIMINATE REPEATS BY "MELTING SNOWBALLS"

The buzzword in customer service and, in particular, in technical support is "first contact resolution" (FCR) or its twin, "one and done." These expressions just mean that the customer got what he needed in one contact with the company. First point resolution (FPR) takes this further by measuring whether the first person could resolve the issue without transferring the customer to another specialist. All these ratings are admirable but flawed in at least three respects: (1) they are very hard to measure accurately from the customer's point of view; (2) they can easily be "gamed" by pressured agents (see again the earlier section on targets) who report resolution when it has not occurred; and (3) they avoid focusing on or analyzing their complement: the percentage of calls or contacts that are repeats. We think the repeat rate is a much better measure of resolution, as it identifies the lack of resolution, or failure, and the consequences.

High FCR rates also produce a false sense of security. Even if you achieve 92 percent FCR, by most surveys a high rate, this still means an 8 percent error rate, which for a two-hundred-person contact center means that more than nineteen thousand contacts a month are repeats! This is far from the "4 9's" accuracy that companies who have adopted Six Sigma are now striving to achieve in their manufacturing and other departments. Again taking a page out of the Lean manuals—that is, viewing most customer contacts as defects in the company's products and services and operations—there is a lot more to be gained by looking at the repeats, so we're going to use a simple analogy, familiar to almost everyone: snowballs.

When a snowball rolls downhill, it gathers speed and gets bigger and bigger, such that if you're at the bottom and can't avoid it, you'll be crushed (or at least very wet and covered in white fluffy powder!). The objective is to help each agent do whatever it takes when he or she gets a repeat contact to prevent it from rolling farther downhill or, to extend the metaphor, to melt the snowball. Amazon's snowball results were impressive: repeat contacts were reduced by over 80 percent in four years, such that they represented a negligible percentage of customer contacts; happier agents not having to deal with upset customers; happier customers because the company did not need to speak with them again or get another e-mail from them (on that issue at least).

Let's describe snowballs, snowball ratios, and the total cost savings that can be achieved. Whenever the second (or third or even fourth) agent encounters the same issue coming back at the company, whether because the earlier agent didn't take enough time to diagnose the underlying causes or because he simply made a mistake, that new agent needs to take as much time as needed to melt the snowball so that it doesn't continue to roll downhill. This means that the CRM system needs to have a flag or marker to indicate "snowball" so that the new agent's metrics are adjusted. After the new agent believes that she has solved the problem, she needs to send a "snowballs report" to the earlier agents' supervisors and to training and quality in order that the underlying reason for the snowball can be analyzed and the earlier agents counseled immediately so that they no longer provide the wrong answers to customers.

The company can then quite easily construct "snowball ratios" comparing agents, teams, groups of teams, centers, and enterprises (in cases where outsourcers are being used)—which ones are starting the snowballs, which ones are melting them, and which ones deserve special attention publicly, one of the rewards and consequences introduced earlier. Amazon's first outsourcing partner worked very hard to ensure that it melted more snowballs than the newest internal center, and once it achieved that plateau, it went after each of the more experienced centers one by one!

You might wonder if the payback for taking extra time to melt the snowballs is worth the effort. Rest assured, it is. The company gets a benefit merely by stopping additional contacts on the same issue (in essence proving FCR). By capturing and analyzing the data, the company can also reduce the original snowball causes, whether they are individual or more generic problems (for example, processes that are hard for staff to understand or implement). Other benefits of melting snowballs include higher levels of customer satisfaction and more positive word of mouth when issues are quickly solved.

SUMMARY

In this chapter, we introduced the first Best Service Principle: instead of simply coping with customer demand and using tired old metrics, such as more contacts per hour or shorter AHTs (which exacerbate customer service upsets for agents and customers alike), companies can benefit greatly by taking pages from the Lean approach (attack product or service defects at their root), from Amazon's proven track record, and from a growing number of organizations that are challenging customer demand.

Following this fundamentally different approach yields huge benefits:

- Happier agents who will do a better job, stick around longer, and convey their happiness to your customers
- More satisfied customers who no longer need to contact you, who get handled in the first contact thanks to your having eliminated the reasons behind the first snowball, and who have more appropriate automation options to use and simpler processes to follow
- Reduced customer support operating costs when viewed on a CPX basis (again, the cost per contact might rise, but if part of this overall "challenge demand" formula, that is a good thing)
- Greater engagement across the enterprise and with third-party suppliers in addressing and fixing problems on behalf of the customers
- The beginnings of viewing and treating customer service as a value center instead of as a cost or revenue center (unless it is equipped for telesales), and of challenging whether cross-selling and up-selling are the province of customer support or are better suited to marketing campaigns, sales forces, and Web sites geared specifically for that purpose

Survey Questions

Please score your company for these four key questions covering the idea of challenging customer demand for service, and refer to Appendix A to check your progress from Basic Service to Better Service to Best Service.

1. How many possible customer contact codes or reasons does your frontline contact center or customer service staff capture for each contact?
   a. We do not capture or track contact codes or reasons in the contact center.
   b. Fewer than twelve.
   c. Twenty to thirty or so.
   d. Hundreds or maybe thousands of possible combinations.
   e. I have no idea.

2. How do your other customer-facing employees and how does the Web site itself code customer interactions?
   a. Differently than the way we do it in our contact center.
   b. We do not collect reason codes outside the contact center.
   c. From our Web site we do capture and log which pages our customers view; they appear as "contacts" juxtaposed with agent-handled contacts.
   d. We capture Web logs, but they're buried in our data servers and are used to analyze Web page speeds.

3. What is the chief driver for your customer contacts?
   a. I don't know.
   b. Customer orders, necessary life events of the customer, critical things we need to know from customers, shipments, and other key issues.
   c. A bunch of reasons outside our control.
   d. Mistakes that the customer service department made in the first place.
   e. Customer complaints.

4. How widely do you share CPX (contacts per X, where X equals customers, accounts, orders, transactions, and so on)?
   a. We capture and know CPX, but do not share it inside the company.
   b. We do not know CPX or have never measured it.
   c. CPX is widely known across the company.
   d. We share CPX within the company and discuss CPX trends with our investors and shareholders.

CHAPTER THREE

CREATE ENGAGING SELF-SERVICE
Instead of Preventing Contact

Customer self-service is everything. What I said in the past wasn't totally right; quality, service, and fast response are important but the customer must be in the driver's seat.
—TOM PETERS, *EAI JOURNAL*

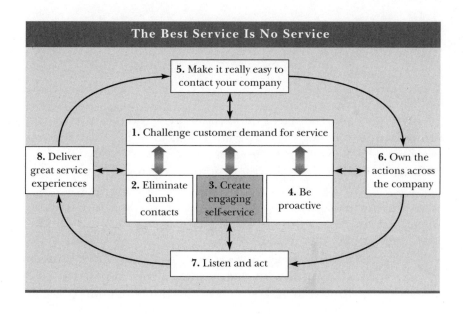

THE PRINCIPLE

Not every customer contact can be eliminated, and, as we've shown, some contacts do need the human touch. However, a significant percentage of customer requests and issues can be handled by offering customers the opportunity to find the answers themselves, whether online or using an interactive voice response (IVR) system or an interactive kiosk—together, self-service. The Best Service is self-service for these types of contacts and for many customers who would rather operate this way.

When organizations get self-service right, customers love it: they find it more convenient than waiting on hold to speak to a customer service agent (some of whom know less than the customer, but that's another story entirely); it puts them in control of their interactions with the organization; they can do it any time (not just when the company is open for business); and with Web-based self-service, they can print details for future reference.

Furthermore, as technologies have evolved, customers have come to expect and demand that organizations provide a range of channels, including self-service, through which they can interact, and they expect to be able to switch between them. Take Alaska Airlines, for example—this feisty competitor introduced kiosks at airports for busy travelers to select or change seats and print tickets, avoiding standing in lines; later, the airline introduced the capability of printing one's boarding pass at home before heading to the airport in the first place, and customers love it! Many other airlines now do the same.

Remember when you had to go inside a bank to withdraw cash from your account and, because of limited hours, couldn't do so 66 percent of the time? Now ATMs are everywhere, including movie theater lobbies, casinos, sports stadiums, and outdoor festivals, enabling customers to access their money any time they want—a solution that is more convenient and puts the customer in control.

Unfortunately, many organizations haven't figured out yet how to provide engaging self-service and have committed three "deadly sins" that undermine this critical option.

The Three Deadly Sins Preventing Against Self-Service

1. **Limited choice.** The first sin is to limit choice for the customer. Rather than giving the customer control, these companies limit the frequency and format of self-service customer interactions, forcing the customer to rebel against these constraints and go elsewhere, to other channels or other organizations. A major global airline demonstrates choice-limiting behavior. This company allows most customers to use self-service IVR to check flight details and even change bookings. But for its most valuable customers, its top-tier frequent flyers, the phone number provided goes straight to an operator, and the customer has no choice. The most valued customers get less choice than others? That doesn't seem right to us.

2. **Poor usability design.** The second sin involves design—self-service that is hard to use and ignores the basic science of

usability. Many organizations appear not to understand the processes and techniques for building phone, Web, or kiosk self-service that customers find easy to use. Often these companies are so stuck in their arcane terminology that they create self-service that customers can't figure out how to use. Examples of bad design abound. For instance, several insurance businesses make buying online hard. Rather than asking the key questions up front and validating them, they capture all the information they might possibly need, only to inform you, several screens later, that you really need to talk to someone in any case. Then once you do, the agents can't view the information you've already provided, so you have to start again. In short, the design of the online experience fails to connect all the moving parts, causing more work for the customer.

3. **Channel disintegration.** We refer to the third sin as channel disintegration, whereby the self-service and staffed channels wind up in conflict rather than collaborating, something that is all too obvious to the customer. Once you have entered your account number and other data in the IVR, why doesn't the information follow the call should you subsequently need to speak to an agent? Often the staffed channels don't promote, can't support, or in some cases actively undermine the self-service channels. In these cases, customers either don't get to hear about self-service or are supported inadequately in their attempts to use it. A major health insurer exemplified channel disintegration when its branch staff actively discouraged Internet applications because use of that channel made it harder for them to hit sales targets.

We'll describe how to overcome these three sins with the opposite strategies and show how to

- Put customers in control.
- Design effective interfaces by exploiting the science of usability.
- Integrate channels so that the customer is supported in adopting self-service.

Today, new generations of organizations are shaping their whole market offering around the self-service capabilities that they provide, thereby disrupting the industries in which they compete. Companies like U.K.'s first direct have forced traditional brick-and-mortar financial services providers to rethink their business models; other self-service specialists like eBay have created new markets by providing a shop front for small specialized retailers and importers to reach far bigger markets using the opportunities that self-service provides. Even in traditional industries like banking, self-service specialists, such as first direct in the United Kingdom and Juniper in the United States (now known as Barclays Bank Delaware), are winning the lower-cost customers with a propensity to self-serve and leaving the others in the industry with a high-maintenance, high-cost customer base. So getting self-service right isn't merely an option: it is a key strategic imperative.

EXAMPLES OUTSIDE CUSTOMER SERVICE

Self-service and automation are being used in many industries, demonstrating the convenience and choice benefits that are also possible in service interactions. We will cover diabetes self-testing, orienteering, and automatic meter reading.

DIABETES SELF-TESTING

There is now far greater understanding of the impact of diabetes on health. Once patients are diagnosed with the condition, many need to monitor their blood sugar levels. Initially this was impossible for patients to do without regular visits to a doctor or clinic, but today digital equipment is available that has made self-testing and daily monitoring feasible. Diabetes sufferers use a pinprick of blood and digital test equipment to monitor their blood sugar levels at home and can therefore assess the impact of their diet and lifestyle and treat themselves with insulin if required. They are also in a position to refer themselves to a doctor if needed and can monitor themselves several times a day. The testing equipment thus makes them independent of health specialists.

ORIENTEERING IN THE DIGITAL AGE

The sport of orienteering, invented in Scandinavia, involves navigating at speed between a series of checkpoints, typically in forest terrain. The largest events involve more than twenty thousand participants competing on a variety of courses. The difficulty for organizers is that they need to verify that competitors have visited all the checkpoints; manning them would be an arduous task and would also make the checkpoints too visible and easy to find. For many years, the sport used a system of punch cards and punches at each checkpoint. Each checkpoint punch had a pattern of small needles that left a pattern in the card. However, organizers then had to inspect each competitor's card to check that he or she had been to the right checkpoints.

The digital age has revolutionized the sport. Competitors now run holding a small digital memory stick. At each checkpoint, they insert the stick into a timing device that stores the time and location on the data stick. At the end of the course, details from the stick are downloaded and can be verified by the associated software. Organizers no longer have to check punched cards; the software takes care of everything. Competitors also win, as punching at each control is faster, and at the finish they are almost instantly provided with a printout of their course time and split times to each checkpoint. The new technology also enables organizers to set more complex courses and reuse checkpoints multiple times on multiple courses. Automation has enabled radical changes and simplification for competitors and organizers of the sport.

AUTOMATIC METER READING

For many years in many countries, gas and electricity use has been measured using meters, and the meters need to be read. The streets of the developed world are being pounded by readers of meters for water, gas, and electricity. But automation is changing the picture. First the meter readers themselves were equipped with handheld devices that saved paperwork and enabled rapid download of readings to centralized computers systems. Today, thanks to satellite and mobile phone technology, automation has gone a step further: automated meters are now being installed in many countries across the Americas, Europe, Japan, and Australia that never need to be "read" in person. These meters "read themselves" and send their readings to central computers, avoiding the expense and street-pounding or customers having to learn how to read their own utility meter.

BAD CASES

General neglect and misunderstanding of self-service manifest in many different ways. To make it easy to spot which manifestation you have encountered or most closely matches your business, we have given them these names to help you: the restrictors, the neglectors, the incompetent, the nonsensical, design by committee, channel wars, wasting the customer's time, and sales prevention.

THE RESTRICTORS

Restrictor organizations decide for customers which channel is available for them to use, often in bizarre ways. Rather than let customers choose, these companies try to force their customers down a given path regardless of customer preference. For example, a major credit card company forced customers down a very prescriptive path when they received new or replacement credit cards. Customers had to call the contact center to "activate" their card. Receiving it in the mail was not enough. Some customers got a simple IVR interface where entering their date of birth and phone number was considered to be proof of identification, and the card was duly activated. Now remember that these customers had already validated themselves when ordering a new or replacement card, so this was in effect a repetition for them. But it didn't stop there. If a customer was one whom the bank thought it wanted to sell to in some way, the bank would not route the call to the IVR but put it straight through to an agent. The agent would complete a similar activation process but then force the customer to stay on the line and listen to the agent attempt to cross-sell additional products and services. The more valuable the customer, the more likely she was to be subject to additional sales attempts. This bank made it fast and simple to get a new card for low-value customers but hard and complex for valuable ones.

THE NEGLECTORS

Self-service neglectors strive to put in place customer self-service and then don't update it, stranding the customer in the equivalent of "voicemail jail" with no means for escape. One high-tech company in the United States offered an option on its IVR system for callers to find the closest retailer featuring its sought-after products; at a later point, someone in the IT department deleted the database because it was out-of-date, yet the company kept the option on the menu. Callers tried the option, heard nothing, and wound up speaking to an agent, who often heard "The menu isn't working" but never passed this news to the IT group, thus perpetuating these dumb contacts.

A major utility forced its customers to navigate through out-of-date messages, confusing menus, and delays from step to step—for example, keeping old organizational structure mentions and broadcast messages that were no longer relevant. The customers suffered extended navigation times and long waits before being offered the next IVR menu or being connected to an agent for additional support.

It is not uncommon for divisions within companies to create their own customer phone numbers with different IVR menu options for specific products or promotions and then simply leave them after the promotion has ended, further confusing and upsetting customers.

THE INCOMPETENT

Incompetence in this area takes many forms; here are some of the classics. The incompetent organization hasn't figured out that it has a Web site that covers many of the questions that customers are asking its staffed channel. Many of its agents and their managers have never used their company's self-service and have no idea how it works. Despite a corporate strategy to "grow the Internet and self-service," the staffed channel remains ignorant; in addition, some agents feel threatened by self-service and decide not to advise the customers that self-service is available. Incompetent companies also don't know how to get self-service right. They design solutions that suit the company but not the customer—or in some cases, neither party.

For example, a prominent IT company had to go through the difficult process of recalling a key component. This meant letting all its customers know that there might be a faulty component but then asking them to ascertain whether or not theirs was faulty. The main channel for doing this was the Web site, where customers were given instructions on how to validate the part numbers on the component. Although the basic process worked, there were several flaws in the solution, suggesting that the company had not had time to test its usability. The main goal of the solution was to get customers to enter a part number. The system would then check the number against a database of known faulty parts.

This company's self-serve solution had many shortcomings that frustrated customers, caused unnecessary phone calls, and increased its costs tremendously:

- The process was unclear; the company did not explain to customers how to remove the component so that they could check the part number against the recall list.
- It forced dumb contacts; the part number wasn't visible until removed, so many customers called the fault line asking how to remove the part and whether their machines would malfunction if they did so.
- It created random chances. Once the customer managed to locate the device, she then had to enter a twenty-digit part number required for validation; however, even if the customer entered XXXX ????****%%%%$$$$, clearly not a valid part number, the system would come back and say "Your part is fine"; the company ran a significant risk that customers would enter faulty part numbers incorrectly and be told they were fine.

This was a classic case of needing to conduct usability testing so that faults and problems for customers would be caught earlier in the process. Then this incompetent company compounded the problem by drastically underestimating how many people would call with issues, so the call center simply could not handle the requests.

Another form of incompetence is setting up the customer to fail. Unfortunately, many speech recognition technology implementations fall into this category. Speech technologies until recently were best used to capture a limited set of responses so that the software could match the responses to a limited vocabulary set. An implementation at a major taxi company illustrates the point. It used speech recognition to automate cab bookings. Some parts worked well, such as when the system asked the customer to confirm the number of passengers traveling or answer yes-no questions. Unfortunately, the designers then foolishly built in a final open-ended question: "Please tell us where you are traveling to." Customers could answer anything they liked. This caused the self-service to fail to find a match more often than it succeeded. It could match standard requests like "the airport" or "the city," but street names, suburbs, and "Grandma's place" never got a match, and customers ended up talking to an operator. Two years later, the company launched a revised system that didn't ask for a destination, as it wasn't needed to book a cab. It took the management all that time to recognize its own incompetence.

THE NONSENSICAL

Renting a car online should be easy. Pick a make and a model, and that should be just about it. Unfortunately, that is not always the case. A couple of the car companies want to up-sell you some optional extras, such as child seats and tow bars. That's fine, and in theory it's great that you can configure your rental for your exact needs. However, bad usability kicks in when the options are displayed. One of these companies in Germany allows you to choose one, two, three, or four tow bars. It lets you do the same for child seats. Unfortunately, the same company only lets you have one, two, or three winter tires. Clearly these self-service options hadn't been properly tested and reviewed, and the results are usability nonsense.

DESIGN BY COMMITTEE

Design-by-committee organizations attempt to mirror all their departments or divisions in their Web or IVR self-service channels, exposing to their customers how they are organized, and failing to offer convenience for their customers. For example, one high-tech firm in the United States asked its customers, "Software or hardware problem?" and then to identify the "notebook" model so that it could route the caller to the best agent, but many customers couldn't decide between software versus hardware (their unit was broken; that's all they knew) and didn't know offhand what model they owned (it's a laptop; that's all).

A large bank decided to stuff its Web home page with every conceivable department listing in an attempt to offer service online, but with so many bewildering options, customers struggled to find what they wanted. With little "white space" on the page, customers gave up and called the toll-free number in frustration. Perhaps not surprisingly, finding the toll-free number to call was just as hard as working out how to get where they wanted on the Web site.

A software company presented bewilderingly different Web page navigation options depending on the product line and division. Customers felt as though they were visiting different companies when in fact the pages simply represented different product lines. The company was broadcasting its internal structure through its Web site.

CHANNEL WARS

Channel wars organizations reveal that they have multiple owners across the customer's interactions with them by making it hard to do business with them. For example, at one bank, applying for a product online was completely different from going into a branch or doing it over the phone—the bank requested different data, offered unique forms and turnaround times, and produced different checks for the customer, depending on the channel selected. To make matters worse, the company couldn't cope with someone who switched channels, as it was almost like changing banks. None of the channels knew how the process worked elsewhere, and none of them promoted the other channels.

Another case of channel wars occurred in a health insurance business. At a workshop held to discuss improvement opportunities, the representatives of the contact center staff filled a white board with their issues regarding the company's Web site. According to them, the site was a disaster that did nothing but drive calls into their center. This was far from the case, and customers using the Internet were, when surveyed, found to be reasonably happy with the services offered to them. The contact center not only was ignorant about the Web site but also fought against it. A sample of nine hundred calls identified that on not one of them did the agent refer the customer to the Internet site, even on simple transactions that the customer could have completed on the Web. No one had told the contact center staff that their role included promoting and supporting the self-service options. But it didn't just stop there. Branch staff at the same company were not only ignorant about the Internet but also hostile to the contact center. Their perspective was that any customer in the branch was their customer and shouldn't set foot in any other channel. Customers weren't invited to call the contact center or try the Web. These staffed channels actively fought against automation and educating its customers.

In some cases, customer service agents cannot even view what the customers are seeing on the company's Web site, making the customer experience essentially invisible to them and setting up "he said, she said" disputes between the customer and the agent.

Wasting the Customer's Time

For a recent major sporting event, customers were encouraged to buy their tickets online. They registered on a Web site many months before the event and were then e-mailed updates some months later once tickets were "released" for the event. A customer logged in using the e-mail address that the notification had been sent to. It didn't work. Various other formats failed, and the "forgotten password" function didn't work either. The Contact Us screen provided a phone number to call.

The customer called the number, which suffered from poor design. The first menu had five choices, but three options had three suboptions, meaning that the customer was being asked to remember far too much. The customer picked the "buy tickets" option, listened to some additional messages including the "your call will be monitored for quality purposes." In total the navigation took over ninety seconds including wait time. Then the customer got the message "We're open eight A.M. to 9 P.M., so please call back then." He checked and confirmed that this information wasn't on the Web site or available in earlier menus—a classic case of wasting the customer's time with poor channel integration and usability design.

Sales Prevention

You would think that most companies would want to make themselves easy to buy from, but poor usability and self-service design can make the buying experience far harder than it should be.

A customer recently took on the challenge of buying a home building-and-contents insurance package in the United Kingdom using Web sites. He attempted to obtain quotations and then possibly purchase from a range of different providers, but eventually gave up the attempt. Here are some of the problems he encountered along the way:

- On one major site, the second question on the list was, "Where did you hear about this site?" with a list of fifteen options. This is a case of a marketing department putting its needs before the customer's time—and before the customer has even started the process. This was a mandatory field, even though it was of no value to the customer.
- The customer was subjected to technical jargon and asked to select a type of coverage without explanation.
- On the third screen of data on one site (after all personal details and details of the house had been captured, about fifteen minutes of data entry), the customer was asked to enter the amount of coverage. The maximum allowed was £250,000. For many customers that limit is insufficient. Clearly this is a critical yes-no decision point for many customers, and therefore it should be captured as early as possible, or they should be warned, "Only policies less than £250,000 can be captured online."
- Three screens of information should not be needed to get a quotation. Postal code and size of house should be enough, but three companies asked for screens of information earlier in the process.
- Better-designed sites enabled the customer to get a quotation and then modify key parameters, such as excesses and amounts insured. Many companies didn't do this. One company got to a quotation with four minutes of data entry. Others took up to fifteen minutes of data entry.
- Ironically, the worst buying experience came from a specialist online broker that claimed that it made finding the right policy easy. It forced the customer to fill out five screens of information before giving a quotation. The process took ten minutes.
- Some sites had "Call me" buttons, but they didn't work. Some did provide contact details and phone numbers, but

few supported the Web customer outside office hours. In other words, that's "Call us—but only when we want you to."

- When search engines brought up its site, one savvy company advertised how fast its process was, claiming "Get a quote in 2 minutes." Sure enough, it captured minimal data and produced a single simple screen completed in less than three minutes. But once that screen was completed, the system responded that applications were "not available." So even though the process was simple, it still wasted the customer's time.

GOOD CASES

Fortunately, there are an increasing number of good cases in self-service: companies that offer ample choice, apply smart design principles, and overcome the challenges of channel disintegration. We will look briefly at first direct, Amazon, Telstra, Nationwide Building Society, and the New York State DMV.

GIVING THE CUSTOMER CONTROL AT FIRST DIRECT

The United Kingdom's "most recommended" and leading direct bank, first direct, recognizes that customers want to be in control. The bank provides this control in a range of ways. Customers can subscribe to SMS phone-based messaging services to provide a range of messages direct to their mobile phone (for example, when a paycheck has arrived or a balance limit exceeded). Customers have signed up for these services at a great rate, and first direct now sends over 3.6 million SMS messages per month.

first direct encourages and promotes Web site use, but it is not concerned if customers contact the bank by phone. In fact, despite being a direct (branchless) organization, it provides no IVR options, recognizing that Web and SMS self-service are just as convenient for customers who want to self-serve. first direct's main goal in providing the Web site is to provide a service that customers really want to use and find easy to use. That concept is illustrated by the choice of language on the Web site. Rather than list balances under such headings as "Loans and Deposits," first direct customers view their balances under such headings as "What I Own" and

"What I Owe." Use of such friendly language creates an engaging self-service experience that customers are happy to adopt.

SMART DESIGN, MULTICHANNEL INTEGRATION AT AMAZON

We have already described how Amazon's streamlined contact coding and Skyline reporting systems enabled the company's true owners of customer contacts to rally behind or lead change programs to eliminate contacts or deflect others to self-service. One of the best examples for self-service arose after the company's first holiday season selling high-ticket items, such as DVD players and digital cameras. In the earlier years, when customers received a damaged book or a CD that didn't work, as infrequent as this was, Amazon told customers, "Don't worry; we'll just send a free replacement to you, and you can toss or give away to the library the original item." Customers loved this "no questions asked" policy, and it was also smart for Amazon—it cost less than paying to get the item back, check for damage, and dispatch a replacement.

However, Amazon couldn't afford to extend this policy for more expensive and complex products, so the company required that customers call to request a replacement for a damaged or unwanted electronics product or other non-BMV (books, music, video) item. Although the number of these cases was also very low, every one produced a phone call and took a number of cumbersome and time-consuming steps:

1. Customer calls Amazon.
2. Amazon customer service (CS) confirms customer identification and the product or item that needs to be replaced.
3. Amazon CS questions customer for reasons; if approved, agent ticks one of eight to ten boxes in the CRM system.
4. Amazon CS agent sends return merchandise authorization (RMA) to local printer.
5. Another Amazon CS employee pulls the printed RMA, stuffs an envelope, and mails it to customer.
6. Customer gets RMA, sticks it on the original package, and arranges for shipment back to Amazon's "reverse logistics" center.

7. Amazon's reverse logistics gets item, unaware that it was coming, and commences its own investigation to determine "ownership" (that is, determining whether the damage was caused by the shipper or that the product arrived from the manufacturer damaged, and so on).

All in all, this largely manual process had at least three major problems: (1) it made the customer wait; (2) it absorbed agent and employee time; and (3) it didn't provide any heads-up for the reverse logistics operations team. Reviewing the rising rate of contacts for exchanges and replacements (again, the rate was the key metric, not raw counts—here, the number of contacts per order [CPO] was going up), and noting that this qualified as valuable for the customer but an irritant for Amazon (in that it didn't produce any new revenues, but rather ate into product profits), the company decided to attack this as a automation or self-service project.

Representatives from CS, reverse logistics, the most affected stores (Electronics, for example), and Web development met to tackle this challenge and figure out how to achieve the stretch target to cut CPO from exchanges and refunds by 50 percent in the first year, an aggressive but exciting goal for the team. After reviewing the root causes and ticked boxes explaining why (there's that key word again!) customers called to request the return, the group designed a simple Web-based solution that tackled all three drawbacks of the manual process by (1) cutting time, (2) eliminating agent time, and (3) providing timely advice to reverse logistics as to when to expect what items and why the returns were needed. Here's what the interface looks like today, with simple use instructions including printing one's own return label and providing details to enable Amazon to process the return:

Instructions

1 of **Mr. Clean Magic Eraser Cleaning Pads, 8-Count Boxes (Pack of 3)**

1. Print this page.
2. Cut out the Return Label and the separate barcode for Amazon use.
3. Write your return address in the space provided in the upper-left corner of the label, after the word "FROM."
4. Securely pack the items to be returned in a box and include the separate barcode and the original packing slip in the package.
5. Affix the label squarely onto the address side of the parcel, covering up any previous delivery address and barcode without overlapping any adjacent side.
6. Give the package to your letter carrier or take the package to your nearest post office for delivery. No postage is necessary if the package is mailed from within the United States.

Your refund will be processed in 7 to 14 business days once your return has been received. Shortly after it has been processed, you will receive an e-mail regarding your refund.

Continue ▶

Less than six months after launching online returns and downloadable return labels, Amazon had achieved its target (CPO for this reason down 50 percent), and the company had made it easier for agents, customers, and the rest of the operations teams.

TELSTRA'S SMOOTH MULTICHANNEL INTEGRATION

An interaction within Telstra, Australia's leading telecommunications provider, illustrates how an organization can recognize that customers want to be in control and get a number of channels to work together to a successful sales (or service) experience (see diagram in Figure 3.1). This end-to-end interaction involved a number of well-designed and integrated processes across different contact channels:

- The customer searched the Web for products, and the phone number was available for follow-up.
- Speech recognition was used to speed navigation to the right operator when the customer called.
- The customer service center recognized the customer's preference for self-service; rather than sending brochures, it e-mailed the customer links to other offers on the Web site. The agent allowed the customer to control the timing and nature of the interaction.
- The customer compared plans on the Internet.
- The company's system recognized that the customer had not purchased, so it scheduled an outbound call for an agent to discuss options.
- The systems helped the telemarketing staff make an offer to the customer, who accepted it.

This is a great illustration of how contact channels can work together and produce results that the customer and the company wanted while giving the customer choice along the way.

ENGAGING THE CUSTOMER—USABILITY AT NATIONWIDE

A few years ago, Nationwide Building Society, one of Britain's leading mortgage lending institutions, embarked on developing a self-service sales system for customers. Its first attempts using

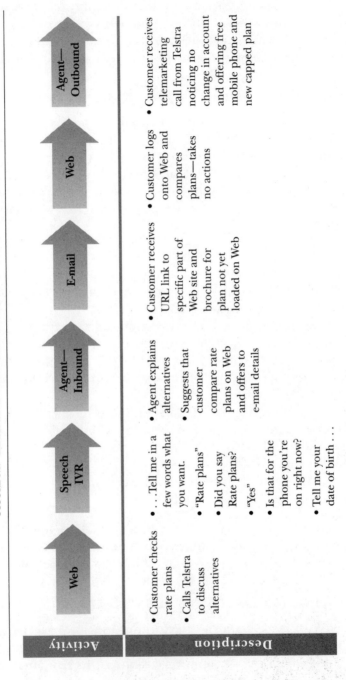

FIGURE 3.1: EXAMPLE OF SMOOTH MULTICHANNEL INTEGRATION: TELSTRA

Activity					
Web	Speech IVR	Agent—Inbound	E-mail	Web	Agent—Outbound
Description					
• Customer checks rate plans • Calls Telstra to discuss alternatives	• …Tell me in a few words what you want. • "Rate plans" • Did you say Rate plans? • "Yes" • Is that for the phone you're on right now? • Tell me your date of birth . . .	• Agent explains alternatives • Suggests that customer compare rate plans on Web and offers to e-mail details	• Customer receives URL link to specific part of Web site and brochure for plan not yet loaded on Web	• Customer logs onto Web and compares plans—takes no actions	• Customer receives telemarketing call from Telstra noticing no change in account and offering free mobile phone and new capped plan

touch-screen technology in a self-service branch had not yielded the results the company was after. Customers seemed suspicious of recommendations made by the technology. So Nationwide started over and decided to involve the customer in the subsequent design.

First it had to overcome the customers' fear of technology in the physical appearance of the devices. It embedded a touch screen into a desk so that it looked more like a TV than a computer. There was no keyboard or mouse—nothing to scare off the technophobe.

In designing the application, the company involved customers every few weeks in usability feedback sessions and posed such questions as "How do you think this would work?" or "What do you think will happen if you press this?" To support the user, Nationwide built a "virtual assistant" using an actress dressed to look like a typical branch service officer. The assistant would help the customer if he timed out or sought help. In each area of the system, the assistant explained what the system did.

Usability testing taught the designers what language to use, how customers would navigate the system, and the circumstances in which customers would accept product recommendations from a computer. The designers found that customers wanted control. They were more likely to buy when multiple products were represented than when there was only one.

When the application was deployed to branches, it was universally applauded by customers and staff. It won numerous awards and helped Nationwide Building Society in its goal of providing innovative and usable technology to all. The application also delivered better sales results than all their previous attempts.

SKIP THE TRIP AND HAVE E-Z VISIT WITH NY-DMV

As do those in most U.S. states, customers at the New York State Department of Motor Vehicles (NY-DMV) have traditionally been required to visit DMV offices regularly to renew licenses or get new vehicle registration plates or tags. The business processes required to handle these transactions were often cumbersome and very time consuming. DMV service throughout the country has historically been a constant source of customer frustration and the butt of late-night talk-show humor; long delays in DMV offices are very common, and there is a strong perception of bureaucracy and poor service.

New York State decided to improve its DMV services. One approach was to launch a NY-DMV Web site in 1996 that provided some online information and the option for customers to e-mail the DMV if they had questions. At that time, the limited self-service facilities had little impact on overall customer service levels.

When the first online transactions at the DMV "Internet Office" were introduced in 1999, they helped ensure that the online office would eventually become the busiest DMV office in the state, receiving tens of thousands of hits per day. The volume of online transactions and knowledge base queries has translated into operational cost savings for the agency and significantly improved service to the state's drivers. In 2002, the NY-DMV Web site attracted over 6 million customers, who have downloaded more than 3.7 million DMV forms and saved hundreds of thousands of trips to local DMV offices.

This sort of take-up wasn't achieved by accident. The NY-DMV recognized that it needed to change customer behavior. It launched major marketing campaigns around the idea of "skip the trip." It invested in self-help learning technologies to help customers self-serve over the Web. It also recognized that some transactions did need physical contact, but that even these could be partly automated. The NY-DMV also promoted a second concept, namely the "E-Z Visit," whereby customers completed details online and merely visited the physical office to sign paperwork or collect details.

The results have been impressive:

- At least 97 percent of customers using the Web site and knowledge base find the information they need.
- Serving more customers online resulted in an 80 percent decrease in the volume of e-mail inquiries.
- Easy access to up-to-date information through the online knowledge base and Web site reduced support phone calls and visits to DMV offices.
- Fewer routine, repetitive questions allowed DMV support staff to focus on customers who truly required individualized attention.

The NY-DMV focused obsessively on building things customers wanted and then promoting them to customers, and yielded great results.

THE FRAMEWORK

Such organizations as first direct in the United Kingdom, eBay, and Amazon are creating their whole business model around a self-service proposition, providing insights into the idea that you can create engaging self-service from the ground up.

Self-service is increasingly being recognized as a critical part of the customer experience:

- In the best self-service operations, nearly 90 percent of customers chose to stay in the IVR instead of speaking with an agent about their issue.
- One in three Americans use Internet banking to pay their bills online, 5 to 10 percent more doing so each year.
- At Amazon, the vast majority of customers place and receive an order without ever having to speak with anyone or needing to send an e-mail message.
- Seventy percent of business and government callers in Hong Kong find their number using speech-driven self-service.

Well-designed self-service works and is now critical to many businesses. How do companies overcome the three deadly sins presented earlier? How can companies ensure that their customers are in control and have choice, that they can use sensible self-service designs, and that all of the channels they use work in unison?

Successful companies have adopted three responses. First, rather than "grabbing control," these companies have created customer-controlled self-service. They are willing to give up some control in return for the adoption and enthusiastic use of self-service that they get in return. They don't try to manipulate customers into self-service use, although they do let them know that it's there and encourage its use. Second, rather than designing unusable applications, they obsess about design of applications that customers can and will use. These companies put themselves in the customers' shoes and apply the science of usability design. When they build self-service, they recognize that there is a science to understanding how customers behave, and address customers' needs and behaviors in their applications. And last, rather than ignoring their staffed channels, they recognize that existing channels must be integrated with self-service and play a key role in customer change management (a term we will discuss further later).

We will now explore each of these "sin avoidance" strategies in more detail.

CREATE CUSTOMER-CONTROLLED SELF-SERVICE

Putting the customer in control is a clear distinction between those organizations who have succeeded with self-service and those who have been disappointed. As customers, we resent being cajoled and forced into use of certain channels even if they are faster and more convenient. One simple case for control illustrates this dramatically. Two private health insurers, Fund A and Fund B, both identified that responding to customers' e-mails by e-mail was typically less efficient than a phone call. E-mail tended to result in dialogues and multiple interactions requiring more agent time. Both companies decided to ask their customers for a phone number as part of the e-mail template that customers filled out. Fund A simply asked for a phone number and then called the customer. Fund B provided the customer with a check box asking permission to call the customer instead and asking for a preferred time of day for the call.

When Fund A called its customers, they were greeted with hostility. "I e-mailed you; why are you calling?" The insurer quickly dropped the idea, as it did not want to annoy customers. Fund B, in contrast, called only those customers who had given permission (and the vast majority did), and these customers welcomed this service and were expecting the call. So the simple "granting of permission" put the customer in control.

Despite this need for control, few organizations today capture or exploit these kinds of customer preferences. When we polled thirty leading organizations in one country and asked how many companies could both capture and use data on customer preferences, only one company of the thirty said it could. This is a significant opportunity. If customers would rather get an e-mail that costs cents rather than a printed and mailed letter, that seems like something companies can easily exploit.

Another classic symptom of organizations trying to keep control is hidden contact numbers on Web sites. Many organizations seem to have adopted a strategy that says "Customers on the Web must stay on the Web." These organizations either don't provide contact details or bury them so deep in the Web site that they are almost impossible to find. Organizations that do this seem determined to keep control of the customer. In contrast, those who are getting it right, far from hiding their phone numbers, make them prominent on their Web sites. Health insurance broker i-select is a great example of this—its phone number is displayed prominently on every Web page, encouraging contact. Virgin goes even farther by broadcasting its web site address in large letters on every plane.

Leading U.S. retailers have started recognizing that they get better results when they let customers control which channels they use. They are delighted if customers want to browse the Web or store and then purchase through another channel. Customers can research products on the Web but buy in-store, or use the telephone to understand how a process works, but then complete their purchase online. Mortgage and insurance purchases are following a similar pattern. Customers research online, but want to talk to someone before closing the sale. Giving up control is an important step in getting customers to adopt self-service.

CREATE USABLE DESIGNS FOR THE CUSTOMER

The self-service leaders recognize that they are building solutions for their customers, and design accordingly. Amazon is a classic case in point as an organization that looks constantly for updates and improvements to the Web site that will help the customer. This was apparent in the early stages of Amazon's development, when such features as book reviews and "Others who bought this book also bought . . ." helped customers select the best products to suit their needs. It would not occur to Amazon to restrict how many pages of a book they could review or organize the Web site according to internal departments (billing, credit, payments, and so on).

Companies that design effective self-service for the customer do four things very carefully:

1. Determine the customers' purpose in using self-service
2. Understand the specific needs and behaviors of these customers and what will make self-service usable for these groups

3. Make self-service easy for the customer
4. Listen and invent constantly for the customer

Determining customers' needs sounds so fundamental that you would think all self-service developers would do it. If that were the case, why do so many Web sites reflect the companies' needs rather than the customers' purpose? On many Web sites, you can almost draw the organization chart from the structure of the site and even tell whether each department designed its own page. How many organizations really ask themselves the question, "What does the customer want to do?" Amazon illustrated this understanding when it recognized that customers don't just want to buy something; they often want to buy something *and* have it delivered before a certain date (birthday, anniversary, and so on). So the date of delivery was a crucial part of the purchase decision for some customers. The buying experience was changed so that a customer could back out of a purchase if she wasn't happy with the delivery date. This was a significant concession for Amazon, but it also reduced a significant volume of contacts in the "Where's my stuff?" contact categories (see again Chapter Two) and demonstrated the importance of understanding the real customer need.

Understanding customer behaviors and detailed needs also seems fundamental. A classic illustration of this is ATM design. At a usability conference, we heard about a Florida bank that was disappointed that its customer ATM use was low compared to benchmarks. It had consciously targeted high-net-worth retirees and had an average customer age higher than most other banks. However, it was these older customers who had the lowest level of ATM use.

The bank conducted detailed research with these elderly customers and found that forgetting PINs during ATM use and thereby losing cards that the machine had "swallowed" was a great inhibitor for elderly customers. They feared loss of access to their accounts and embarrassing processes required to reclaim cards. Armed with this insight, the bank designed ATMs with card swipes rather than conventional card "swallowers." Thus elderly customers retained their cards, and if they forgot their PINs, they kept control and could try again or go into the branch. A machine swallowing a card could be seen as the ultimate form of organizational control. In contrast, customers who hold their cards in their hand are in control. This simple change (which surprisingly few banks or ATM companies have figured out) led to significant increases in ATM use.

Making it easy for the customer is equally crucial as a design element. Making it easy means thinking through the entire customer experience. Let's look at the airline booking experience as an example. The airlines who have this right have thought through their customers' needs and their likely behavior. Self-service check-in kiosks are convenient and fast for customers, and they avoid queues, demonstrating seven key elements of well-designed self-service:

1. Allow for a variety of mechanisms to identify the customer—frequent flyer card, credit card, a booking reference, and also the passenger's name if needed.
2. Have a backup support mechanism for the customer—airline staff always on hand to assist self-service customers where they need help.
3. Recognize a variety of interaction types. Well-designed kiosk interfaces recognize that many customers book and travel together, so the systems prompt for additional travelers where a joint booking exists so that people can sit together.
4. Offer a faster and more convenient process. On short return or multileg trips, customers are able to book and ticket subsequent legs in one go so that they save time.
5. Match or improve the staffed channel experience. The experience is made as good as, if not better than, staffed check-in, as customers can chose their seat as well as make use of frequent flyer preferences automatically. Customers have more control where they sit than they do when they use a staffed check-in.
6. Increase usage with physical positioning. In many airports, the kiosks are well positioned in front of the staffed check-in, with plenty of room for luggage and even an effective exterior design that allows customers to put down a handbag or a wallet, thus freeing their hands to interact with the machine.
7. Enfranchise all customers. The machines are free of keyboards or mice, so they appear usable to non-computer-literate users.

These seven fundamental design features have led to high adoption rates and popularity with customers, but the airlines haven't stopped there. Many have recognized that the Web offers a third check-in mechanism. Customers can now check in from their home or office and print a boarding card before they even get to the airport. The Web facility offers the same choices and options as the airport kiosk, and simple screen-by-screen design, but with options for changing seats and so forth. Perhaps that is the ultimate in customer control; the airline is saying, we trust you to get to the airport, so you can print and bring your own boarding pass.

Dumb Things Done to Customers

CHANNEL MISMATCH

At a self-service check-in kiosk, the machine allows you to check in a second passenger traveling with you. As you do so, a warning appears saying that "you cannot check in a passenger not present at the airport." That sounds reasonable on the surface, except that the same airline allows passengers to check in over the Internet from home or the office—where they are clearly not at the airport. Furthermore, later in the dialogue, the kiosk allows the passenger to check in for the return trip from a city he or she hasn't even flown to yet, let alone an airport he or she hasn't reached. So this warning message about "passengers not present" illustrates a design that doesn't match the experience required.

It's not surprising that some customers hate automated phone interfaces. So many companies ignore basic rules of usability, such as how many options we can remember or even how long a message we can bear to listen to or read. Often the compliance, legal, and marketing departments seem to have won the battle of self-service scope. For example, it may be legally compliant to ask a customer to review a hundred-page terms and conditions statement before downloading software, but does it achieve anything? Who will read a hundred pages of legalese?

The trouble with effective usability is that we don't notice it. We do notice when things are difficult, counterintuitive, or impossible, but effective self-service usability is almost transparent. That is the whole point.

Here are some examples of good usability that becomes transparent:

Usability Feature	Why You Don't Notice It
Short menus on IVRs	They just make selection easy and don't tax your short-term memory.
Consistency across IVRs and Web sites (that is, the features that help you navigate work the same way)	Knowing where things are or how they will work makes sites and menus intuitive.
Correct use of silence (on IVRs) and white space on Web sites	We only notice when we are rushed into decisions or feel crowded and overwhelmed by the content of a site.
Multiple support levels for the user	IVRs should kick into a more detailed level of support when the user has a problem; Web sites similarly should help users recover from mistakes or problems.
Standard navigation features (ability to repeat menus on IVRs or bread crumbs on Web sites)	They are just there, and we find it easy to find our way around!

What many companies don't realize is that there really is a science to usability design. It isn't just an art that some people design self-service better than others. There are rules and tests that can be applied to any self-service design based on an understanding of human factors and psychology and the body of research that exists in that area. There are also far simpler methods that organizations can employ, such as bringing in customers to test any self-service application at any stage from prototype to finalized solution. These usability tests form an invaluable part of the process of designing self-service solutions and frequently reveal to the design team important details that they had not expected.

The designers have to understand usability rules. That means, first off, understanding the customer's frame of reference and language opposed to that of the organization. For example, customers go to a banking site to *borrow* money, whereas banks have *lending* departments. Customers buy computers and software for the home office, but companies often want these customers to distinguish between home and office. Those are just two examples of not seeing things the way customers do. Good usability ensures consistency and uses customers' language and customers' frame of reference to make it easy for them to find what they want.

Other "human factor" rules concern such concepts as customer short-term memory. Most people can remember only thirty seconds of information at any time, so any IVR with a menu of options or messages that take longer to play than that will confuse customers and lose them. There are also rules about how many items a customer can remember (see in Appendix B "the rule of 7 plus or minus 2"). Some companies think they have understood this rule by having just three or four IVR menu options, but then they load each option with suboptions. For example, they ask, "For Department A, Department B, or Department C, press 1." That combination asks the customer to remember four things: three departments and the menu number.

In many channels, some de facto standards have emerged, so customers generally expect these to be followed rather than ignored. For example, hitting 0 should always get you an operator. On the Web, an example is the use of bread crumbs, which show you how you got to your current page (usually a trail of text at the top of the screen showing you the path you have navigated to get to the page) rather than just relying on back and forward buttons for navigation. Usability design also reinforces the ideas in Steve Krug's *Don't Make Me Think:* don't make customers wonder if something is clickable or not, don't hide the most frequently used links, and don't change the Web site "bones" or framework except when absolutely necessary.

These are just a few of the rules of human-factors scientists that can be applied to customer self-service. Academic research can help you understand what will work and what won't work, but there is one Golden Rule: *if in doubt, ask your customers.* It's amazing what customers will tell you if you ask them, or show you when you put them in a usability environment. Just going through the exercise will produce many surprises for the designers in an organization. Often IT and other self-service developers are too close to the action. Of course most IT staff are the worst possible people to develop self-service. They are so familiar with technology that they forget what the rest of the population will understand, or they, as designers, aren't aware of what aspects of the design customers will find hard to use.

INTEGRATE CHANNELS TO MANAGE CHANGE FOR THE CUSTOMER

It seems reasonable to customers that channels should work together and be consistent, yet time and again we see organizations deploy new channels without reconsidering the role of the old ones. Customers often seem to know more about what is available on the Web site than the staff do. Many contact center staff are unfamiliar with how IVR options work, and few branch staff have ever set foot in the contact center, or vice versa. At one health insurer, all the staffed channels seemed to think that they were the only area to get it right. For example, the contact center staff couldn't understand why branch staff didn't complete customer notes on each interaction, because for them that was an essential audit trail. By contrast, the branch staff couldn't understand the shorthand that most contact center staff used to annotate customer calls. This silo mentality seems all too common, yet customers see all service channels as representing the organization.

A critical component in designing self-service channels is to consider the role that other channels might need to play: Are they there to support, promote, or refer, and if so what will they need in order to be effective in this role? The existing staffed channels should go through their own evolution until they become effective in promoting and working with the self-service channels:

Transition and Role of Existing Channel

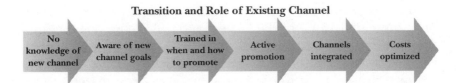

To move the staffed channels through this path takes planning and effort at every stage of the process. For example, they have to be trained in how the self-service works, given incentives to promote it, and monitored on how well they promote and support it. It is also possible to predict how staff will respond, and manage accordingly. Will they feel threatened? How will you check that they educate and promote? How will they keep abreast of what is available on the new channels? Any successful self-service strategy or new channel deployment must consider the role that other channels will play and must be set up to give them the systems and information they need to play that role effectively.

Success stories illustrate this. In the early days of Internet banking, the banks rewarded branch and contact center staff with sales credits for signing customers for Internet banking. That certainly produced an incentive. In some situations, they may have gone too far. In one bank, the branch staff was rewarded equally for an Internet sign-up or for a home loan sale. The sign-up rate was terrific, with 50 percent annual growth in new customers. However, the bank then discovered that many customers being signed up didn't use the Internet. In fact, some of them didn't even have Internet access. So in this case the reward mechanism and channel role were not aligned to the self-service strategy.

One of the defined roles of customer agents at Amazon is to educate customers on self-service features and use. The contact centers used to have posters asking the agents, "Have you educated a customer today?" Amazon considered it a key part of an agent's job to promote its robust self-service options and enlighten customers to learn how to order online or to understand the options they have for obtaining order status. For each of the last four Harry Potter books with hyped Saturday launches, Amazon said to its anxious customers who called or e-mailed to find out when Peter or Dennis would get their new edition, "Did you know that you could find the shipping estimate in Your Account online? It's updated immediately, and you'll know exactly when the truck will arrive at your house."

Amazon is a highly seasonal business with a high proportion of revenue generated in the last two months of the year. Staffing the contact centers to meet this seasonal peak is a key challenge, yet even at this time of year, Amazon staff are still encouraged to educate customers. It would be far easier to drop the education role during such busy times, but the company also recognizes that this is the best time to teach customers to self-serve, as it prevents the holiday rush from getting bigger still.

Managing change for employees is hard enough, but managing the behaviors of customers is even harder, and increasing self-service adoption is a complex task. Too often organizations assume that a "build it and they will come" approach will produce high usage rates, but unfortunately the world is littered with the heroic failures caused by underinvestment in the design and communication of self-service choices.

So how do you get customers to use self-service? We have coined the term *customer change management* to express the methodology that is required. Companies invest significantly these days in getting their staff to use new processes or technology. They wouldn't consider rolling out a new system without masses of communication, training, and support. Yet many companies launch a new self-service application without the same kind of investment, when in fact there should be more. After all, staff have limited choice in using the systems and processes, but customers do have choices. Changing customer behavior involves thinking through both whether customers will be *able* to use self-service and whether they will *want* to use self-service. In terms of this "can't do–won't do" model, usability and the support available from staffed channels impact the "can't do," and convenience and promotion impact the "won't do."

Incentives, penalties, and availability are critical tools in the customer change management approach. Incentives such as Internet-only rates have encouraged airline customers to buy online. Banks have used fees and product design (for example, Internet-only products) to discourage branch and contact center use, and some observers believe that excessive queue lengths in branches and call centers have been used to drive self-service adoption. Getting people to adopt self-service is not just about incentives, however; it also involves promotion, awareness, and creating technologies that customers can use readily.

Whether or not customers stick with self-service is driven by the experience they encounter. The self-service check-in kiosks at airports provide fast and simple alternatives that are easy to control, but if many of them are broken or the screens are complex and hard to use or they have queues, then customers will drift back to staffed channels. The willingness to adopt will quickly be removed.

Dumb Things Done to Customers

CREATING SELF-SERVICE BARRIERS

One major airline created an obstacle to its drive for self-service check-in. The implication of offering self-service check-in is that passengers with luggage will still need to check it on. At an airport we went to recently, the self-service check-in systems have worked so well that the queues for the "baggage only" check-in needed by self-service passengers were far longer than the queues for the full check-in process. If that situation continues, customers will start to vote with their feet and stop using the self-check. Through poor management of the staffed channel area, the airline is in danger of creating a disincentive for the behavior it wants.

The case of the NY-DMV (see "Good Cases") illustrates what is possible to deliver and how much customers relish well-promoted, well-designed, and well-thought-through self-service. The NY-DMV realized that advertising and promoting options for customers were critical to getting them to adopt a new set of behaviors. The NY-DMV's advertising, using such concepts as "skip the trip," recognized the benefits for the customer and promoted things accordingly. This case also shows the amount of effort required in promotion and publicity. As we mentioned, the "build it and they will come" approach usually leads to disappointing results. With effective promotion and support from staffed channels, far more is possible.

Dumb Things Done to Customers

NO IDEA

A customer called her insurance company. She navigated through four levels of messages and options. Then she was asked for her account number, and she dutifully entered it. Next came the message, "Sorry, we're closed."

SUMMARY

Customers will love and embrace self-service if companies get it right. Just look at the success of online retailers or Internet banking and ATMs. First, companies have to give customers choice; grabbing control will not deliver the outcomes companies want. Next, they need to work really hard with their customers to make the self-service usable for them. Finally, companies need to ensure that the self-service channels are tied into and promoted by every other channel. The following list of dos and don'ts summarizes the ideas behind creating usable self-service.

Do	Don't
Involve and educate your staffed channels on how self-service works	Let your customers know more than your staff about self-service
Put the customer in control	Try to put a straitjacket on the customer to get the behaviors you want
Invest in customer change management	Expect "build it and they will come" to work
Design with the customer in mind, using the customer's terms	Design what the organization wants, using company-speak, without reference to the customer's need
Use incentives	Penalize staffed channel use
Apply the science of usability	Let your tech, marketing, and legal teams loose on customer self-service
Start with the end and reuse in mind	Take shortcuts that lead to channel isolation

The organizations that are getting the best value from customer self-service get all these things right because they have recognized that self-service is a great way to ensure No Service by the staffed channel. These organizations let the customer choose how and when she uses self-service; they employ design and usability rules to create self-service solutions that suit their customers and put the customer in control; and they have thought through how all the sales and service channels, both staffed and automated, work together and how they will approach changing customer behavior. They are getting great results and have raised the bar for other organizations.

Survey Questions

Please score your company for these three key questions covering the idea of creating engaging self-service, and refer to Appendix A to check your progress from Basic Service to Better Service to Best Service.

5. Our customers
    a. Love our self-service, and tell us why.
    b. Don't use our self-service as much as we would like or had anticipated.
    c. Are mostly unaware of the self-service we offer.
    d. Would never use self-service even if we offered them incentives.
    e. Self-service doesn't apply in our business.

6. Our sales and service staff
    a. Move our customers to self-service options if the customer prefers it that way.
    b. See the Web site or our IVR system as a source of problems.
    c. Understand what our self-service does and actively promote it.
    d. Know less about our self-service than our customers do.
    e. Have no self-service to promote.

7. Our company
    a. Tracks the extent to which customers are being successful in self-service channels and drives improvements from those data.
    b. Captures the take-up rates of our self-service channels.
    c. Asks customers periodically what they think of their self-service experience.
    d. Sees no benefit in self-service; for us, every interaction needs a human touch.
    e. Has self-service, but doesn't track its use in any detail.

CHAPTER FOUR

BE PROACTIVE
Instead of Waiting to Respond

We hope you enjoy your stay at the Grand Hyatt San Francisco.
Due to high winds we are currently experiencing, you may hear
a "creaking noise" in your room. Please be assured that the
building is reacting to the wind as it should and that this sound
is to be expected.
—CARD IN HOTEL ROOM UPON ARRIVAL

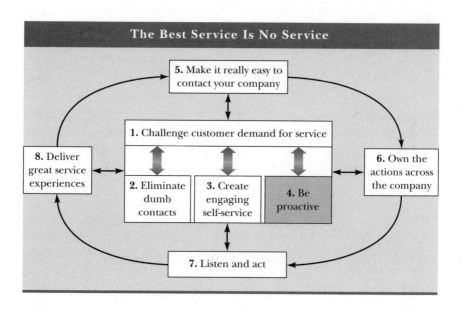

THE PRINCIPLE

We have already covered the process of profiling customer contacts into four buckets using the Value-Irritant Matrix, which in turn leads to eliminate contacts entirely (Chapter Two) and designing successful self-service programs (Chapter Three); there's a third powerful approach that companies can take to pursue the No Service of Best Service. This involves notifying customers proactively whenever contact-creating "events" are known, especially repetitive and critical situations. Being proactive produces other important value for companies, such as "Wow, you remembered" and "They're taking care of me, so why should I take my business elsewhere?" both solid marketing and top-line benefits. Few customers are going to shop around or accept an offer after a positive experience they were not expecting. Being proactive also reduces the need for customers to contact your operations in response to such classic situations as a delayed flight or an order confirmation.

Proactive contact requires making contact with customers to achieve a range of objectives, most of which obviate the need for the customer to contact the company. Proactive contacts can be used in the following four ways:

---

1. Keep the customer informed of progress on task. Examples: estimated arrival dates for complex orders or those with a long wait time; details on registration for shipped products; estimated service restoration during electrical outages; updates on progress for insurance claims or mortgage applications.
2. Manage expectations proactively (rather than reactively). Examples: actively soliciting complaints instead of asking post-contact or post-visit, when response rates tend to be much lower; rebooking cancelled or delayed flights, thus eliminating the need for the customer to contact the company to rebook, a classic insult-to-injury situation.
3. Anticipate the customer's need. Examples: sending virus or update alerts directly to the customer's computers (maybe also automatically downloading the patch); performance monitoring software; notices when securities sold at the requested price or time, along with net profits for the customer.
4. Surprise the customer with new or valuable information. Example: proactive retention campaigns, including customer-wowing "down-selling," as Telstra does today and MCI did in the 1990s, calling customers to inform them that they are on the wrong calling plan based on recent usage, with recommendations (the most advanced version being moving the customer without them even asking) for better-suited plans. USAA Insurance also practices down-selling as part of its customer-centric strategy: "'We try to understand individuals' needs and offer appropriate solutions rather than trying to sell them products and services that aren't in their best interest,' said [President Robert G.] Davis. It's not uncommon for a USAA representative to inform a member that he or she

has too much insurance or offer alternative products that can save added dollars. 'As long as we continue that bond with them, that's the difference between us and most other companies,' he said."[1]

The benefits of these proactive contacts are (1) improvement of the customer experience and (2) a clear cost savings for the customer and the company. One thousand outbound letters or e-mails are far cheaper than handling one thousand inbound phone calls, and proactive outbound calls are far cheaper than handling the same number of irate customers' inbound phone calls after the event.

How does a company go from being reactive to proactive? We will start by explaining the benefits to being proactive and the capabilities needed to enable proactive contact. Next we'll show how a company can find the triggers in the relationship, in service, and in sales that enable this proactive response. Then we'll look at long-running processes and how you can build proactive response into the process design to prevent contacts along the way. Finally, we'll describe how a company can close the loop and ensure that a customer can return the proactive contact, or request more of the same. As in other chapters, we'll begin by looking at examples outside customer service and then at bad and good examples.

EXAMPLES OUTSIDE CUSTOMER SERVICE

Being proactive is well accepted and well understood outside the world of customer service, as our examples—the German Autobahn, leak tracing, health care and personal safety, and stay-home messages—will show.

THE GERMAN AUTOBAHN

A great example of proactive alerts has been operational since 1974 on the German Autobahn, the (in)famous no-speed-limit interstate highways crisscrossing the country. Radio stations started sending the ARI signal that notifies car radios to unmute or stops the music cassette or CD player with for warnings about traffic congestion or accidents ahead so that the driver can get off the Autobahn onto local roads, seek another highway, or at least be prepared for a slowdown. Today digital radio services continuously feed the GPS system with traffic warnings and dynamically adjust the route chosen.

The following description of the systems is from the English-language Web site guide "Getting Around Germany":[2]

> In addition to radio traffic reports, many sections of Autobahn are equipped with traffic monitoring systems and electronic signs to warn of downstream incidents or congestion and to reduce the speed of traffic as it approaches the jam. . . .

> Traffic reports use one of several terms to describe varying levels of congestion: *"Stau"* usually means a colossal traffic jam where you'll probably get to know the people in the cars around you, *"stockender Verkehr"* indicates the only slightly more tolerable stacking or slow-and-go type traffic, while *"dichter Verkehr"* or *"zähfliesender Verkehr"* denotes the hardly-noteworthy heavy or sluggish but moving traffic.

Leak Tracing

The TraceTek leak detection system, invented by California-based Raychem Corporation, has demonstrated the value of proactive monitoring and reporting. Oil or water pipeline leaks are very expensive to isolate and repair, in some cases causing significant environmental damage and often threatening human and animal lives. With Raychem's solution, minute leaks are detected and reported to a nerve center that can dispatch a repair and restoration crew, ideally before any damage has been done. The company's recent online promotional materials describe its process.[3]

> TraceTek has been the most reliable and accurate liquid leak detection system for Commercial, Industrial and Environmental applications for the last 20 years.

> A leak detection system may be installed and operating continuously 5, 10, 15 years before being called on to provide the earliest warning of a leak. And after all that time, the system must operate perfectly, providing positive detection of a small leak, and accuracy

in the leak location. There are few systems in any facility that must perform as well as the leak detection systems, and even fewer tasked with protecting the most critical systems and equipment.

HEALTH CARE AND PERSONAL SAFETY

Proactivity abounds in the fields of health care and personal safety. Much of this we learn in childhood and no longer need to remember consciously ("Look both ways before you cross the street"); there are also some more recent inventions or exhortations (sunscreen or SunGuard clothing with the catchy tagline picturing visitors to the pyramids: "If you meet the Egyptian sun god, Ra, you'll want to be wearing protection"). Other examples are part of our everyday activities (seat belts and air bags). Together with admonitions about the dangers of smoking, drinking before driving, and other personal habits, these proactive actions have cut death and injury rates in many countries.

In the 1980s, the links between skin cancer and sun exposure became clear. Until that point, the iconic image of the bronzed Australian sunbather or surfer was common. The Australian Cancer Council and various government organizations faced the challenge of reeducating the Australian public on the dangers of long exposure to bright sunlight. The marketing and education campaign they launched in Australia has since become an icon in its own right. The "Slip-Slop-Slap" campaign was brilliant for its memorability and simplicity. The message was simply to "Slip on a shirt, Slop on some sunscreen (or sunblock), and Slap on a Hat," easy to remember for adults and children alike.

The effects of this program have been quite remarkable. Australian beaches these days are filled with children wearing hats, UV screening, and lightweight nylon bathing shirts that cover shoulders and much of the arms but still enable swimming and surfing. Twenty years later, "Slip-Slop-Slap" is still a well-understood message, though the TV ads are rarely seen anymore.

STAY HOME MESSAGES

Cities can't control the weather, but thanks to proactive messaging they can at least warn employees or students to stay at home when bad weather is on the way. Text messaging is an ideal vehicle for these alerts, routinely used in Asia, the United Kingdom, and across Europe and now with great success in the United States as well. "The evening before an ice storm swept over the University of Texas at Austin, in January [2007], administrators sent an urgent message to its 67,000 students, faculty and staff: 'Stay home tomorrow'. . . . students instantaneously received the alert as text messages on their cell phones and via email on their PCs. . . . Building managers received a similar message on their pagers. . . . The next day, the campus was empty, and there were no weather-related incidents."[4]

BAD CASES

There are many cases in which companies have not sufficiently thought about the benefits of proactive alerts and communications, and in which their reactive behavior costs them dearly in terms of customer loyalty, higher costs, or both. Let's stroll through some of the more egregious examples, the last one also demonstrating a competitor's proactive approach.

NO PLANE STRAIN

Airlines have suffered customer upset and irate calls to their service centers whenever travelers arrive at the airport, often through heavy traffic, only to discover that their flights have been delayed three hours or cancelled. With proactive technologies that we'll describe in the next section, there is no excuse for this anymore—the airline knows when flights are delayed and who is traveling, and can contact them beforehand, but doing so is often viewed as an "additional cost" to the company. Yet the total cost for the support resulting from a lack of communications far exceeds the investment in proactive alerts.

BREAD AND BATTERY

Not too long ago, many PC companies issued laptop battery recall notices to their customers. Although on the surface this could be regarded as a "proactive" step to prevent one or two customers from experiencing a problem, the mechanisms used by some of these companies were far from proactive. One manufacturer told its customers to go to a Web site or call their contact center in order to check if they had a faulty battery. The company knew which batches of batteries were potentially faulty and knew the range of ID numbers involved, but, amazingly, they didn't know which customers had those batteries (those data were deleted soon after those PCs had been sold). Despite the fact that the company had customer product details stored for many components of a PC, they simply did not know which customers to contact; instead, they left it to the customer's initiative to find out whether his battery had to be replaced. This left the company exposed: many customers would not check, and others would execute the checking procedure incorrectly (we commented in Chapter Three on how poor one of the solutions was that was put in place). It would have been far better if the company had been able to contact all those customers with batteries in the problem batches and deal with them directly.

WALKING ON RAZR BLADES

The Motorola Razr mobile phone has been a top seller in the United States and elsewhere, but unfortunately some of them allowed dirt to enter the casing and make it hard to view the phone's screen. Two of the U.S. mobile companies that sold the Razr demonstrated different philosophies of proactive versus reactive contact. AT&T Wireless (then known as Cingular) knew which customers had purchased the affected phones, so, according to Dana Cogswell, director of customer life cycle management, the company decided to tell them, "Your unit may be affected; please bring it to a retail outlet. We'll check it out and, if necessary, replace it for you free of charge!" Company B adopted the opposite strategy, even though it too knew which customers owned the affected units. The company did not inform its customers; instead, it waited for problems to develop and then dealt with them. Either the company didn't have the data to reach out to the at-risk customers or it thought it better to deal with the problem only when the customers experienced it. Clearly neither of these excuses is Best Service. Customers would rather know there is a potential problem and choose how to address it rather than suddenly experience a failure and face a more difficult issue. Full marks to AT&T Wireless; think again, company B.

Good Cases

Fortunately there are many useful examples of companies that have applied proactive alerts and have enjoyed fewer customer contacts and, in some cases, increased revenues as well. We will cover examples from Amazon, Alaska Airlines, Puget Sound Energy, XM Radio, first direct, Medibank Private, and AOL France.

Amazon Keeps the Customer in the Loop

Probably the best-known examples of Amazon's proactive alerts are order confirmations and shipping confirmations. Amazon created order confirmations soon after launch because customers nervously called or e-mailed the company right after placing the order online. (These were the early years of e-commerce when customers didn't know if the system would work or if they'd get Ann's present in time to wrap it and surprise her.) After implementing order confirmation, often sending the e-mail while the customer was still online, Amazon sliced almost to zero an entire category of customer contacts, and now every online retailer has followed suit with order confirmation alerts. Similarly, Amazon's shipping confirmation messages were instituted in response to customers calling or e-mailing the company with "Where's my stuff?" demands (covered also in Chapter Two), which became more complicated as customers started to order more than one item at a time and Amazon occasionally faced splitting the order into multiple shipments. Over time these shipping confirmation alerts have gotten more precise, stating when customers can expect their package to arrive, further reducing the need for them to contact Amazon.

Amazon also developed holiday missed-promise e-mail messages with links to cancel the order or items within the order if the company found, for some reason, that it might not meet the delivery promise made at the time of order. These messages usually shocked Amazon customers (in a good way!), sometimes generating unexpected but positive replies from customers, such as

"No, it's for little George's birthday in two weeks, so please get it to us when you can, thank you" or "I can't find this item anywhere else [which is also an example of very useful information for Amazon to get—see also Chapter Seven], so I'm happy to wait until you can get it to me."

SORRY WE'RE RUNNING LATE AT ALASKA—BUT WE CAN HELP YOU GET THERE

Another Seattle company, Alaska Airlines, pioneered using proactive alert technology to notify its customers about flight delays or cancellations, accompanied by the ability for customers to speak to a reservations agent if needed. According to Steve Jarvis, Alaska's VP of sales and customer experience (a title we heartily endorse!), "being proactive means taking care of our customers." If Alaska is running late or needs to cancel a flight, the company sends an automated alert notifying travelers and, on occasion, telling them that they have been booked on the next available flight. "We know that our travelers' time is very valuable, so we tell them as soon as we know about schedule changes, always allowing them to speak to our reservations specialists if they would like to make other arrangements." Alaska has not only scored high on customer satisfaction surveys but also reduced operating costs and improved its service levels—another win-win-win!

WEATHERING THE STORM WITH PSE

In a recent ice and windstorm in Seattle and its suburbs, two of the largest public utilities had opposite systems in place—one, Puget Sound Energy (PSE), with an almost ten-year history of providing proactive alerts, reassured its customers about service restoration, neighborhood and street-by-street situations up to the minute, and what to do during the cold weather outage; the other, with no alerts in place despite previous storms and its neighboring utility's contrary practices, suffered public outrage and regulatory pressures afterwards. Wes Pitman, former manager of customer service integrated technology at PSE, notes:

> [C]ustomers basically just want whatever information is available so they can make necessary living adjustments to "weather the storm." Power restoration during a major storm is very complex,

so providing specific details to individual customers isn't always possible. However, by leveraging the IVR to inform the customer of the details that are known, particularly in their own neighborhood, there is much less chance the caller will stay on the line to speak with a representative. The key data fields that must be quickly updated for the IVR to speak back to the customer include recognition that power is out to their house, how many others in their neighborhood are affected, what caused the outage, and, of course, the estimated time of power restoration. By deflecting the general outage status calls to automated service, the representatives are more likely to be available to quickly respond to emergency calls that are received during the storm.

WE'RE DOWN BUT NOT OUT AT XM NATION

Subscribers to broadcast or technical services who can no longer access their service are an unhappy lot, often canceling the service with the first unexpected interruption, deluging the service provider with questions about service status, or simply clogging the lines to inform the company that they're experiencing a problem, something well known to the company (we hope). A recent XM Radio service interruption shows how proactive alerts can stem the tide while also keeping subscribers up-to-date. XM is one of two U.S.-based satellite radio providers, charging a monthly subscription fee to access more than 150 advertisement-free stations offering a wide range of music, news, sports, and commentary.

In early 2007, XM suffered a systems outage, but in a series of three clearly worded messages to subscribers' e-mail addresses, the company kept everyone informed about the outage, the estimated time for service restoration, and when the service was operational again. The messages worked as planned, proactively telling customers that the company was aware of the outage and keeping them informed.

GETTING THE BALANCE RIGHT WITH FIRST DIRECT

first direct, like many banks, figured out that some of its customers called nearly every month to ask about their account balance, presumably to make sure that their mortgage check or some other large payment would clear with sufficient funds. As we mentioned in Chapter Three, the bank decided to provide an ingeniously simple solution to help these customers—it enabled them to opt into a service whereby balances would be sent via text message to their mobile phones either at regular intervals or when certain limits were exceeded. Over 3.6 million customers have opted into this proactive service.

An American bank found a different proactive answer to the same problem. For many customers who called regularly to check balances, it identified them through its analytics technology (having recognized the caller's originating phone number and bouncing it against prior calls' reason codes and collecting the customer's balance automatically). When these customers called, the message announced the balance to them before subjecting them to listening to the bank's IVR phone tree—an example of engaging self-service plus proactive messaging.

HEALTH CHECK FOR MEDIBANK HEALTH INSURANCE

Proactive messaging can also lead to increased revenues and deflected future contacts. Health insurance is a grudge purchase: a healthy customer pays premiums all year but receives no benefits (if she has had no treatments or illness). Medibank Private, one of Australia's larger health funds, contacts customers who haven't previously contacted the company in the last ten months, figuring that these customers are at risk of switching to a lower-cost product at another fund or of lapsing from private health care altogether. Medibank made outbound calls to these customers to "check" that they were on the correct product. In some cases the customers retained the same level of coverage. Those who were at high risk of lapsing altogether were down-sold to a lower level of coverage. The fund was able to prove that customers who had been contacted had far lower defection and lapse rates and that these proactive retention calls were very valuable. Dean Tillotson, Medibank Private's general manager of direct sales and service, has said that the proactive customer calls proved to be a worthwhile investment: "Customers can go a whole year without seeing a benefit from our product. They are amazingly grateful that we have taken the time to call them and advise and support them. We have proven that it prevents defection and helps our customers understand our products and services better."

TAKING THE INITIATIVE AT AOL FRANCE

Broadband Internet has been booming in many countries in the last couple of years, particularly in France. An early adopter of broadband in France was enjoying the benefits of high-speed Internet connection. This customer was satisfied with his ISP until the following happened: he had lost his connectivity for three days, so he decided to contact the ISP customer service line. There was a twenty-minute wait and then the agent logged the case. The customer's connectivity issues continued for a month, during which time he called customer service six or seven times. At this point, the customer was upset and frustrated. During one memorable call, the customer explained that he had had no Internet connectivity for a month, and was told, "I understand, sir, but you know, five years ago no one had Internet and that was fine, so you can surely live without it for a little while longer." Evidently, customer service had no control (see Chapters Two and Six), only the pain of having to deal with hundreds of frustrated customers every day.

After that response, the customer asked to cancel his subscription. He then received a call from the retention team the next day, trying to convince him not to cancel and promising that the problem would be solved within a week. Recognizing the issues involved with changing his ISP, the customer was prepared to give the company another chance. The problem was not resolved, however, and the customer cancelled the subscription.

The customer looked for a new ISP and selected AOL France this time, subscribing to an offer that did not include a modem, as he already owned one. Two days later, he received the welcome pack, with ID and password to connect. The customer entered the details and tried to connect, but it did not work. He called AOL France customer service (with little wait time) and explained the problem. The agent repeated the connection procedure, which was correct but still failed to work. The agent tried two or three other parameter changes with no success. Then the agent said, "I'm sorry, sir; I cannot get it to work. I believe your modem is not compatible with our services. I know you want to use your own modem and not rent one of ours, but I can propose to ship one of our modems for you to keep and use, free of charge. You can have the modem within two days. Is that OK for you, sir?" This was a great example of a proactive solution; clearly, staff were free to own issues and problems and fix them.

Two days later, the new modem was up and running, and the customer had Internet connectivity. The cost to AOL was a modem, but how many long technical calls were avoided? More important, the company won the customer and his business. This is a great example of a moment of truth when the customer can be won over with proactive service.

The Framework

The techniques that companies can apply to be proactive comprise four parts; we'll look at each in the next sections and describe how to

1. Build the case and capabilities for being proactive.
2. Find the triggers for launching proactive alerts.
3. Design proactive contact into long-running processes (including the technique of stapling yourself to an issue).
4. Close the loop so that the customer can tell you when to be proactive and if proactivity is working.

Build the Case and Capabilities for Being Proactive

Customers who get nervous about pending events will pick up the phone and call, fire off an angry e-mail message, or otherwise find some way to make contact, so companies need to figure out which of these potential contact-causing situations has high priority and is very urgent. The method for working out whether being proactive is worthwhile has three parameters:

1. What is the cost of the contacts that can be avoided by proactive contact?

2. What are the revenue and retention benefits in surprising the customer proactively?
3. How much will the proactive contacts cost?

These calculations might sound easy, but of course this isn't a simple process. It is very hard for a company to tell exactly what percentage of an inbound contact type will be deflected by any form of outbound contact. However, over time this deflection percentage becomes more and more predictable. This is an ideal area for experimentation with sections of the customer base or the contact types that a company thinks can be most easily prevented.

The revenue benefits are even harder to calculate than the deflected costs, but in most companies the cost equation alone is enough to justify certain types of proactive contact. The revenue issues are more pertinent to revenue-focused contacts, such as retention calls or suggestions for an alternative product. In this area, successful companies have also used retention models.

Telstra, the large Australian telecommunications provider, monitors the plan usage of its mobile phone customers. Customers who significantly overuse or underuse their plans (and are therefore paying too much) get a phone call from the company. Telstra reps then suggest alternative plans that would better suit the customer's calling patterns and usage levels. Some companies might see this as extraordinary behavior "cannibalizing" the company's own revenue, but in reality, in both of these cases the company will lose the revenue: customers whose usage is under their monthly plan are paying for calls they never make, so they are apt to switch providers for a cheaper rate; those who exceed the plan cap are often paying penalty rates for additional calls, so they might switch to a more attractive deal. After a series of experiments, Telstra learned that customers who had been moved proactively to a new plan were grateful and loyal—their attrition rates were far lower than a control group of customers who had also over- or underused their plans but had not been contacted. Therefore, the company was able to prove the net revenue benefit of this proactive contact strategy.

The cost of making the outbound contact is another important part of the equation. E-mail and SMS messages are cheap to generate. Letters are more expensive and also somewhat less timely (and therefore not useful for an urgent issue). Outbound phone contacts or rep visits are more costly again. A company assessing the benefits of generating proactive alerts needs to assess the benefits and the effectiveness of the proactive mechanisms, some of which might require little or no subsequent contact with an agent. In some cases, companies just do what is necessary for the customer. Firewall software providers, for example, will update their software, and virus-checking providers will update the virus lists on a customer's PC without asking the customer for permission or requiring her to do anything. These are good examples of "background" proactive alerts.

Another good example comes from IT help desk guru Ivy Meadors, who has many stories to share and a clear vision of how employee support programs should operate to be more proactive and not wait for problems to occur. Meadors cites such "be proactive" best practices as HP's network monitoring programs that can identify when commercial printers are running low on toner, write trouble tickets, and dispatch an administrative assistant to replace the toner cartridge or place an order for new toner if needed. "Few internal help desks are proactive because, unfortunately, they're considered overhead," Meadows explains, "but companies forget all of the hidden costs of employees trying to fix problems themselves, the opportunity to solve many issues at the same time, and the plain fact that 15 to 20 percent of calls can be eliminated when the company takes action proactively." She also concurs with points that we will raise in Chapter Six— namely, that charging technical departments that cause problems with the costs to fix those problems is an excellent way of aligning the help desk, which is responsible for resolving the calls, with the departments that are ultimately accountable for fixing the problems once and for all.

There are two critical capabilities that companies need in place in order to be proactive: (1) the analytical capability to work out when to do it, including using the Value-Irritant Matrix we described in Chapter Two; and (2) the mechanisms to launch the alerts.

To determine when it is appropriate to use proactive alerts, there is a well-honed process that has been used for many years for software programming bug fixes. Information Technology

Infrastructure Library (ITIL) helps companies understand priorities and can be easily adapted to customer support. ITIL helps developers assign standard definitions for priority and urgency so that the entire organization can use the same language, expressing the voice of the customer if only he could participate directly.

Figure 4.1 illustrates a simple way to view this process in action. The impact-urgency matrix generates five levels of priority, which correspond to five service levels.

Using the system shown in Figure 4.1 or something similar, from ITIL or an even simpler high-medium-low priority identification system, will enable the company to focus its launch of proactive measures to save the customer from leaving or to advise her when situations merit early notifications.

The next capability that a company needs is the ability to launch proactive alerts. Most companies know their customers'

FIGURE 4.1: PRIORITY MATRIX AND CORRESPONDING SERVICE LEVELS

Priority Matrix

H	3	2	1
M	4	3	2
L	5	4	3

Impact to Company

L　　M　　H

Urgency to Consumers

SLAs for Problems

Pri	Acknowledged and assigned	Fixed and confirmed
1	10 minutes	1 day
2	1 hour	3 days
3	3 hours	7 days
4	8 hours	14 days
5	24 hours	21 days

Definitions

Impact
H = I have canceled service
M = I will cancel service
L = I am upset with your service

Urgency
H = My service isn't working
M = My service slows me down
L = My service frustrates me

home or office phone numbers and are able to contact them by mail or by phone, but there are cheaper and faster methods using e-mails, calls to mobile phones, or text messaging. Companies are only just starting to gather and store these data about their customers, but others lack the infrastructure to make mass e-mail contacts with customers or send SMS messages simultaneously to large groups.

In some industries, such as online banking, it is natural to capture the customers' e-mail addresses. However, in some countries, spam legislation prevents companies from sending e-mail messages to customers without permission. So this whole area of proactive contact is one where ideally a company would capture and use permissions and preferences from customers. This means that when a new customer is set up or a new account opened, the company will need to ask the customer for permission to use some contact types or to express his contact preference. Many customers are also looking for reassurance that their e-mail address or mobile phone numbers will not be used inappropriately.

We have looked at why using proactive alerts are valuable and the techniques involved; now we need to consider when to be proactive.

FIND THE TRIGGERS FOR LAUNCHING PROACTIVE ALERTS

Once you have established issue priorities from the customer's point of view and built the capabilities to communicate proactively, it's time to address the triggers to evoke the proactive messaging. As we introduced in the preceding section, it is important to have registered the customer for "opt-in" notifications, getting the customer to specify the devices by which she wants to be alerted (home or office phone, mobile device, e-mail, and so on), ideally in an escalating fashion ("e-mail me first, but follow with a call to my cell within thirty minutes"). Companies also need to confirm an "opt-out" path in case the customer no longer wants to be contacted.

Where are places to look for appropriate triggers? Table 4.1 lists eight "trigger types" with examples.

Table 4.1: Proactive Contact Triggers

Trigger Type	Examples
Unexpected problem or failure (outside the customer's expectations)	Delayed flight notification
	Product recall
	Utility outages and faults
	Downtime of an online application
Expectation management for long-running processes	Stages of insurance claims
	Order progress and delivery
	Cable TV installation
	Mortgage application and approval
Concern for customer's best interest	Exceptional behavior on credit cards—for example, use of a card outside normal geography
	Approaching a limit or trigger of additional cost—for example, usage levels on a broadband account that will trigger additional charges
	Mobile phone use exceeding plan limits
	Health insurance customer nearing claim limit
Reminder of required activity	Telling a car customer that a service is due
	Monitoring products under warranty, and warning that warranty will expire
Retention triggers	Renewal notifications prior to anniversaries
	Too much or too little activity on a given product
	Fees or charges that will be triggered
Customer contact history and behavior	Identifying that a customer always asks for her balance
Providing information to customer in a way he can control	Proactive balance notification

Each of these triggers requires careful analysis. Deciding if a process or reason justifies some form of proactive contact requires an assessment of the following:

- The volume and cost of inbound contacts (Is it a well-established and high-volume contact reason?)
- The percentage of customers who do and don't contact the company about this reason (Is it worth being proactive if 99.9 percent of customers seem happy with reactive contact?)
- The level of accuracy and hit rate that the company will have with the proactive contact. For example, Amazon knows that order status e-mails will be read by the customer; if a company were trying to call customers for the same thing, it would have a lower hit rate.
- The importance and urgency to the customer and company as described in the ITIL methodology.
- The available contact channels and their likely success rate.

When considering these triggers, a company must determine how many proactive contacts are needed. Is it enough to tell a customer that her electricity is off, or does she also need to be told when it is turned back on? Does an airline need to notify of a delay and, later, of the revised flight time? Amazon identified multiple proactive contacts that were necessary on each order. On some long-running processes, proactive contacts may be needed at many stages, and they will be even more necessary if problems arise.

There are many triggers that an organization can consider using. We will now look at some of the most complex processes and how they need to be handled.

DESIGN PROACTIVE CONTACTS INTO LONG-RUNNING PROCESSES AND "STAPLE YOURSELF TO AN ISSUE"

Several years ago, in their *Harvard Business Review* article "Staple Yourself to an Order," Shapiro, Rangan, and Sviokla argued that company executives are not paying enough attention to how their customers often wait—and wait—for status information on orders or other internal company operations because too many parties are involved with insufficient role definitions. We have adapted this concept for customer support with these six steps:

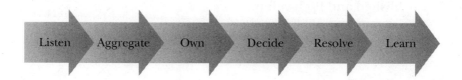

Companies can assess where in their complex processes these steps are performed, and who performs them. We call this process "stapling yourself to an issue." The idea is to follow a cutomer issue through all the steps that it goes through and note who does what and when, covering all the issues raised by the customer and handled by the company. The same approach can be applied to any complex process, such as

- Insurance claims
- Mortgage applications
- New utility or phone service connections
- Passport applications
- Broadband or pay TV installation and connection

The idea is not only to understand the process but also to consider at what points proactive contact is needed (to get or provide information) or what delays or exceptions would justify proactive contact. If a customer expects a credit card application to be processed in a week and it gets stuck partway through the process, should someone call the applicant? For sensitive processes like insurance claims, our answer would be yes of course. How much goodwill and extra time is bought by a call to a customer saying that the process has been delayed and revising the customer's expectations? A great deal. Customers are more tolerant if they are informed. Ignorance is far from bliss.

Companies' failure to "staple themselves to an issue" results in incomplete assignment of roles and responsibilities, often leaving the customer in the dark during the life cycle of doing business with the company. Let's look first at the "before" picture using the RACI framework to display and compare each player's roles. (The RACI methodology aligns Responsible, Action, Consulted, or Informed roles.)

◯ Responsible   ◯ Action   ● Consulted   ● Informed   ◯ No role

Customer	Steps	Customer Service	Operations	Marketing	Development	Sales	Executives
●	Listen	◯	◯	●	●	●	●
	Aggregate	◯	◯	●	●	●	●
	Own	●	◯	●	●	●	●
	Decide	●	◯	●	●	●	●
●	Resolve	◯	◯	●	●	●	●
	Learn			◯	●	●	●

This analysis reveals several big problems. First, there are redundant responsible roles at the start of the process. More critical, however, was that customer service and the customer were not informed along the way until, voila, at the end of the process, marketing created the solution and informed the customer. No learning, no executive or customer service involvement—and therefore a recipe for unwanted future contacts.

The next chart illustrates a completely different story, one of engaging the right parties in each step and keeping the customer fully in the loop, being proactive at its finest!

The RACI framework can be extended to each stage of complex processes. In a mortgage application, for example, it might be needed for each critical stage, such as credit assessment and property evaluation.

○ Responsible	◔ Action	◑ Consulted	● Informed	○ No role

Customer	Steps	Customer Service	Operations	Marketing	Development	Sales	Executives
◔	Listen	○	○	○	●	○	●
	Aggregate	○	○	◑	○	○	○
●	Own	●	●	○	○	○	●
●	Decide	●	●	○	○	○	●
●	Resolve	●	○	○	○	○	●
◔	Learn	○	◑	○	●	●	●

On the sales and retention side, the issues are a little different. Proactive contact is driven less by the processes being followed and more by intimate knowledge of the customer and the relationship. Shoshana Zuboff's concept of "deep support" reinforces this essential point of being proactive with one's customers, especially those in critical or urgent situations, on the sales side as well as service. Denis Pombriant explains this idea:

> As long as we think about the sale as discrete from service, Zuboff argues, we will always face the question of how to engage the customer to make the next purchase. We ought to be building service into the relationship, not adding it on. Bringing the two together is what should constitute the vendor-customer relationship (don't they have software for that?), and it is what Zuboff calls "deep support." That's the new paradigm we need to shift toward. The highest form of service is found in knowing your customers so well that you can anticipate their needs and be ready with proactive solutions. Deep support is not free. It has to be paid for out of the margin a vendor gets for the product, or it needs to be provided under a separate agreement. Done right, the process of creating a service center that can reliably generate revenue is a no-brainer. It is an act of faith in the customer and a demonstration of commitment to building long-term relationships.[5]

As we have seen in the good cases, some companies are assessing the stages in product use and the value that they see in the relationship with the customer and, drawing from their deep knowledge of customer behavior, deciding where proactive contact is needed.

CLOSE THE LOOP

As the two RACI charts demonstrate, it's critical that senior managers not hide from the customers while an issue is being resolved. Equally, companies need to provide the opportunity and avenue for the proactively contacted customer to express his dismay at what he's hearing or, more positively, conduct another transaction with the company immediately upon receiving the alert. For example:

- When the airline sends an alert message to the passenger's mobile device to inform her that her scheduled flight has been canceled, but that she has been booked on the next flight to the same destination (let's say that means a three-hour delay arriving), the airline needs to ask the passenger, "If this is acceptable, say or press one; if this is not acceptable to you and you would like to speak immediately with one of our reservations rebooking specialists [perhaps a higher-level or sanctioned position], say or press zero." At that point, if the customer does say "zero" because a three-hour later arrival means she will miss the planned meeting, then she is placed at the head of the queue to speak with an agent who can cancel the reservation or rebook for a future date.
- When the online retailer sends an e-mail confirming that the order has shipped, it also should provide a link for the customer to return to the Web site to shop for another item.
- When the securities firm calls with a message such as recorded message stating that the prearranged stock sale has been conducted successfully, it should also provide a message such as "Do you want to speak to our investments manager to discuss how we can distribute or reinvest your funds?", thus extending the revenue cycle.

Don't expect proactive contact to be one-way. Ensure that you think through how customers are likely to respond, and be ready for it. Some customers will just delete a notification e-mail, others will respond and say thank you, and some might send an e-mail that needs a response. In all cases, you have to be prepared that a proactive contact may generate a series of responses. You'd better be ready!

Summary

Being proactive on the customer's behalf launches this three-stage rocket:

1. Understand all customer contact-causing events using the Value-Irritant analysis (Chapter Two) or the impact-urgency matrix (Figure 4.1).
2. Classify the events with a focus on two key types in particular—critical life cycle and revenue-bearing—and then focus on where the customer needs to be more in control. Work through the principal steps in the process, stapling yourself to the issue so that the need for proactive contact becomes clear.
3. Create appropriate solutions using prearranged media that are chosen based on what the customer needs, and be sure to close the loop (for example, offering an option to speak to an agent).

Being proactive produces multiple benefits ranging from renewed sales rates, fewer unhappy customers, happier agents who no longer have to provide rote answers or updates, and lower costs—all in all, well worth the efforts to install the triggers and closed loops.

Canada Post president and CEO Moya Greene described the proactive approach we recommend this way: "What is your customer service mantra? We certainly have a very important value, which is that we know we have to work to earn our customers' business. We can't be complacent. We can't rest on laurels thinking that we have some God-given right to be in the market. We don't. Our mantra is to know that it takes proactive effort [to] make sure that you're continuously meeting your customers' expectations."[6] We agree, and would add that it also often saves the company a great deal of money, time, and effort.

Survey Questions

Please score your company for these three key questions covering being proactive, and refer to Appendix A to check your progress from Basic Service to Better Service to Best Service.

8. What is the ratio of proactive communications and alerts to inbound customer-initiated contacts in your company?
   a. We do proactively contact our customers, but I do not know this ratio.
   b. We do not provide any sort of proactive alerts.
   c. Approximately 1:10.
   d. Close to 1:2 or 1:3.

9. How often do you set priorities for customer issues along some sort of impact-urgency matrix?
   a. Never
   b. Some of the time
   c. All of the time
   d. Only for big issues

10. In our company,
   a. Proactive contacts do not apply.
   b. We use proactive alerts in exceptional circumstances, such as for a product recall.
   c. We have a range of issues or reasons that trigger our reaching out to the customer.
   d. Rather than wait for our customers to contact us, we use proactive contacts wherever possible.

CHAPTER FIVE

MAKE IT REALLY EASY TO CONTACT YOUR COMPANY
Instead of Dodging the Bullet

When asked why he didn't throw to the cut-off man, [Seattle Mariner right fielder] Ichiro said, "I knew I didn't have time to look, then throw. I knew where the base was and I got the ball and threw it right away."
—J. HICKEY, "ICHIRO IGNITES M'S," SEATTLE POST-INTELLIGENCER, MAY 21, 2003

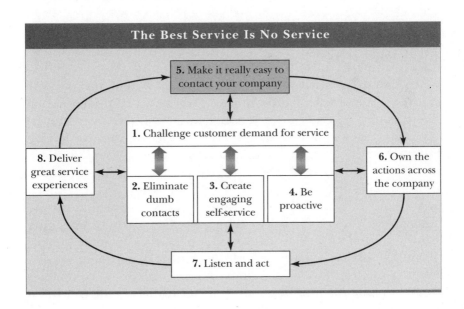

The Best Service Is No Service

5. Make it really easy to contact your company

1. Challenge customer demand for service

8. Deliver great service experiences

2. Eliminate dumb contacts

3. Create engaging self-service

4. Be proactive

6. Own the actions across the company

7. Listen and act

THE PRINCIPLE

Isn't it amazing how some companies change between the time that you are a prospect and when you become a customer? When you're a prospect, they can't do enough to get your attention through marketing, special offers, and an array of mechanisms for buying products or services. The marketing side of many organizations would have us believe that they are really easy to do business with and are accessible night or day. But after you've been seduced by the spin of many of these businesses and have signed on the dotted line, doesn't the story change? Suddenly, you're searching around to find anyone to help you; you're stuck in some eternal queue for service or have to find the returns department hidden away on the top floor of the department store. Some companies seem to want your business but not want to deal with you when you are a customer. The really incompetent companies take it even further by making it hard to become a customer in the first place. For example, a major department store cut staff numbers to such an extent that customers complained that there weren't enough people to answer questions or even take their money; it's a ludicrous state of affairs when revenue walks out the door for marginal cost cutting.

By some accounts, only one out of ten customers who experience problems with a company's products or services complain to the company. Lurking among the remaining 90 percent of unexpressed frustration are gems that the company needs to hear and interpret so as to figure out what to do to improve its current and future offerings. Further, those in the "quiet majority" will tell seven or more of their friends about the bad service they experienced; the spread of negative information can spiral out of control, as customers now can post their frustrations on the Internet in blogs or other places, influencing vastly greater numbers of prospective and current customers.

Therefore, every organization needs to take a major step before it is in a position to challenge the demand for service. This step will feel like a step in the wrong direction because it is likely to result in more customer contact rather than less. It involves making it really easy for customers to contact you, opening the floodgates to contacts that were previously suppressed. We think of it as opening the tap or widening the contact funnel.

Unfortunately, many organizations, as we will illustrate, have made themselves so hard to contact that they have ignored their customers' true wants and needs; others have ignored feedback that they really need to hear—thus papering over the real issues with their processes and products. Customers may have given up on the organization, found their own work-arounds or solutions, or be in the process of leaving. Being hard to contact is very dangerous, all too similar to the ostrich with its head in the sand saying, "No, I can't see any lions."

If your customers find it hard to contact you, they can't tell you (1) what makes them unhappy, (2) why your products or services didn't meet their expectations, (3) what they like and dislike, and (4) what would make them interested in buying more or buying less. Some companies are so determined to control how and when customers contact them that they appear prepared to risk disaster—or aren't even aware of the danger. Restricting customer contact is the path to self-destruction because it promotes "groupthink" that causes companies to lose touch with their customers and with their own business. Customers are very valuable eyes and ears that can give you vital insight into how your products are working, how your staff is behaving, and even what your competitors are doing. In this chapter, we will emphasize how to widen the customer contact funnel and how to benefit from making it really easy for customers to contact your company.

We've identified three "maturity levels" in producing this increased customer contact:

---

1. Build the tap. Lay the foundation by establishing the basic mechanisms you'll need to have in place so that customers can contact you.
2. Open the tap. Go beyond making it possible for customers to contact you and move to actively encouraging customer contacts in order to foster the kinds of contact analysis and challenging of demand that we described in Chapter Two. One of our basic premises is that it is critical to encourage more contact so that you can challenge it, and we'll explain why.
3. Let go of the tap. Start to shape and mold the mechanisms of customer contact by putting yourself in the customers' shoes. At this mature level, you give customers more choice and start to consider how they will want to contact you in different situations and what choices you can give them. Few companies have achieved this level, but we hope that more will aspire to reap its benefits, including what we call two-way control: on the one hand, customers feel in control of the way they can deal with a company and feel they have choices, with their preferences always available and used; on the other hand, the company is using mechanisms that are simple and inexpensive for it to use.

We'll describe each of these levels in more detail and illustrate with examples.

Examples Outside Customer Service

Let's first spend time outside the customer service world to learn how to produce greater value for all parties by making it really easy to encourage contacts.

Wikimania

One of the better-known and widely read examples of building or opening the tap is the wiki-based content development engine, led by Wikipedia, darling of Web 2.0. Wikipedia (www.wikipedia .org) has become legend in its short history—a collaborative process for anyone and everyone to contribute content that each person edits and, over time, improves and perfects. With Web sites in English, French, Chinese, Dutch, German, Polish, Italian, Portuguese, Spanish, Finnish, Swedish, and other languages, chock full of over five million articles (as of October 2007), Wikipedia is used more than any other online encyclopedia, often appearing first in search engines thanks to its timeliness, currency, and links to supporting sources. Similar bodies of knowledge used to be published by a core group of "experts," laboriously in book form, costing many hundreds if not thousands of dollars; as soon as they appeared they were out-of-date, and the annual supplements were awkward and confusing to find what you needed. The Internet has produced much advancement over the book editions, some also produced by experts but others by enterprising business managers or software companies like Microsoft Encarta. But the Internet also spawned open-source software, producing the easy-to-edit Wikipedia and several spin-offs and variations, such as Wikitravel (www.wikitravel.org) and the Encyclopedia of Life (www.eol.org), which aims to chronicle online all living flora and fauna, thanks to contributions from amateurs and experts alike all over the world.

One of the most impressive aspects of Wikimania is the egalitarian nature of content entry and editing—if a world-renowned expert in stained-glass window construction submits an article, someone whose favorite pastime is taking pictures of Gothic cathedrals in France can edit that article and upload her favorite pictures and descriptions, and yet another person can challenge the expert with a different perspective—all within minutes, visible to everyone. Moreover, the "community" (as we will expand this concept later in the book) winds up agreeing on the format and structure for presenting content—for example, the sequence in which to present a movie star's biography or a rock musician's discography or, in the case of Wikitravel, how to share details on a city or other popular place. (The standard ten-point content is "understand; get in; get around; see; do; buy; eat; drink; sleep; get out.")

Because all "voices" are heard and applied in the wiki worlds, everyone benefits (well, maybe not travel guidebook or hardbound encyclopedia publishers) from updated information vetted by multiple parties, in real time if needed—a clear case of being easy to contact.

THE CHARRETTE PLANNING PROCESS

In many countries of the world, town planning is a very secret process. Although town or urban planning departments might publish their plans and involve a certain amount of local participation, it appears at times that the consultation is not really wanted. Any alternatives or objections put up by those who review the plans or attend consultations are treated more as obstacles to getting the plans through than as a necessary part of coming up with plans that everyone likes. Occasionally plans are leaked to the press, forcing councils and planning groups to fight rearguard actions to defend their plans, which somehow become more sacred in the face of criticism.

But in the new urbanist movement, the "Charrette" process (named after a French word for the carts used to collect designs from architecture students in the nineteenth century) is the equivalent of our service idea of opening the floodgates. Rather than suppressing and fighting citizen ideas, the Charrette process invites and embraces feedback from the community in the development of new urban plans. Typically the Charrette process lasts four days and involves multiple rounds of significant public input and reviews; as a result, the urban design or town plan is embraced by the community (there's that word again!).

This Charrette process is similar to the philosophy we're advocating: make it really easy for customers to contact you; they will tell you useful information, and if you have the appropriate processes in place, the nature of their demand (see again Chapter Two) and their feedback (see Chapter Seven) will help you improve the business.

"Do You Know Where Your Child Is?"

On American television in the 1960s and 1970s there were frequent public-service advertisements asking parents of teens "Do you know where you child is?" and now that we authors have preteens (David) and teenagers (Bill), this is hitting close to home. There's a new way to make it really easy for teenage drivers and their cars to keep in touch with their parents—no, not the ubiquitous mobile phone, but a new program based on global positioning system (GPS) technology called Teensurance, being offered to Safeco Insurance customers.

The Teensurance system also includes 24/7 roadside assistance, safety assessments, and parental resources, but the Safety Beacon™ Safety and Protection System's built-in GPS lets the vehicle communicate directly with parents. Among the features designed to help young drivers avoid problems and get out of jams are speed reminders, an instant locate service, safe driving zones, remote door unlock, stolen vehicle retrieval support, arrival and departure notifications, and driving curfew reminders. With real-time notification to the parent's PC, the teenager can obtain directions more clearly than calling home with "Dad, where am I?" and having to describe cross streets or landmarks.

Bad Cases

Unfortunately, customer service is full of bad cases that are the opposite of "making it really easy to contact your company," frustrating customers and robbing the company of valuable ideas. Some companies offer customer contact channels that don't work; others eschew such channels as e-mail or SMS because they don't think that their customers want to use them to contact the company, or vice-versa. Perennial surveys, such as the one whose results are graphed here, underscore how easily customer contact mechanisms can become blocked and unworkable, in this case because one of the foundation pieces (e-mail responsiveness) is missing, and getting worse:

PERCENTAGE OF COMPANIES RESPONDING TO E-MAIL WITHIN TWENTY-FOUR HOURS

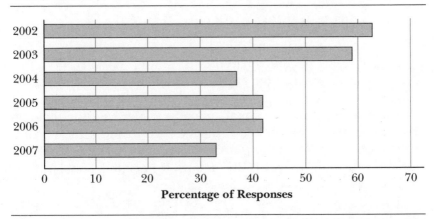

Source: Computing Technology Industry Association; cited in *Baseline,* June 2007

We will summarize numerous bad examples under two broad categories: the consciously incompetent and the unconsciously incompetent.

THE CONSCIOUSLY INCOMPETENT

Consciously incompetent companies set out to make it hard, by design, for their customers to contact them, whether to cut costs, make their lives easier, or "game" the performance measurement systems. They might also resort to this off-putting behavior in a crunch when replacing systems or adding outsourcers or operating during peak seasons, but none of these cases is acceptable or excusable. There are two types of consciously incompetent companies—call chokers and channel prisons.

Call Chokers

Call chokers deliberately turn off communication channels or limit the number of customers who can use them at the same time. During its recent customer service operations expansion to a new facility, a large U.S. airline played this message every time a customer called its toll-free main reservations line: "Due to heavy volumes, all of our agents are assisting other customers. Please call back later." Amazingly, there was no mention of going to the Web to book a reservation or check status or do any number of activities that the airline offered, and of course there was no way to ask for a callback, which we will cover later as a preferred alternative.

Another consciously incompetent company illustrated call choking by shutting off demand in an effort to meet service level targets. This company, like many others, measured how many calls were answered in twenty seconds. (A typical rule or target is "80-20," meaning that 80 percent of the calls should be answered in twenty seconds, the equivalent of three rings.) Often, as in this case, this was seen as the key measure of service delivery (which it isn't, by the way, but that is a whole different story). The contact center technical staff found a way to game, or beat, the metric: they choked demand by restricting the number of lines (or trunks) into their contact center, which meant that many callers simply got a busy signal. The number of callers who got a busy signal wasn't measured, so the contact center staff were able to declare that they met their targets. As a result, on the calls that were measured, they hit their service level targets, answering the calls in the prescribed time. To the company's board of directors, everything looked rosy, but the company failed to measure the number of customers who got a busy signal and had to try to work out when to call back or simply gave up. So, to use our analogy, some people in this company did their best to hide the tap.

Channel Prisons

A second form of conscious incompetence results from the channel wars that rage in many organizations—for example, Web sites that have been created by IT staff determined to keep customers there at all costs. At one major telecommunications provider, once customers selected "self-serve," they became stuck—finding a phone number to call, a major search exercise in its own right, produced failed searches or irrelevant information. The assumption of the Web designers seemed to be, "If you've gotten this far, we'll keep you here." An older example is "voicemail jail" or its more recent incarnation—interactive voice response (IVR) systems that provide no "escape" to an operator or live assistance. As we already debunked (in Chapter Three), self-service doesn't need to be this complicated, but many of these dead-end IVR systems are designed for that reason—for "call prevention." There's even a blog available now to guide customers in bypassing IVR systems and reaching a real person quickly, a sad indictment of the industry.

THE UNCONSCIOUSLY INCOMPETENT

Although the aforementioned cases may seem like extreme examples—and believe us, they are not unique—at least they involved planned and conscious moves. Many other companies make it hard for their customers to contact them without meaning to do so; in these unconsciously incompetent cases, companies seem to be unaware that their marketing, contact mechanisms, or Web sites are making it hard for their customers to reach them. Let's review four classic examples, which we refer to as overwhelming options; policy shields; missing at the moment of need; and not your hours, ours.

Overwhelming Options

One major IT company tried hard to give the customers many ways to call it for support; however, it had "unconsciously" taken this idea to extremes by offering over thirty thousand phone numbers worldwide. On the surface, that seemed like giving the customer choice, but in reality it was almost paralyzing. In each country, the company could have more than a thousand numbers that the customer was supposed to figure out how to use, placing the onus on the customer to divine how to do business with the company and making it extremely difficult to find the right place to call. The odds of hitting it right the first time? Very low!

Bowing to customer feedback about being unable to pick the right phone number to call, this company recognized the problem, but its initial solution was hardly any better: it constructed elaborate, multichoice IVR menus to "help" customers navigate to the department they needed. In reality, however, this meant putting every customer through the same complex IVR system, and the jungle of options was spaghetti-like in its complexity; on average, customers spent five minutes wading through the IVR before being placed in a queue, as all agents tended to be busy. Many customers simply gave up (the abandonment rate in IVR systems is a key metric, often not captured or reported), and many more got through to the wrong type of support and had to be redirected. The net result was a dreadful customer experience, more work than the company needed (with all the wasted transfers), and many unhappy customers (who bought less, reducing the company's formerly heady growth rates significantly). This "solution" also caused confusion in the company as to how many customers were really calling and for what reasons; the options that customers chose certainly weren't a reflection of their needs but, rather, of desperation.

Policy Shields

A second form of unconscious incompetence exists when organizations don't recognize how restrictive their options have become. Take the example of a leading cable TV company. One day, a customer called up to request support for a faulty set-top box and told the agent that he had already been through the suggested steps in the manual for broken boxes; he had performed the various reboots, and the box still didn't work. Here's the painful dialogue that followed:

"Sorry," said the agent, "but you'll have to repeat those with me on the phone."

"Are you sure?" asked the customer, "because I've done all those checks."

"Sorry," replied the agent.

The customer repeated the process and, not surprisingly, got the same outcomes.

"OK," said the customer, "now what?"

"Well, we'll need to send someone around to fix it," said the agent.

"Good," said the customer. "How soon?"

"Is tomorrow OK?" asked the agent.

"Great," replied the customer, "but it will need to be early morning or late afternoon so someone can be around."

"Well, we can offer you nine to twelve or two to five," said the agent proudly.

"So I have to wait in all morning or all afternoon?" said the customer. "Why can't you be here at nine A.M. or four P.M.?"

"We can do nine to twelve or two to five; that's how it works," said the agent.

"Well, that's not good enough," said the customer, now getting agitated.

The customer asked to speak to a supervisor but didn't succeed. After much argument, the customer dug in his heels.

"So what if I decide not to have it fixed? I'm sick of this, and I just want to terminate my dealings with you."

"Well, I'm sorry to hear that," said the agent. "If that's the case, we'll have to collect the box."

"That sounds fine," said the customer. "If you want to send someone around to collect it, I can offer you nine to twelve or two to five."

"Sorry," said the agent, "but we tell you when we're going to come."

"No, you don't," said the customer, who then explained, "I can't be sure when I'll be there between nine and twelve or two and five, so the field rep can wait on my porch out of the rain."

The long and the short of this true story is that the call was eventually escalated to a supervisor, and the customer was able to arrange for a guaranteed early morning repair visit. But it took the ingenuity of the customer to flip the situation on its head to show the company how ludicrously restrictive its process was.

Missing at the Moment of Need

Possibly the worst case of unconscious incompetence we have seen occurred at a major insurance business. None of us likes paying for insurance, but we buy it for the peace of mind that if something goes wrong, we are protected. So the critical moment of truth for an insurance business comes when we make a claim, when we judge whether all the premiums we have paid have been worthwhile.

Poor claims experience obviously leads customers to switch to another provider, yet this is a delicate juggling act for all insurance companies; on the one hand, they want to satisfy customer needs, but on the other hand, their claims expense is by far the biggest expense line item. (In the typical insurance business, the cost of managing the business and serving customers can be less than 10 percent of the costs, whereas the claims line can represent the other 90 percent.)

In this particular insurance business, the company had not set out to create poor experiences, but the end results were distressing to watch:

- The company established a claims process whereby customers called a contact center known as Teleclaims. The idea was that this dedicated Teleclaims unit would log claim details and then act as a channel for contacts to the departments that would process the claims—for example, claim assessors for burglaries, or repair shops for motor claims.
- However, the net result of the execution of this model was a claims process that made it hard for the customer to make contact. Lodging a claim was straightforward enough and something the Teleclaims area could do; however, for any calls after the initial lodgment, the process fell apart. If customers wanted to know whether a claim had been assessed or when the next stage of a process was to occur, the Teleclaims area would look up the status of the claim, but often had no idea when actions were occurring or what decisions had been made. At some points in time, the other claim-processing teams would fall behind in their work, and that caused even bigger problems. As processes took more time, more and more customers would call to ask about progress or issues, but the Teleclaims team could do little to help. It got so bad that the wait times for the Teleclaims contact center were being measured in minutes rather than seconds. One customer called and said she had set her alarm for three in the morning so that she could call when no one else was waiting in the queue.

This example of unconscious incompetence illustrates a model by which the company had narrowed the funnel of contacts to an area not able to deal with them. In theory its concept of a "one-stop shop" to handle customer claims sounded appropriate; however, in reality, the company had restricted demand and was unable to deal with the customers' real needs. The departments causing the issues, such as assessing or payments, didn't feel the pain of the issues they were causing for customers (this was a core argument in Chapter Two). Worse still, the senior manager responsible for the contact center was blamed for delivering poor service. This case illustrates a company that had not only made itself hard to contact but also managed the demand for contact very poorly.

Not Your Hours, Ours

Another form of unconscious incompetence is exhibited when hours of operation don't match customers' needs for service, similar to the policy shields dialogue earlier. Major sellers on a well-known auction site have determined that they get their best results (that is, the most bidders) when their auctions close on Sunday nights, one of the more popular ending times. An hour or two prior to the auction closing is the point at which they receive the most contacts about their products—last-minute bidders e-mail with questions to clarify pricing or ask feature questions. Many sellers find this customer behavior very frustrating: "The nearer to the close of the auction, the more likely we are to get stupid questions about things that are already written up in the product listing." These sellers may be irritated, but this behavior on the part of customers seems to us to be very predictable. In the panic and frenzy of an auction about to close, customers have less time to read product descriptions and payment or shipment rules. With the large number of auctions closing on Sunday night, you would think that these sellers would have someone on a special support shift to deal with the last-minute flurry of questions, but fewer than 10 percent of the sellers recognize this need. They all work regular nine-to-five shifts during the weekdays, despite the fact that the critical customer sales support need is on Sunday evenings. Therefore, the tap is wide open on Sunday nights, but unfortunately the water is flowing straight down the drain. The sellers don't know how much more business they would obtain if they were available to deal with the last-minute questions!

GOOD CASES

The companies that are good at making it easy to contact them also make this skill look easy to do; when you observe these businesses, it seems so obvious that they clearly "get it." Nevertheless, they represent the minority of the companies that we see today. We will touch on USAA Insurance, Apple, i-select, Virgin, Bank of America, and Amazon.

PICK A NUMBER, ANY NUMBER, AT USAA

One of the most successful U.S.-based insurance providers is USAA, originally serving current and former U.S. military officers but now open to senior enlisted ranks as well. USAA's biggest reason for losing customers is death, not competition or poor service, and USAA "members" (as they are called, and in full disclosure, Bill Price has been a USAA member since 1972) have enabled the company to win coveted quality awards year after year. One of USAA's hallmarks is making it easy to contact the company. Figure 5.1 is a screen shot of a small portion its Contact Us Web page. In addition to sharing its contact information broadly, USAA connects its own contact centers with third parties that provide specialized services

FIGURE 5.1:   USAA CONTACT US WEB PAGE

USAA Federal Savings Bank

Banking Services

1-800-531-USAA(8722)
(1-800-531-USAA(8722) in San Antonio)
Monday - Friday, 7:30 a.m. - 10 p.m. CT
Saturday, 8 a.m. - 6 p.m. CT

Lobby Hours
(210-498-7979 in San Antonio, Texas)
Monday - Friday, 8:30 a.m. - 5 p.m. CT
Saturday, 8:30 a.m. - 1 p.m. CT

Drive Thru Hours
(210-498-7979 in San Antonio, Texas)
Monday - Friday, 7 a.m. - 6 p.m. CT
Saturday, 8:30 a.m. - 1 p.m. CT

Mailing Address
USAA Federal Savings Bank
10750 McDermott Freeway
San Antonio, TX 78288-9876

ABA/Transit Routing Number: 314074269

such as credit cards or business insurance, making it seem to the USAA member that he is still working with one company when in fact he might be touching different enterprises.

APPLE: GENIUS, PURE GENIUS

Not only has Apple revolutionized product design with easy-to-use computers, iPod MP3 players, iPhones, and other products, but the company has also led the way in making itself really easy to contact. The Apple Stores mushrooming across the United States, Canada, the United Kingdom, Italy, Australia, and Japan fulfill the promise on the Apple Web site: "Innovative, approachable, and designed like no place else. The Apple Store is the best place to learn everything there is to know about the Mac or iPod. Wondering what products are best for you? Let our Mac Specialists answer all your questions. Need a hand setting up your Mac or want to get the most out of your iPod? Visit the Genius Bar for one-on-one support and advice. Free workshops—for beginners and pros—are always available. Welcome to the Apple Store." Steve Jobs, Apple's CEO, has managed this rollout brilliantly where other companies have failed, partly because he imagined a completely different customer experience: welcoming customers. "He set out to create the conditions most likely to convert museum visitors into actual customers, and then to make those customers feel that they were being pampered long after the sale was consummated."[1]

WHERE TO CALL ON EACH i-SELECT PAGE

i-select is a rapidly growing health insurance broker in Australia. Its whole business model is built around the proposition that health insurance is a highly complex product and that customers and prospects find it very hard to compare the features and benefits of different companies. By making their products complex and hard to compare, the insurance companies themselves opened the opportunity for a broker like i-select. The company also recognized that customers and prospects were researching and comparing products online and that visiting a half dozen Web sites was too time consuming. The company knows that making it easy for the customer means that its customers need to be able to talk to someone as well, so every page of the i-select Web site has the number to call in very large letters. Rather than hiding the number or making the customer hunt for it, i-select actively seeks the calls.

By comparison, many of the health funds whose products i-select sells are much more restrictive about publishing contact details on their Web sites; their mind-set seems to be, "Well, you're using our self-service now, so we don't want to tempt you with those expensive staffed channels, even for sales." This "protective" behavior opens the door to i-select and others like it to intermediate between the customer and the manufacturers of the products (health insurance, mortgages, and so on). Ironically, by being concerned about the cost of contact, the companies who manufacture the products give away much more money in sales commissions to a company like i-select that makes itself really easy to contact.

VIRGIN: CAN YOU SEE ME NOW?

In many markets in the world, the Virgin airline brand is competing at the budget end of the market; self-service sales enable Virgin to keep its costs and fares competitive by avoiding travel agent commissions and reducing the cost of person-to-person channels, such as contact centers. Many customers have come to expect that if they want the cheapest fares, they will have to complete the booking themselves on a Web site. Virgin prefers this customer behavior, and works hard to make sure that the Web site offers a simple and easy booking experience; it offers such features as storing and reusing returning customer details and allowing frequent flyers to progress quickly through booking screens.

However, Virgin doesn't try to restrict the customer to this self-service mechanism; phone numbers are readily available on every screen, and when customers print their boarding passes at home or work, the phone number is printed on the pass so that the customer can easily call at any stage. Virgin also uses its airplanes to encourage contact: the company's web address is emblazoned in big letters across its planes. So even in this case where the low-cost business model would seem to encourage restricted contact, Virgin takes the "open the tap" approach.

BANK OF AMERICA: WHERE DID YOU GO?

Sometimes companies surprise us when they take the extra effort to make it easy to contact them. Here's a short summary of one such experience with Bank of America (this story came to us by e-mail): "This morning, I was put on hold while being transferred to another agent, and I realized I didn't have time to wait, so I hung up. A minute later, the original agent called me back and apologized that the call had been dropped, and tried to get me back in the queue. Not all companies would want to implement that, but for a bank, it makes great sense, and emphasizes the 'personal, caring' stuff they try to project."

AMAZON CHANNELS OPEN FOR BUSINESS

Amazon is a case in point of not wanting to restrict contact. Customers certainly have many self-help choices and can fire off e-mail inquiries if they need anything. Amazon piloted and has expanded a "click for callback" feature that exploits the latest Web-based phone technologies to support the customer. The Amazon agent who then calls the customer knows the entire history of the customer's visits to the Web site and is already able to figure out why the customer needs help, which (1) improves the connection between customer and Amazon and (2) shortens the handle time.

Even Amazon has suffered challenges to ensuring that it is easy to contact. For a period of time, the company emphasized its vaunted self-service, FAQs, and rapid, complete responses via e-mail messages, and made the toll-free number harder to find. The number never changed, and it was easily found on Google and other search engines, but Amazon's systems frustrated some of its customers with contradictory order status where a quick phone call would have been very helpful. In the run-up to a recent holiday season, Amazon e-mailed U.K. customers (several times) to remind them that December 18 would be the cutoff date for orders to ensure that they would arrive before Christmas. However, Web site messages were somewhat mixed: pages for some items stated that the product would normally be shipped within twenty-fours hours, but a message appeared at the top of the screen stating that all orders could not be guaranteed for delivery before Christmas. Following the site's e-mail process only compounded the confusion: there were automated replies stating, "If you've explored the above links and still need to get in touch with us, you will find all our contact details in the online help guide." Fortunately, Amazon listened to its customers, synchronized the systems' messaging, and restored easier access to the phone channel.

THE FRAMEWORK

The main reason for making it easy to contact your company is that your business needs to hear from your customers. As we will discuss in Chapter Seven, customers love to tell you what isn't working that you need to fix or what they need from your company. Burying their issues will merely frustrate them and drive them to your competitors.

Being easy to contact, though, doesn't just mean making different mechanisms available; equally, if not more important, is making those mechanisms easy to use when customers get there. Companies should question every extra option they offer customers on the phone or every queuing decision they ask them to make in a branch. Companies must constantly put themselves in the customer's shoes: How would *you* want to be treated as a customer? What options would *you* want to have available? How would *you* feel if options were not even offered? Further, as we'll cover in more detail later, companies need to adopt and scrutinize new performance metrics with regard to being easy to reach.

The amazing thing is how much customers appreciate easy contact and how it also makes life easy for support staff. When customers are pleasantly surprised that someone answers the phone and is available or, when online, they find on the first or second page exactly what they need, they are happier and do not need to push the company overly much. However, customers who spend a frustrating five minutes trying to get contact details on a Web site, two minutes navigating poorly constructed IVR menus or speech recognition (that doesn't recognize them) and then an additional sixty seconds waiting for an agent are hardly in a favorable mood by the time the agent finally comes on the phone.

Therefore, it is very important for your company to determine what it needs to do to get to the mature stage on the contact maturity path. Do you need to lay the foundations, or are you ready to open the floodgates, or are you already letting go of the tap and by doing so exhibiting two-way control? Let's explore each in turn so you can decide. However, we should make it clear that any business may need to be at all stages simultaneously. As a new contact channel emerges (for example, video phones), you may be laying the foundations. Meanwhile, in another part of the business you may be widening the funnel, while with some customers you may have already let go of the tap.

Step One: Lay the Foundations (Build the Tap)

The first step of making your company really easy for customers to contact is laying the foundations. If the tap is broken or impossible to use, there is not much point in offering it to your customers. So this stage is all about making sure that the contact mechanisms you offer to customers work properly and consistently once customers choose them. For example, there is little point in inviting customers to send you e-mails if you don't have the staff or technology in place to respond in a reasonable amount of time—where the customer defines "reasonable." (A company we once saw had one person processing e-mails with an average response rate of over twenty days. Recall too the graph earlier in this chapter illustrating the decline in e-mail responsiveness.)

Laying the foundations is about making sure that the contact mechanisms available to customers work in the ways that satisfy their needs, typically by addressing each of these three elements:

1. How the contact will be handled
2. When the contact will be handled
3. What will be achieved as a result of the contact

Addressing each of these elements requires that companies understand quite a lot about their customers and their needs. Some companies kick off a big "industry benchmarking" exercise looking at their direct competitors, but that often produces cases of the blind leading the blind. Instead, we always recommend one or both of these two approaches: (1) last contact benchmarking, which means analyzing the most recent customer support experience that your customers had, largely outside your direct competitors (for example, they might have just had a terrific call with FedEx or made reservations without any hiccups on www.alaskaairlines.com), and making sure that your contact experiences match or exceed it;

(2) conduct customer research on which channels customers want and their expectations for when contact can occur, how quickly, and for what purpose.

We recommend these two approaches instead of the typical fallback—namely, asking around the senior executive table what they would want—because those inside the company may well be unrepresentative of the customer base. The senior executives of large businesses often understand little about the behaviors and needs of different customer generations. Try this experiment: ask customers how they would score the importance of a number of classic items, such as speed of service, pricing, technical features, and customer contact programs, and how they would rate your company's performance on those items; then ask the executives to score those items from their customers' point of view. The results will almost invariably demonstrate huge gaps.

How the Contact Will Be Handled (Is It a Tap?)

The "how" question raises complex issues, such as "In what languages will customers want to interact with us?" as well as "Which channels do they want to use?" Some companies are great at doing this, offering language choices on their IVR systems and on their Web sites. In North America it is almost a standard for contact

WIKIPEDIA

English
The Free Encyclopedia
2 109 000+ articles

Deutsch
Die freie Enzyklopädie
672 000+ Artikel

Français
L'encyclopédie libre
589 000+ articles

Polski
Wolna encyklopedia
446 000+ haseł

日本語
フリー百科事典
441 000+ 記事

Nederlands
De vrije encyclopedie
382 000+ artikelen

Italiano
L'enciclopedia libera
378 000+ voci

Português
A enciclopédia livre
342 000+ artigos

Español
La enciclopedia libre
304 000+ artículos

Svenska
Den fria encyklopedin
263 000+ artiklar

center menus to ask for language preference. In other countries—Canada, for example—there is a legal requirement to offer choice among two or more languages. Wikipedia, the collaborative online encyclopedia, offers an excellent "window" for its readers and editors on its landing page, as just shown.

Offering the right channels is harder than offering languages, because channels exist in a continuously changing landscape. For example, mobile phone technology has reached a mature level of use so quickly in some economies that it has caught some companies flat-footed. In many Asian economies, SMS text messages are the prevalent communication mechanism used by generation Y customers, but few organizations offer text as a service or sales channel. Over 90 percent of Australians have mobile phones, but only one Australian bank allows customers the option of receiving balances by text. The experience is better in the U.K. and Europe, as the first direct and egg examples demonstrate.

E-mail use has also become problematic for many companies and can require a retooling of the contact taps. This contact channel has changed the rules of the game for companies that have set up the entire infrastructure needed to take calls and have trained staff in how to talk to customers. Now written skills are important again (as they were in the days of letters), even with the typical practice of creating a library of prewritten partial responses, and tone in writing is different from tone and manner over the phone. Managing inbound e-mails, as opposed to inbound phone calls, requires a different set of skills and tools.

Each wave of technology has a faster take-up rate, a function of customer education and, generally speaking, of reduced component and system costs. Computers at home were adopted far more quickly than typewriters, and the pace of mobile phone take-up has been faster again. The next wave of technologies appear to be mobiles with visual capability, so voice calls may soon by replaced by video calls. This rapid change means that companies need to question constantly whether they have the right taps, and you can easily get stuck with a set of older "legacy" taps while your customers are busy at another sink!

The "how" question also must address how easy it is to use that particular mechanism. We discussed this in Chapter Three when we described self-service. Laying the foundations involves making any mechanism you offer for customer contacts as easy as it can be. This entails questioning every menu layer you ask customers to navigate or button you ask customers to push: Why is it there? Is it really necessary?

To illustrate, the new VP of customer service at a major utility asked his team to explain to him how his IVR worked. The next day, they took him into a room where two walls had been decorated with the complicated flowchart that represented the navigation paths through the IVR. The technical team talked the new VP through the chart, and he then asked, "So I assume that we do all that so we can send the customer to different teams or skill sets?" The technicians shook their heads and said that all the calls went to the same people; the customers were subjected to IVR spaghetti just for reporting purposes. Part of laying the foundations is making it easy by getting rid of unnecessary complexity in the way customers connect with your taps.

When the Contact Will Be Handled (When Will the Water Flow?)

The "when" question has two aspects that serve as the foundation or structure of the contact tap. The first is about hours of operation. Companies need to think through when customers want and need to contact them. This is such a fundamental notion that we shouldn't need to state it, but there are many cases where companies' hours of operation don't align with the needs of their customers. This doesn't mean 24/7 availability for every type of contact and every customer, but if your customers are buying or using your product outside of normal business hours, then you should find a way to support them during those hours. In the "Bad Cases" section, we described a situation in which online sellers did not support auctions closing on Sunday nights; interestingly, some sellers were doing so—one savvy seller told us that he didn't bother working his team on Tuesdays but had a special shift operating on Sunday evenings.

We once observed an unusual instance of a company recognizing when it needed to provide service in, of all places, a cab. The taxi driver in question always worked night shifts, but his cab also had a separate headset for a second mobile phone—he acted as the evening order taker for a singing telegram company that recognized that many of its potential customers would decide to send a singing telegram while at a party or drinking in a bar. Having a voicemail-based message service would have lost business for the company, and a full-time receptionist would have been uneconomical, so its phone diverted to this cab driver, and he took the orders during the night.

The second aspect of "when" is "How quickly?" which is also an issue of understanding customers' expectations and needs. Unfortunately, many companies don't think through this very carefully. The concept of answering in x number of rings or handling 80 percent of calls in twenty seconds dominates the contact center industry regardless of the type of call or need. Many boards of directors monitor this kind of standard as their only measure of customer service quality, but they are failing to acknowledge that customers' time tolerance varies by process, need, and channel. A recent study at one organization showed that customers often abandoned calls after 120 seconds. Contrast this with the Teleclaims area we described earlier; customers' needs were so great that many were prepared to wait fifteen minutes or more before being answered. In some technical support areas, customers may be prepared to wait even longer (but that doesn't mean that they should!).

We are not saying here that Best Service is to make customers wait this long—far from it. What we are suggesting is that priorities within the business need to be aligned with customer needs. Some calls or e-mails are urgent and need to be answered quickly; others can wait longer. The real trick is understanding this variation in need and setting up your operations (taps) to respond accordingly. Amazon divided customer e-mail (the larger channel compared to phone calls) into six or seven distinct categories; it responded to some as quickly as in real time, and the other response times ranged up to within twenty-four hours. At Citibank, customer service agents used to ask credit card customers how long they would be willing to wait on hold before speaking to an agent when they called the next time, adjusting up-front routing systems to match customer requirements.

In the case of the online sales businesses we described earlier, many sellers were applying a blanket turnaround time. They tried to respond to all e-mails within twenty-four hours (a common standard). This seems misaligned with needs. A prospective customer about to bid on an auction has an urgent need and may require an answer in minutes or seconds; a customer who has just purchased an item and is asking about payment methods may be delighted if she receives a response in twenty-four hours. Laying the foundations involves understanding these needs and establishing operations capable of responding appropriately by customer and by issues.

What Will Be Achieved as a Result of the Contact (What Comes Out of the Tap?)

The last foundation element that companies must consider is what services and outcomes customers are expecting from the mechanisms and channels that are available. Failing to understand this can make contact channels totally ineffective and, worse yet, can create snowballs (repeat contacts for the same issue, as we showed in Chapter 2). For example, a major computer manufacturer established a pilot retail outlet to compete with Apple's highly successful retail stores. Unlike Apple, this company didn't provide any form of post-sales service or technical support in the stores, nor could customers buy new computers or hardware or get machines fixed or upgraded. The pilot failed to generate the sales figures the company wanted, and after a few months it closed the store. Imagine if Apple had done the same thing. How would customers have reacted if they couldn't return their precious iPod or get a new laptop battery just before heading out on vacation? Each contact channel needs to deal with the expectations of customers.

The Teleclaims example further illustrates this step. Customers called expecting to obtain the status of their claim and to be able to influence the timing in some way. Imagine their dissatisfaction when this didn't occur, a clear example of a contact channel set up to fail. Once again this comes down to management of expectations; if customers are aware that each contact channel performs functions in certain ways, they won't be disappointed by those outcomes.

Laying the foundations includes promoting and making clear the role that each channel can perform and defining how it works. For example, pretending that a certain phone number will allow customers to have person-to-person service when it only enables automated transactions will frustrate customers. However, if a number is clearly advertised as "our automated payment" line, the expectations are set appropriately. This isn't just about telling customers what they will be able to achieve; it's also about understanding what they *want* to achieve.

One further negative example illustrates the danger in not understanding how customers expect to interact with you. A new budget airline launched recently in the United States and proudly advertised that customers would be able to book only through the airline's Web site. Despite all the evidence that personal interactions can be highly effective in closing high-value sales, this company is determined to box its customers into one channel. We'll wait with interest to see if that works, but we suspect it won't.

STEP TWO: OPEN THE FLOODGATES (TURN ON THE TAPS)

Assuming that a company has laid the foundations and has contact mechanisms in place that work, are available at hours that suit the customer, and perform the roles that customers expect, what do we mean by "open the floodgates"? To open the floodgates means encouraging rather than suppressing customer contacts. The following is a list of some classic suppressive behaviors:

Mechanism	Suppressive Behavior
Web site	Phone numbers are not available.
Contact center	Exit to an operator is not available and promoted.
	Standard exit process, such as hitting 0 or saying "Operator," are not enabled.
Automated e-mails	Automated responses don't promote other mechanisms, such as contact centers.
Branch operations	Staff don't promote other channels to close sales or transactions.

Bills and letters	Only a limited range of mechanisms are advertised, as the company wants to pressure the customer to use the cheapest channels.
Customer-initiated blogs	PR or legal department shuts them down.
All channels	Companies cherry-pick which contacts to respond to and ignore others.

Some companies might have trouble recognizing the need to change: they might worry about the cost involved if customers call or start using more expensive mechanisms, or they might fear the sheer volume of contacts they will have to deal with if they open the tap.

However, the consequences of *not* opening the tap may be more damaging. Let's consider again the example of the Teleclaims company that had unconsciously restricted the customer to one tap and had also turned down the supply of service to the tap. In doing so, senior management pointed the finger at the contact center management team as the problem area. They saw contact center service levels at all-time lows and called in the contact management team to "please explain." But what they really needed to do was open the tap. Had they been able to listen to all the issues that customers were describing to the agents and the reasons for their calls, management would have gotten to the bottom of the real issues that were disappointing customers. Instead, the executive team made an incorrect link between the poor customer satisfaction ratings and the wait times in the Teleclaims contact center—in essence, they attacked the symptoms and ignored the disease.

If the tap had been open far enough for them to be able to categorize and identify the true nature of customer needs and their sources, management's actions would have been far clearer and much more comprehensive. Backlogs and mismanaged expectations in the "downstream" departments who processed claims were the real issue. Had management been able to get the calls to the departments that really needed to handle them, they would have been able to see where extra investment of people was really needed. A narrow tap and a lack of focus on the drivers of customer needs hid the problems for far too long.

This mechanism of opening the floodgates is unpleasant short-term medicine to swallow. Although it might mean more people or more investment in customer contact (offset by eliminating dumb contacts and enhancing self-service), the issues and information that flow from the process lead, as we explained in Chapter Two, to a much better position in the long term. Taking our insurance example again, if the company had had the tap wide open, it would have been able to analyze where the worst bottlenecks were in the claims process. Applying some form of SWAT team to clear backlogs and help employees get on top of their workload would have had an almost immediate impact on contact volumes, making unnecessary the temporary additions required in the contact center to "cope with demand."

So what does opening the floodgates really involve? We've boiled it down to these five key actions:

1. Encourage contacts.
2. Match the contact channel to the need.
3. Provide choice.
4. Extend the hours of operation.
5. Remove the cost and barriers of contact.

Encourage Contacts

Actively encouraging customer contacts means, quite simply, that you want customers to contact you whenever and however they need to do so. This often represents a mind-set shift for organizations that have spent years attempting to control customer behavior, often taking the form of invitations and publicizing contact mechanisms on all correspondence, marketing, and media. But it's also about customer-facing staff feeling comfortable inviting further contact or use of other channels and feedback mechanisms, and educating the customers about all the options available, including self-service channels.

Many organizations do this as a matter of course. Utility bills, for example, provide Web addresses and phone numbers to call. But it is often in the midst of change that companies find it hard to stick to their guns. It may be that they are changing a product or service or reconfiguring a Web site. These types of transitions are "resource hungry" in any organization. Ironically, they represent the very moment when contact with customers is most valuable. These are the times when companies need customers as their eyes and ears to tell them what they think.

A major international bank created a new service platform for its corporate customers' treasury and finance departments to manage their accounts and currency exposures. In effect it was a self-service banking system for the bank's largest customers. The bank knew that it wouldn't get the design right the first time; realizing that it faced a long and complex design and development cycle, it needed ways to fine-tune the new system once customers started using it. The bank decided to deploy the new system with listening "baked in":

- The Web-based application included a feature that allowed customers to provide feedback on any part of the application and on any page.
- Clicking on the feedback button opened a structured survey whereby customers could choose the feedback topic and provide as much or as little information as they wanted.
- Each area of feedback was linked and reported to different owners within the bank.

The bank then used the feedback to decide what to change, how to change it, and how to set priorities. The frequency of customer ratings and feedback in different areas gave it information on what mattered to how many customers. The company was surprised that the customers' perspective was very different from its own. Features or problems that had been thought to be high priority turned out not to be important to customers, whereas others jumped up the list. (Note: we see this happen all over the place, and will come back to this point later in this chapter.)

Thus the bank rolled out, amended, and improved its new platform. The listening process it applied reduced the risk of customer defection as the bank steadily removed imperfections, and over time it created an even more symbiotic relationship with its key corporate customers, who felt that the bank was responsive and had their interest at heart, and that they had a system they liked and had helped fine-tune. During this potentially risky time, the bank lost no key customers, and the process of dialogue continues to this day. Using a self-service channel, the bank has found a way to open the tap for customer contact.

Prior to the phone and Internet age, it was harder for companies to provide ways for customers to contact them. Today there are no excuses. Mechanisms like blogs and Web- and phone-based feedback tools provide companies with many taps from which to choose. Market leaders, such as Dell, are creating blogs to ask customers what they want (described further in Chapter Seven), and others are using wiki software to collect the latest practices and knowledge from their customers and their frontline agents instead of relying on out-of-step centralized "knowledge bases." In these examples and many more, companies are encouraging contacts and benefiting from the increased flows.

Match the Contact Channel to the Need

Widening the funnel requires a little more sophistication than merely making contact mechanisms available. Customer contact channels have to be appropriate to the need; for example, if a customer is using an Internet-based interaction method, supporting her can involve a number of mechanisms, such as phone, e-mail, and Web chat, but the applicability of each channel will depend on the nature of the interactions. Phone and chat are likely to be more effective if the customer needs help in working out how do to something, but e-mail may be entirely appropriate where reference information is needed. An example of how companies ignore the nature of the need is in technical support situations where the customer's very problem may be that his computer isn't working or can't connect. In these situations, the customer will almost certainly need to talk to someone, so chat and phone are more appropriate. Yet many "self-help" tech support Web sites don't make these options readily available. In France, many retail food stores are open on Christmas Day, providing fresh produce and bread on one of the most popular days of the year, yet in most other countries, all stores are shuttered that day, forcing mad dashes the day before.

Part of matching channels with customer needs means being thoughtful, such as by automatically enabling a customer to talk to a person if she gets stuck in an IVR menu or if she unsuccessfully enters the second set of security data. On a Web site, a company might offer customers choices if they repeatedly fail to complete a form. There is nothing worse than being stuck in a problem loop on an IVR or trying to overcome an issue on a Web form and feeling stranded. Too few Web sites offer "If you are having difficulties, please call . . ." It is so easy to measure "dwell time" on key Web pages, yet this sort of support—a classic example of opening the tap—is provided all too rarely. Really smart companies do this and then can analyze and answer why so many customers are getting stuck on screen x or in menu y.

Provide Choice

Choices for customers need to be obvious and easy to access. Customers who need to send an e-mail shouldn't have to hunt high and low on a Web site for a Contact Us button; phone numbers should be a click away on any Web page and listed prominently; and talking to an operator should be available from every menu level on every IVR. It's amazing how reassuring it is to hear such a message on the IVR: "Welcome to Company X; if at any time you need to talk to an operator, hit zero." It shows respect for the customer and openness to service. As we discussed in Chapter Three, if the self-service works and the Web site or phone provides what customers want in a usable way, then customers won't take this option. It seems at times that companies live in fear of customers abusing these options, but the flip side of not providing these simple choices is that customers will find another way that is even more damaging. As we mentioned elsewhere, Web sites exist today telling customers "which options to press to talk to a real person." These sites shouldn't need to exist. Companies should be striving to make it both easy and unnecessary to talk to a person.

Providing choice takes many forms, so here's a handy checklist.

Mechanism	Choices
Web site	Phone numbers on every page Talk to Someone buttons enabling chat Contact Us buttons that make it easy to send e-mails and state how quickly they will be responded to

Phone IVR menus or trees	Web site alternatives advertised
	Options to leave a number for a callback
	Ability to hit 0 to exit to an operator advertised up front and when the caller seems to be in trouble
E-mails	Phone number provided on all e-mails sent to customers
	Links provided to the pages of the site that will help explain the issue
Branch operations	Phone provided to talk to the contact center
	Self-service devices, such as ATMs or information kiosks
	Web PC provided for self-service in branch
Bills and letters	All channels advertised: Web site, numbers to call, automated services, alternative payment methods (including information about cost and timeliness of payment methods)
Customer feedback	Feedback surveys post-call or on Web site
	Customer-initiated feedback from the Web site at any stage ("Tell us what you think")
	Option to record a message after an IVR interaction
	Blogs

Extend the Hours of Operation

Isn't it amazing how few companies are available when you need them? It seems such a basic issue. Of course we understand that staying open 24/7 is not an economical proposition for all companies, but there are lots of ways to do this, such as the following:

Expand the Organization We've already described the option of finding another business that has hours or seasonality that might complement yours. For example, gift provider 1-800-Flowers has a collaborative arrangement with a major hotel chain and a major rental car company, matching their respective customer demand peaks and valleys. Another way to expand the organization is to outsource to a company that provides scale and capability not available in-house, as well as times of day or days of the week.

Go Somewhere Else It may be uneconomical to run your operation onshore, but "follow the sun" strategies may enable you to set up operations offshore or use other parts of your organization. One hotel chain we know handles their English-speaking calls on the opposite side of the world rather than have expensive night shifts in each English-speaking location. Using a third-party outsourcing company or even a contact center within the enterprise but in another country can also help during holidays—Amazon used to offer U.S. contact center agents the day off on the Fourth of July, yet could still, ironically, service customers by having their contacts handled by Amazon's U.K. operations.

Capture the Demand and Shift It Many new contact center technologies enable companies to get a customer to leave details and be called back at a later date. The most primitive are simple message banks, but these are expensive—someone has to listen to each message. More sophisticated technologies allow the customer to leave a number and state when he wishes to be called. This can be an excellent way of filling quiet periods earlier or later in the business day or when the agents are available.

Shift the Demand to Another Channel A compromise strategy may be to make it clear how the customer can meet her needs in another channel. Web sites and many kiosks and ATM machines are typically 24/7 even if call centers and branches are not. However, do watch out for the issue that customers may expect more immediate turnarounds of e-mails if there is no one available by phone.

Remove the Cost and Barriers of Contact

Opening the floodgates won't work if your pricing signals keep the tap firmly closed or your taps don't work for your customers. Some companies charge customers for technical support; they are so driven by the desire to sell additional warranties and maintenance contracts that they charge customers to get help fixing problems with equipment they have sold them. Although the economic drivers of this behavior are clear, it is a dangerous way to block issues that the organization really needs to learn. If such a company puts a new model into the marketplace but then restricts the likelihood that customers will tell it about faults and design issues, then critical aspects of quality control are at risk. Furthermore, the company won't receive the feedback that it needs to further the development of the next product, and so forth.

Price is not the only contact barrier. We've already described availability and publicity as obvious barriers, but design can be another important barrier. IVR spaghetti, impenetrable Web sites, and call number proliferation are other examples of design barriers; we covered fixing those issues in Chapter Three.

The most critical barrier, though, isn't about cost or design; rather, it is in the mind-set of the organization. What we've found really makes a difference is a company's *wanting* customers to contact it. That mind-set shines through in how the company advertises, how it designs, what it offers, and how it deals with the contacts that do occur. There are huge differences between companies that think "We'll restrict them" and those that say "We'll make it easy." This attitude difference came through when we looked at a number of Internet sellers. Those with the highest satisfaction ratings saw every e-mail as a chance to build a relationship with a customer; they say, "Yes, we answer every e-mail, even though many are about things that we have already told the customer." This contrasted with the approach of sellers who saw e-mails as frustrating and annoying; they tend to say, "If it was on the listing, we tell the customer to go look at the listing."

STEP THREE: ALLOW TWO-WAY CONTROL (LET GO OF THE TAP)

The most advanced level of maturity beyond opening the tap involves making the channels work and available to customers with choices tailored to customer needs. Best Service companies also place increasing choice and trust in the hands of customers and find mechanisms for them to contact you in ways that make it easy for them to give you the feedback you need. Operating at this level demands certain critical ways of thinking and acting:

- The more critical the problem, the more freely available human support needs to be.
- Match the channel to the need.
- No channel is too hard; if it's logical for the customer, then you have to be there.
- Find ways to make it easy and convenient for customers to use the channel that suits their needs.
- Tune in to the preferences of customers and stay tuned to the channels customers are using.

Let's review each of these more advanced skills one by one.

The More Critical the Problem, the More Freely Available Human Support Needs to Be

Certain aspects of technical support are a good illustration of this principle. Software and hardware organizations have worked hard to provide self-service support, and at times that service can be invaluable. But there is something perverse about being expected to contact the Internet for some remote Web site at a time when a particular piece of software or a communication link is failing. Even obtaining a phone number is hard when your Internet connection is down or your hard drive is dead. Anyone with a bug, hard-disk crash, or systems failure is in critical need of expert help, so the customer needs to talk to someone. This means that these companies need to think ahead and provide phone numbers in places that the customer will be able to access easily, such as phone directories, software packages, and even the user manual. The company needs to think through the scenarios that the customer might experience and make them easier to deal with. That could be as simple as providing a sticker for a laptop computer with key phone numbers or ensuring that a public Web site has all the numbers a customer might need in a crisis.

Match the Contact Type to the Need

The most sophisticated companies don't even have to think about matching contact type to customer need, but it's surprising that many organizations match the intensity or availability of contact to the value of the customer, regardless of need. A common model is to have account managers assigned to highly valued customers but make the masses fight for attention in contact centers or branches. Many organizations have adopted segmentation models that assume that the availability of human contact should increase as value to the company increases.

At a major bank, one contact center agent serviced roughly three thousand mass-market customers. However, in the "premium" segment, there was a designated "personal banker" for every three hundred customers, and in the "private bank" (that is, for high-net-worth customers), this ratio fell to one to fifty. The strange thing about this situation is that both the private and premium customers were the most likely to use self-service channels such as Internet banking, to such an extent that the bank thought of withdrawing the service from private banking customers so that they really did have to talk to someone. How perverse is that? The more valuable you were to the bank, the less choice you were given.

How should a needs-based model work? Matching contact type to need does not always mean contacts with a person. Energy utility Energex operates in storm-prone areas of Australia. One season produced severe damage across the utility's power network, and within one week it received one million phone calls, what the company normally receives over the entire year; not surprisingly, the utility was not resourced or equipped to deal with that situation and couldn't cope. As it mopped up the damage, Energex resolved never to get into that situation again—it invested heavily in technologies to identify the caller and area from which she was calling to enable outward SMS messaging to mobile phones and to be able to deploy rapidly different IVR messages depending on where the caller was located. Should the company ever run into such a storm event and an avalanche of calls, it now has automated systems in place to keep customers informed and to notify several hundred thousand at a time of known storms and recovery times. So Energex has matched the need for rapid information with the technologies best equipped to satisfy it.

No Contact Channel Is Too Hard

Best Service companies recognize that they cannot dictate the contact mechanism that customers should use. If it makes sense for the customer to contact you by phone or in person, then you should be there for them. Some organizations have tried hard to deny this to their peril. In Australia and the United Kingdom, the major banks spent much of the late 1980s and 1990s shrinking their branch networks. According to the Australian Bankers Association and the Reserve Bank of Australia, between 1994 and 2001, the number of bank branches in Australia fell from 7,064 to 4,789, over 30 percent of the network. In the United Kingdom, the ratio of branches per million inhabitants fell from 290 to 220 between 1983 and 1994 (with a relatively stable population).

In Australia, this branch closure trend also opened the door to the second tier of banks to enter "local" markets that the major players abandoned. The most famous of these is a small bank called Bendigo Bank, based in a small regional town in Victoria, Australia. Bendigo created the idea of a community bank that could open in small towns and suburbs that the other banks had deserted. It was often seen as the savior of small country towns left branchless by the major banks. Bendigo was so successful that it opened 190 community branches between 1998 and 2006. Bendigo also has the highest satisfaction rating of any bank in Australia and is the only bank where more than 90 percent of customers are either satisfied or very satisfied.[2] It demonstrates that providing the channels customers want can be a successful strategy and that denying them is a very high risk strategy. In the last few years, the larger banks in Australia have responded by opening additional branches, and overall branch numbers are now climbing again.

Find Ways to Make It Easy for Customers to Use
Channels That Suit Their Needs

Some companies truly focus on customer needs and go the extra mile to make it easy for customers to reach them. The technologies to do so vary in type, but here are three examples that illustrate that it isn't hard.

First, a small health fund is too small to be able to guarantee rapid response to every call, and its research showed that customers were very likely to abandon calls after more than sixty seconds. As a result, if the wait is longer than thirty seconds, customers are given a choice: they can wait in the queue or leave a phone number, maintain their place in the queue, and get called back by the fund. Many customers take this option. The phone number is dialed automatically and "popped" to a contact center agent as though the customer had called directly. Everybody wins: the health fund has fewer customers waiting in the queue and pays lower call costs for toll-free numbers; it needs less capacity in its phone systems; customers are delighted that their time is respected; and the staff are happy, as they have much happier customers to deal with.

Second, several leading taxi companies have made equally smart use of technology to simplify booking cabs. They use call line identification (CLI; in the United States, this is called ANI) to associate the customer's incoming phone numbers with the pick-up address. Automated messages ask if the customer is leaving immediately from her home address with four passengers or less; if the customer answers yes, a cab is dispatched. The customer has to answer one question, requiring less than thirty seconds, and the call is done. The company benefits, as its agents have to deal only with more complex bookings or customers not at their home addresses. The technology can even deal with mobile phones that are always used from the same address. All in all, this improves customer experience at lower costs.

Third is the use of biometric voice identification. In most countries, privacy legislation requires that customers identify themselves using three to four items of information, such as date of birth and phone numbers. This annoys customers and uses up valuable time, so Australian health insurer ahm now lets its customers record their "voice print." If they go through this process, this voice print is used to identify them on all subsequent calls. The first person who left a recording was a seventy-three-year-old who was delighted that she no longer had to identify herself using her date of birth. It saves customers and the company forty-five seconds on every call.

Stay Tuned to Customers

Few companies have taken this "easy to deal with" concept to its ultimate state, as it means recognizing, capturing, or "sensing" the contact channels that their customers prefer. At its crudest level, this means capturing the contact mechanisms that customers say they prefer and then using them. That could mean calling rather than e-mailing or e-mailing a bill rather than sending it through the mail. As we mentioned earlier in the book, first direct, the successful U.K. online bank, enables this to a certain extent by allowing the customers to opt in to various services, such as having their balances sent via SMS to their mobile phones. However, going beyond asking the customer for preferences and acting on them would be for the company to divine preferences and act on them without even having to ask. We've yet to see this business, although the data warehouse and analysis technologies exist right now to enable this approach.

Summary

Best Service may mean no need for service, but that doesn't mean that an organization should be hard to contact; in fact, companies need to make themselves easy to reach however and whenever customers want and need to do so. For many companies, having to make themselves available and give customers choice is a frightening prospect, but they need to open the floodgates in order to gain insight into the issues in their business and finds ways to tap into the feedback from customers that they need to hear.

A common customer complaint is that companies are hard to reach. How many times have you been trapped in the IVR of no return or searched desperately for a phone number on a Web site where the Contact Us option seems really to be saying, "Please don't contact us the way you want to"?

It's a shame that phone numbers are buried or even not revealed on Web sites, that e-mails sent by customers disappear into the ether, and that options to talk to an operator aren't available on automated phone menus. Companies need to provide to customers the freedom to choose the contact mechanism that suits them; companies need to reinforce that they truly value their relationship all the time, not just when attracting customers' business in the first place. At the same time that organizations need to strive to become the No Service company, they must also strive to become the "easy to reach" company.

Survey Questions

Please respond to these three key questions covering the idea of making it really easy to contact your company, and refer to Appendix A to check your progress from Basic Service to Better Service to Best Service.

11. Our customers
    a. Have no choice in how they contact our company.
    b. Can decide how to contact us, but have few options.
    c. Are free to use any contact mechanism they wish.
    d. Are using contact channels that we would prefer they didn't use.

12. Our Web site
    a. Has a Contact Us section that allows customers to send a structured e-mail.
    b. Provides access to a phone number if customers look hard enough at the bottom of the Contact Us section.
    c. Gives our customers as much information about other contact mechanisms as possible, including a phone number on almost every page.
    d. Has a "click to call" function that links them to an agent in seconds.
    e. Hides our phone numbers, because we want customers to remain on the Web site.

13. Our organization's customer contact channel strategy is focused on
    a. Ensuring that our customers use the mechanisms that we want them to use.
    b. Maximizing the amount of information flowing from customers to us.
    c. Using the cheapest possible channels.
    d. Nothing—it is not really discussed very much in our company.

CHAPTER SIX

OWN THE ACTIONS ACROSS THE ORGANIZATION
Instead of Blaming Customer Service

Customer experience is the job of everyone in the company.
—MARK HURST, CITED AT GOODEXPERIENCE.COM

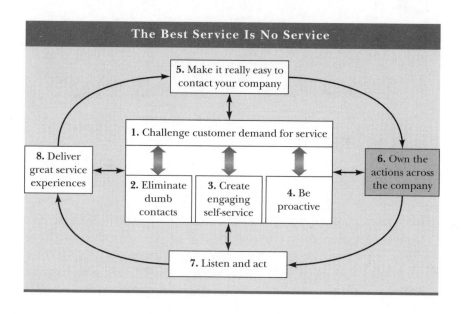

THE PRINCIPLE

Pervading many organizations is a strange myth that managers who run the customer service (or customer care) operations are accountable for the level and quality of service delivered by the customer support function. The manager of the contact center is therefore called to account and is placed under the spotlight if call queues are too long or if backlogs develop in responding to customer e-mail or in processing claims. That seems logical, right? After all, those managers recruit the customer-facing support staff and direct their performance. But if you look a little deeper at why the customer contacts are occurring and what the staff needs to do to handle these contacts, then accountability or ownership appear less clear.

In reality, contact centers "cause" very few of their own contacts. In studies we have performed in over forty organizations across ten major countries, we have yet to find a contact center that has generated more than 20 percent of its own contacts (calls, e-mails, chat sessions, or letters). Similarly, Customer Service units "request" few of the letters or forms that customers send to the company, and branch staff rarely stand outside inviting people to come in and join the queue at the transaction counter. So who is really generating all this activity? Why is this myth of accountability so pervasive?

If we start to consider why the contacts are occurring—in other words, why customers have to bother themselves to call, write, or appear in person—the issue of who is really accountable becomes a little clearer. Let's consider a typical customer contact center. Customers contact utilities for a variety of reasons, as illustrated in the following graph.

Root Causes of Call Volumes (Utility)

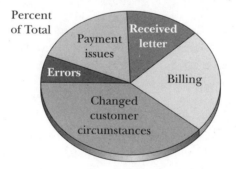

If we look at these major reasons that customers contact the company, few of them are within the control of the contact center management: (1) they don't control the letters sent to customers; (2) they aren't responsible for producing the bills; (3) they typically have nothing to do with payment problems; (4) they certainly can't control how many customers move, struggle to pay bills, or want to get access to the Internet (the changed circumstances category). In fact, the only causes that the contact center management control are the number of errors, and even then many errors may be for reasons outside their responsibility, such as systems complexity or process adherence. These simple points illustrate that ownership of the contact demand, as we described in Chapter Two, often sits outside the areas that handle the customer contacts.

It isn't just the ownership of demand that is misplaced. Let's also consider who controls the processes and tools that help frontline staff process customer requests. A typical branch manager can't control the quality of the IT systems that his team has to use—he is told that he must use these tools. Similarly, the processes and policies that frontline staff execute aren't in their control, either. Processes are usually controlled by product or policy groups sitting in the head office. Therefore, the frontline people can't control how they are expected to perform the work or the amount of work that occurs. In practically all companies, those who appear accountable for service to the customer shouldn't be held accountable at all.

So how can we tackle this problem? We believe that there are three critical steps that companies need to take:

1. **Tear down the walls.** Rethink who is accountable for causing contacts and for handling them, then identify and engage the real owners of the issues. This involves understanding the nature of contacts and demand as we described in Chapter Two, then working out where in the company responsibility sits—in other words, finding the root causes of issues so that the real owners can be identified and encouraged to take action to support customer service—then customer service can indeed support the customer.

2. **Make accountability stick.** Ensure that the issue owners have the appropriate incentives and encouragement to analyze and resolve the root causes. This is much harder than it sounds, because it challenges department silos and traditional roles within companies. Before they take action, many department leaders will deny their new role or plead ignorance or denial unless confronted with incentives or pressure.

3. **Liberate the front line.** Enable customer support teams to do the right thing for the customer; allow them to make decisions and take actions—with minimal permission or oversight—that produce the best results for customers.

When companies follow these three steps, dramatic service improvements will occur. After visiting examples of this challenge outside customer service, we will present cases of companies that have tackled ownership of customer issues, some badly and some well, and then lay out in detail how to implement these steps.

EXAMPLES OUTSIDE CUSTOMER SERVICE

There are several classic examples outside the world of customer service that demonstrate the challenges of assigning ownership for customer, or citizen, issues.

THE MYTH OF MINISTERIAL RESPONSIBILITY

In the Westminster system of government, there is a well-established mode of operating called ministerial accountability. Under this model, the ministers in the British cabinet are held accountable for all the workings of the departments that report to them. The ministers are political appointments by the prime minister, but these individuals may not have any specialized experience in the area under their control. For example, the minister for defense may not have a military background, and the minister for trade and industry need not have been in business. By contrast, their departments are full of public servants who typically have spent their careers in that specialized field. Ministers are shuffled between roles, and governments come and go, but the public servants continue in their roles and therefore are able to provide stability and ongoing knowledge to keep the government ticking. However, if something goes wrong, it is the minister who "carries the can" (gets fired), producing strange issues regarding accountability.

For example, in the 1960s, spies were discovered to have been operating in Britain, some of whom defected to the Soviet Union. Even though these spies had been in place for many years and had gone undetected by the responsible Home Office department, it was the minister of the day who was forced to resign when the scandal broke. He really hadn't "caused" the problem, but he was seen to be accountable when the issue emerged on his watch. Although the system is very honorable and has been copied in other countries, such as Japan, it quite often fails to place accountability where it really belongs: the public servants survive while the politicians take the blame.

ISLAND HOPPING WINS THE WAR

The Americans were caught by surprise at Pearl Harbor on December 7, 1941, and soon faced world war on several continents and oceans at the same time. In the Pacific, Fleet Admiral Chester Nimitz and his staff designed the grand strategy, but decided to leave the local strategy and tactics largely to his Navy admirals and Marine generals "on the ground," close to enemy action; had he micromanaged from his offices, he could not have imagined the numerous programs to outmaneuver the dug-in Japanese. One of these programs, called island hopping, was a critical reason why the Allies won the war in the Pacific. It was Admiral William F. "Bull" Halsey who conceived of the idea to bypass strongly held Japanese positions as he raced westward to the Philippines, with General MacArthur advancing from Australia. Nimitz exercised an excellent example of ownership—tearing down walls, making accountability stick, and liberating the front line—that minimized U.S. and Japanese casualties and prevented many Japanese-held islands from slowing Allied troops and ships.

"MR. GORBACHEV, TEAR DOWN THIS WALL!"

On June 12, 1987, at the Brandenburg Gate in West Berlin, but also heard across the wall in Communist East Berlin, U.S. President Ronald Reagan delivered one of his most powerful and memorable speeches. He recounted the proud German history, the travails of wars and reconstruction, and the pressures that the Cold War brought to the world, and then he identified the true "owner" of the "two Germanys" and exhorted Mikhail Gorbachev, the general secretary of the Soviet Union, "if you seek peace, if you seek prosperity for the Soviet Union and Eastern Europe, if you seek liberalization: Come here to this gate! Mr. Gorbachev, open this gate! Mr. Gorbachev, tear down this wall!" It took another two years for the Berlin Wall to crumble, to the eternal benefit of mankind.

BAD CASES

Let's now turn back to the customer service and support world, and examine a group of bad cases that show the perils of not assigning owners who need to fix underlying root causes.

SHOOTING THE MESSENGER

A recent example from a U.S. utility paints a bad case of shooting the messenger rather than addressing what caused the problems. Electric and gas utilities' contact centers handle calls regarding network faults and local outages, as well as billing and provisioning issues. Storms often topple power lines or poles, burn out transmitters, and disable street and traffic lights; customers call to report these outages, but also offer, "Did you know that I don't have power here at the office?" Utility contact center managers are measured on two areas, often with tight regulatory standards: (1) the percentage of calls answered in thirty seconds (also called grade of service, or GoS), and (2) customer satisfaction with the service provided. If a large number of customers suffer outages at the same time and call to report them or ask when they will be fixed, the contact center struggles to answer the calls with its noncrisis staff levels, creating an avalanche and frustration for customers and for the agents.

In this example, customers called with increasing intensity, demanding, "How quickly will my power be restored?" but the only people who knew the answer were network engineers who controlled the databases to record and upload information about local service restoration status. This utility had not suffered serious outages for many years, so the data servers could not keep up with the demand, and the contact center agents only had access to old data, further frustrating residential and business customers. The agents could not isolate outage or restoration details for areas where some houses or offices still had power while others in the same block were in the dark. After the storm finally cleared, the public utilities commission landed hard on the utility for missing mandatory customer service GoS, not for the clogged data servers or the understaffed network engineers. In essence, the commission shot the messenger.

The contact center manager wasn't the owner of any of the drivers for the service levels—the volume of calls (the demand) was caused by the network outages and the data system limitations. Because the maintenance crews and engineers failed, and because the company underinvested in its systems development, the calls flooded in. If the company had created a real-time informational IVR system, a proactive alert system like the one we described in Chapter Four, or a geographical mapping system pinpointing service status, customers could have obtained timely updates without bothering to contact the center; if those messages were supplied quickly and were accurate, they could have deflected a significant volume of the calls—in fact, over 80 percent.

Unfortunately, customer satisfaction was equally hard, if not impossible, for the contact center to influence. Post-contact surveys asked, "How satisfied were you with how the agent helped you today?" but it's hard to imagine the customer granting a high score if the agent didn't have access to the outage restoration data, or the customer encountered a sixty-minute wait time to speak to that ill-equipped agent. The utility's customers were dealing with inherently dissatisfying experiences: either the power was off or the streets were impassable, so naturally they often said they were dissatisfied, particularly if the contact center had provided them with inaccurate information (provided or not updated by other areas) as to when the power would be restored or the streets reopened. Note that accountability for customer satisfaction resided outside the contact center; the network engineers and IT developers held the keys to satisfaction and the call volumes that drove the GoS and speed of response. The only parameters the contact center could control were (1) having the right staff levels in place to handle predicted pre-storm call volumes and (2) following the largely useless processes accurately and efficiently. Naturally the contact center manager and staff were stressed out; they should not have been held accountable for areas outside their control. The key question today is, "Has the utility learned its lesson and beefed up server capacity, built proactive alert systems, and shifted ownership to network engineers and IT and away from the beleaguered customer support manager?" Time will tell, when the next disaster hits.

CONTACT CENTER BEARS THE PAIN OF POLICY AND TECHNOLOGY

A U.K.-based telecommunications company demonstrates another bad case example of misplaced ownership. Customers often run low balances on their mobile phone accounts (while on vacation, testing another service, and so on), but there is usually a minimum charge per month. In one famous case, the company produced an invoice for zero pounds (no payment due), with five pages of detailed backup all adding up to, you guessed it, nothing.

The same inane automated system that generated the zero invoice sent ding notices to customers who didn't owe anything to the company, prompting (you probably guessed this already) calls of protest to . . . the contact center, not to the billing department (see again the cartoon that opened this chapter). In this case the company had, fortunately, scanned all invoices and associated them with customer records so that when customers did call, at least the agent could reassure them that they didn't owe anything and to ignore the collections notices. Not all companies scan customer invoices or other communications, however, so in most cases the agents are flying blind when customers hammer them for explanations, prompting some agents to hide behind the "policy shield," which we introduced in Chapter Five and will cover again later. The key questions are (1) Did the customer service group feed back customer concerns to the IT and billing departments to stop the disturbing zero invoice practice? and (2) Did the company stop any credit report incriminations?

SYSTEMS SPAGHETTI

An insurance company case illustrates how IT and other departments need to understand their accountabilities and their impact on service performance and service quality. This company had considered investing in new information systems, but had never been able to justify the investment; meanwhile, the frontline staff grappled with systems spaghetti. The contact center agents had to keep open twelve different systems that they needed to be able to access, delaying their shift until all twelve could be opened and made ready to go. (Note: you can easily determine this number by counting the number of open programs on the agents' desktop tile bar; in some cases they created a two-level display, not what Microsoft intended.)

For many transactions, the agents had to type the same information into three separate systems, taking extra time and introducing possible errors; only a few of the agents had become proficient in cutting and pasting. These disconnected and non-integrated systems affected the customer in several ways: (1) straightforward transactions, such as updating bank details on a direct debit, could take ten minutes to complete instead of three minutes (or zero minutes if the company had offered and promoted self-service on the Web site or the IVR system); (2) customers with more policies—in other words, the most valuable customers—actually got worse service because the slow and cumbersome processes had to be repeated for each policy; and (3) over 30 percent of customers were put on hold while the agents filled out the multiple screens as fast as possible. Despite the obvious IT spaghetti issues, this company held the customer service manager accountable for customer satisfaction and the speed of the process.

Thankfully, this bad case has a silver lining. The customer service manager protested being placed in the corner, and got attention from the IT department; once the IT staff sat down and observed the convoluted process, they began to understand it. After analyzing the way the center worked, the IT staff developed "fixes" to some of the more cumbersome processes and, with help from the customer service department, built the business case for replacing some of the IT spaghetti. Within months the technologies had improved, and clumsy, time-consuming customer experiences became the exception and not the rule.

MATRIX MANAGEMENT: NO ONE'S IN CONTROL

In the 1970s, matrix management, meaning that a manager had two bosses to whom he reported, was all the rage. For example, product managers would take direction from marketing and from IT. Peters and Waterman decried matrix management in their book *In Search of Excellence,* arguing for unambiguous direction instead of the supposed advantages to having two bosses.

However, many companies still practice matrix management to enable, they claim, multiple experiences for junior managers. The inherent flaws of matrix management have not changed, and we continue to view it as a scapegoat answer compared to finding a single owner per issue. This is analogous to a confused team of baseball players all converging on a pop fly to shallow center field, all calling for the ball; invariably the ball drops, and the adroit batter is already headed to third base. Ownership is key to providing Best Service, just as it is to sports victories.

Policy Shields, Up

A customer had been with a mobile service provider in Hong Kong for five years. Rather stupidly, he was paying five-year-old rates, too—about four times what he really needed to be paying. Mobile service competition in Hong Kong was very effective in reducing prices. The customer realized that the mobile vendor had relied on his lethargy. He checked out current packages on the company's Web site and found the one he wanted. He called the vendor to get the package changed. He was prepared to sign a new contract for eighteen months. However, he was told that the new packages were for new customers and that he didn't qualify. This was not a great way for the company to repay the customer's many years of loyalty. He said he would leave and become a new customer of the vendor's main competitor. Rather than say yes to switching him to a new package there and then, the company claimed that it would have to go through a tortuous process of getting approval from the "marketing department" for the new package, and that this would take ten days. The customer agreed to wait for this approval.

Two weeks later, no one had called the customer back, so he called the mobile service provider; unfortunately, no one seemed to have any recollection of the request. He gave the company two more days to approve the package and call back. Two days later, there was still no call.

The customer went down to the competitor's store and signed up for its current pricing package. As part of the process, the new company had to fax (yes, fax) the old service provider, asking it to transport the mobile number to the new service provider. Thus the old provider knew that the customer had just signed up for the new provider's package. About an hour later, the customer received a call from the old service provider, saying the new package had been approved.

GOOD CASES

In the following examples at Amazon, a health insurer, McDonald's, Nordstrom, and a major financial services company, each company has designed or stumbled into assigning customer contact ownership and aligning accountabilities with specific tasks. In each situation, two themes emerge: (1) finding the real owner and (2) responding clearly with "Yes, that's my problem."

PHOENIX RISES IN AMAZON

Amazon grew so quickly and achieved such significant scale in the new world of online retail that few, if any, contact center suppliers could support the company's need for its three core systems: (1) Web site management and order taking; (2) warehouse fulfillment and shipping; and (3) customer relationship management (CRM), the desktop software that agents use to interact with customers. As a result, Amazon's talented IT group, led by CIO Rick Dalzell, built and managed all three of these critical systems and produced impressive "best in class" systems that played a major role in the company's resounding success. The CRM system was the weakest of the three, as it was built for Amazon-employed customer service representatives who became adept at its codes and jargon, but was not scalable or easy to teach to third-party outsourced agents or new hires outside the core teams.

Amazon's customer service department (CS) lobbied for a new CRM system, but the original replacement proposed by IT lacked an Internet protocol (IP)–based user interface and other advances, so the whole issue was set aside to manage the holiday season. Amazon exhibited tremendous community and spirit each holiday season, when over 30 percent of the orders and revenues poured into the Web sites around the world: many managers and headquarters staff worked their main shift or even a second one packing books or other products in the distribution centers, while others, including all CS alumni, worked in CS as "elves." One year, an IT group led by former Microsoft software engineering manager Ben Slivka decided to be elves. They not only answered customer e-mail to help eliminate the queues but also suggested immediate fixes to the older CRM system to enable all agents to work faster. But perhaps most important, Slivka recognized that the old CRM system and the proposed new one were both underpowered for the emerging needs of the company, so he proposed building an entirely new system from scratch using IP technologies. Code-named Phoenix, this system revolutionized how Amazon conducted CS.

Slivka and the CS leadership team then "cracked the code" (from an ownership perspective) by harnessing twelve of Amazon's CS veterans, including floor supervisors, to work closely together to design Phoenix from the user's (agent's) point of view so as to support Amazon customers more efficiently and effectively. This CS team helped design, test, improve, and document Phoenix and, critically, share with the rest of Amazon CS that agents would benefit from this new system. As a result, agent adoption was high and the results impressive—within a matter of months, all agents had exceeded previous productivity levels, and customer satisfaction rose even higher. (It was at this time that the ACSI started to survey American customers' satisfaction and ranked Amazon number one among U.S. services companies, and second only to the H. J. Heinz company among all U.S. companies.)

Bringing Amazon's Shippers in Line

As described previously, Amazon cut its customer contact codes from 360 frequently changing reasons to 30 never-changing "why" reasons, the former ownerless and the latter with one MECE owner. One of Amazon CS's methods to keep owners apprised of customer issues and of the true voice of the customer (VOC) was the "bcc [blind copy] program," whereby managers outside CS opted in to have real customer e-mail threads sent to them every morning to their Outlook inbox. CS provided as much detail as the managers wanted, and enabled side-by-side observations with agents if managers visited one of the contact centers, thus obtaining even deeper insights.

On some occasions, however, Amazon needed to "push" e-mail to certain owners who had not requested to be blind copied, usually with the same results: the owner would move from anger to denial to resignation to acceptance and, finally, to evangelizing. In one case this also led to a significant reduction in Amazon's costs by extending ownership and accountability outside Amazon itself, to one of its suppliers. For several months, Amazon CS had played its role as canary in the coal mine, reporting problems with one of its outbound shippers and presenting in the Skyline report (see again Chapter Two) and in weekly operations meetings. Despite these spotlights on the culprit, Amazon's shipping department wasn't doing anything to investigate or remedy the situation, so CS decided to send all the e-mail with that shipper's name to the logistics VP's inbox every morning. At first he reacted angrily ("You're sending so much e-mail to me that I can't do my job," to which CS responded, "That *is* your job"), then he rejected CS's claim that this vendor was out of line ("They're my best partner," which CS interpreted as "They're the cheapest provider"), and only after seeing so much e-mail accumulate did this VP react positively ("Wow—they're doing *that* to our customers?"). He then assigned his process improvement team to work with CS to figure out possible root causes and confirm the true depth of the problem (because Amazon knew that not all effected customers were complaining to the company).

In short order, this joint team concluded that the shipper was indeed at fault, upsetting enough customers that the logistics VP lodged a protest with the shipper, who exhibited the same reaction that the VP had shown (anger, denial, resignation, acceptance, evangelizing). What cracked open the shipper's cooperation was the VP's subtracting CS support expense from the next monthly invoices to convey Amazon's resolve to get the shipper to fix the problem. Amazon might not have been "whole," because customer experience temporarily suffered, but the combined CS–logistics department–shipper effort did eliminate the problem, proving that Best Service means getting rid of all dumb contacts, even if they are caused outside the company.

PHYSICIAN, HEAL THYSELF

The management team of one health insurer saw the contact center as a problem—hold times had risen to unacceptable levels—and the contact center manager was asked to explain what was going on. Headquarters dispatched an internal consulting "fix-it" team to sort through the issues that went into the center, listen to calls, and analyze them. One thing stood out: the number of people calling to ask why their claims hadn't been paid. On each of those calls, after the contact center agent had checked the customer's status on the systems, the agent called the claims department. That's when the trouble started. The claims department didn't have enough people to staff its phones and also pay the claims, so the contact center staff could wait up to ten minutes to get the query answered. The internal fix-it team calculated that at any time, up to 30 percent of the contact center staff was tied up trying to determine claims status.

The team quickly decided that accountability for the call center's woes really resided in the claims department and that the latter area was really the one that needed fixing. The company then attacked the claims backlog, and within a month both the claims operation and the contact center had caught up, at least in the short term. The company also needed a long-term solution to prevent the problem from reoccurring, so it established same-day processing. Under this concept, the owner of the claims and administration area agreed that all requests received would be turned around the same day.

Not only did this minimize wait times for customers, but it all but eliminated the calls from customers asking for the status of their requests; once the ownership of the problem was put in the right area, it was easily fixed.

McDonald's Lives Its Motto

McDonald's has been perfecting owning the problem by living its motto, coined in 1957: Quality, Service, Cleanliness and Value (QSC&V). The company's U.S. customer satisfaction department, led by VP Terri Capatosto, is able to slice and dice customer contact codes from calls, e-mails, and letters coming into its customer contact center and mine through customer verbatim comments to provide critical customer insights to other McDonald's departments and to key supply chain partners. This partnership across its extended enterprise includes providing customer feedback in real time directly to the independent franchisees and the managers of company-owned restaurants, who are obligated to respond to the customers within specific time periods depending on the criticality of the issue. As Capatosto points out,

> We take our role in improving QSC&V and making McDonald's our customers' favorite place to eat very seriously. We provide detailed customer insights to assigned owners across every major function in our business, who then study problems and fix them, once and for all. For example, when we first launched our line of salads, we identified a unique issue from customers who complained about dirt on the salad that should have been removed through the normal lettuce quality assurance steps. Our supply chain experts traced this issue to lettuce fields in California where the workers were cutting the lettuce too close to the ground. Once the growers changed the cutting height, the issue was completely eliminated. We received no more complaints, but did get more contacts—praise for our excellent salads!

Another McDonald's story demonstrates using customer feedback to eliminate a problem; the solution included a universal procedural improvement that had operations benefits. Says Capatosto,

> Another example is when we launched our Fruit 'n Walnut salad. Customers told us they were not receiving their walnuts. Our food improvement team went to work on this issue and developed a preassembled "condiment bag" that contained a napkin, utensils, and the walnut packs. Restaurant operations procedures were changed to ensure each customer receives this condiment bag with their salad order. This became so successful in reducing these "missing condiments" complaints from customers that the condiment bag became the new standard operating procedure for all products that had additional condiments or toppings that go with them. And, we achieved an added benefit of simplifying operations in our restaurants!

NORDSTROM SHUTS SERVICE DEPARTMENT

One of the best-known names for customer service in the United States, clothing retailer Nordstrom has been quietly closing its formal customer service departments in its stores. Instead, "it will offer services provided by the department, including the return of items purchased online, at each sales register throughout the store."[1] According to the company spokesperson, "We're always looking for a way to enhance service." By "pushing" service to the floor where associates interact so closely with its customers, Nordstrom can consolidate its listening posts with its selling stations.

WITHIN CUSTOMER SERVICE, TOO

The twin issues of accountability and ownership don't just apply between departments or with key suppliers; they also apply across a customer service organization. The customer service department itself can produce poor results and deliver unacceptable performance levels if its internal measures and accountabilities are incorrect; getting these accountabilities right can enable rapid turnarounds in performance and agility when under pressure. A major financial services company experienced this turnaround.

The company's contact center had been underperforming for many months, and it appeared on the surface to be a basket case: (1) speed-of-answer targets had not been met for many months; (2) complaint and escalation levels were rising; and (3) staff turnover and absenteeism were at record levels, such that vacation and training had been cancelled in an effort to meet the service level targets. The general manager of customer service appointed a new contact center manager to solve the problem, and this individual quickly got to work. The manager reviewed such key data as the forecasting and planning for the center and the variations in the level of staff use ("occupancy") and then spent time observing how staff behaved, what team leaders did, and the way everyone was measured.

The new manager concluded that there was an accountability problem inside customer service. Staff measures emphasized handle time, the time spent performing "after-call work" (preparing notes after the call), and the quality of calls, but only paid lip service to how well staff adhered to shift schedules. The manager listened to calls and found it painful to observe such perverse behaviors as cutting short a customer in order to get to the next call because the "wall boards" all around the center were flashing red, indicating large numbers of customers waiting in the queue.

The manager calculated that over the previous year as the pressure had increased, the customer support staff spent more and more time in after-call work, but in reality agents were using this time to relieve the stress of taking call after call with no break. The company's emphasis on speed led to an increase in the number of calls, as poorly handled calls snowballed into repeat calls with more and more complaints.

Over the next week, the manager met with each team in the contact center, one by one, to lay out the new accountability rules: contact center agents were to be accountable for only two things: (1) being at their desks ready to take calls at the time assigned to them; and (2) minimizing the time they spent in a "not ready state" that made them unavailable for calls. The manager told them not to worry about the speed of the calls or how many people were waiting in the queue, and promised that under this new system they would get breaks between calls and their normal leave and training times. It was equally important to make team leaders responsible for the same measures as the agents and for the quality of call handling—their role was to make sure their teams were available for calls at the right times and to teach the skills needed to handle the calls well.

Naturally, there was cynicism among the teams that anything would change, but the manager's job wasn't done yet. The forecasting team had to revise its planning assumptions to accommodate this new order. After a week communicating the desired new behaviors and accountabilities, the center "went live" the following week. The turnaround was almost instantaneous. After being 50 to 60 percent outside their targets in the previous week, the center hit or exceeded targets three days out of five. As the accountabilities became clear and the agents adhered to them, performance improved even further. In week two, the center hit its targets every day, and the feeling of relief was palpable. The agents started to have gaps between calls, team leaders had time for coaching and development, and absenteeism dropped dramatically as the work stress declined. By week three, the center was able to reintroduce training that had been skipped, and the center hit their targets predictably from that point forward.

What this contact center manager understood was how to apply correct accountabilities within customer service, just as companies need to do across owner departments. In essence there are only two things that agents can control (shift adherence and availability to take calls), and team leaders must help the agents achieve these targets and then coach them for quality. The contact center manager also had to forecast and plan accurately, and have the right number of people available to take the calls, but productivity and speed were owned elsewhere. As a capstone to this turnaround, the now seasoned customer service manager later spent time with the process and system design teams to design changes that improved productivity.

The Framework

Assigning accountability and ownership requires these three steps, introduced earlier: (1) tearing down the walls, which includes resolving the issues that prevent managers from finding out who is accountable, and working back through root causes to find the real owners of issues; however, tearing down walls (also called eliminating the stovepipes or silos) alone isn't enough, so it is important to (2) make accountability stick and (3) liberate the front line such that the agents interacting with customers are given the freedom to be effective.

Step 1: Tear Down the Walls

The two most common barriers we see that prevent accountability for Best Service are lack of information and ignorance. Unfortunately, many company departments are blissfully unaware of the issues that they cause because there is limited information flow among the departments. This lack of information can take many forms. Contact centers and administration areas typically report the number of interactions they handle, how fast they handle them, and sometimes how well they are handled. As we discussed in Chapter Two, there is surprisingly little emphasis *why* the contacts occurred, who is accountable, and whether there are better ways for the company and the customers to obtain the information or solutions. There are four states of lack of information, all of which result in limited accountability:

Lack of Information	Issue
Contact reasons not reported	The customer-facing areas track and report volumes, not the nature of contacts.
Too few reasons captured (fewer than ten)	Use of "top ten" categories that are too generic, such as billing, credit, or payments, often driven by customers' selection in the IVR. These reasons often span many departments (that is, they are not MECE).
Too many reasons captured (more than sixty)	The nature of contacts is reported at such a granular level that it is perceived to be unreliable, incomprehensible, or too complex.
Reporting "what," not "why"	This process involves reporting what was done for the customer—for example, "Updated system x," rather than why the contact was necessary. Only the "why" helps an organization understand accountability.

In Chapter Two we explained how Amazon set up effective contact tracking using thirty unchanging "why" codes that produced effective reporting and management of contact categories, thus removing the interdepartmental information barrier. A critical part of the process was making sure that each contact category had a clear owner within the company; for Amazon, that meant an executive who reported to CEO Jeff Bezos.

Sometimes, ascertaining the owner is straightforward, but this is not always the case. In many situations, companies need to investigate the root causes of contacts before they can work out who owns them. For example, Amazon had to learn to distinguish between the four different types of "Where's my stuff?" issues before ownership became clear:

"Where's My Stuff?" Reason	Root Cause	Owner
Item not in stock when customer placed order	Inventory systems not providing correct information to Web site	VP of supply chain
Item delayed or stuck in warehouse	Warehouse team not staying on top of orders	VP of fulfillment
False expectation— order still in shipment	Web site not conveying when customer will receive item	VP of Web development
Late by shipper	Shipping companies not delivering to promised service levels	VP of shipping

Because Amazon's product inventory and order tracking systems were so accurate, the agents handling the contacts in these cases were able to deduce quickly the root cause of contacts by checking the order dates and status of items.

It's not always that easy to identify the owner of a customer contact or problem. For utilities, a common contact category that seems unnecessary occurs when customers who have already paid their bill in full receive disconnect warnings. On the surface, this would seem to be a problem for the owner of the credit management processes, as this department defines the rules about when customers are sent letters to warn them of impending disconnection or to remind them to pay. But in fact there could be several root causes and owners of this problem:

Problem	Root Cause	Owner
Letters take too long to be mailed.	Logistics of letter production, batching, and sending	VP of operations
Payments are processed too slowly.	The customers pay (or think they have), but for some reason it takes several days to update their balance.	VP of accounts receivable
Business rules are too crude or are set improperly.	The credit department is driven by bad debt ratios and wants to get the money in the door ASAP.	VP of credit and collections
There is no recognition of customer payment history and type.	The systems are not clever enough to work out that this customer always pays on the last possible date and always uses a mechanism that takes x days to reach the company.	VP of systems

Each of these problems could be happening at the same time, but note that each has a different owner in the business. As we have emphasized earlier, the head of customer service or contact centers isn't accountable for any of them—his or her job is to figure out why the customer did get the incorrect letter, apologize, and move on to the next customer contact—*and*, as we have also stressed, feed back these situations with clear reporting so that the underlying reasons can be fixed. The department responsible for credit or the other root causes may be blissfully unaware of the amount of contacts it is causing and the frustrations for the customer. There may also be a complex equation on the net benefits of relaxing business rules to delay when to send reminder and disconnection notices in order to allow for predictable customer behavior.

This is a clear example of a company that needs to understand the nature of its customer contacts, analyze the root causes, and then hold the real process owners accountable for implementing lasting solutions. In this case, the VP of credit and collections is probably the most logical owner for poorly timed credit letters and warnings. He or she may need help from other departments to figure how to fix the issue, but if designated, the owner needs to lead the process (collecting debt) that has driven the contact.

If there are issues in identifying accountability for contacts, we recommend applying the "Five Why's" technique. This analysis process drills down through the layers of causes to reach the real root cause and therefore clarify the accountability. Here's an example:

Why Question	Answer
1. Why did the customer call (or e-mail or send us a letter)?	She received a letter warning her that she would lose her power, when in fact she had already paid.
2. Why did she get the letter from us?	Our payments system did not know she had already paid.
3. Why didn't the system know she had paid?	It takes three days to update certain payment types after payment.
4. Why doesn't the system make allowances for payment methods?	The system doesn't analyze the payment history to look at previous payment history and timing. If no payment is received, we send the letter to get the money in the door.
5. Why doesn't the system vary business rules by payment history?	We have a one-size-fits-all business rule, because it's a simpler way for us to manage the wide range of customer types.

The Five Why's technique can get to the bottom of who really owns the contact; once you understand the root causes, the solutions are more apparent. In this case, a range of solutions might be feasible, such as

- Delay reminder notices for customers with a sound credit history.
- Fine-tune the system to examine typical payment types and history.
- Have a different reminder period for customers who always use the payment methods with long update time lags.
- Provide an automated way for customers who think they have paid to be able to check that their payment has been received (something that all companies should provide anyway; see Chapter Three).

The lack of information on contact types is the first barrier to effective owenership, and understanding root causes is the second barrier. Next, the company needs to appoint appropriate owners. To do this, conduct both of the following simple tests of ownership:

Ownership Test	Description
Ownership of root cause	Does this person own the area that causes the issue or drives the contact type?
Fix-it test	Does this person have the authority and budget to fix the root cause?

If a company assigns owners who do not pass these two tests, nothing will change. If the company can't answer the root cause question, then further analysis is needed. In most companies, we have found that the most effective owners are direct reports to the CEO or business unit head. That level of owner has the requisite authority to make change happen and can be held accountable.

The same issues of accountability and ownership can be extended to other problematic types of contacts, such as the drivers of repeat contacts and the drivers of complaints. We sometimes see these as a hierarchy of contacts, as illustrated in Figure 6.1:

FIGURE 6.1: HIERARCHY OF CUSTOMER INTERACTIONS

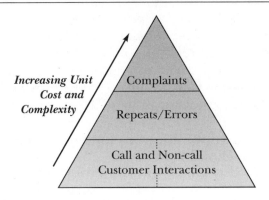

Analyzing root causes and identifying the owners of those root causes apply equally to complaints and repeats, but many parts of the company will be in denial that they are the causes of these more serious issues. We have seen many organizations address this by setting up "complaints forums," where ownership and accountability are allocated to those who have caused the problem. These complaint forums examine the root cause of complaints and put in place solutions to fix these root causes. The goal of the forums is to get rid of the issues that cause complaints rather than merely react to the symptoms of each individual complaint.

Some organizations' reporting structures make it harder to assign accountability. Unfortunately, many organizations are proud of their so-called matrix management structures, which we described earlier as antithetical to the MECE rules—how can two people be responsible for the same thing? It is appropriate to describe those situations both as "everyone's accountable" and as "no one's accountable." If your company does have a structure like this, you will need to fix the structure before you can determine any true accountability.

STEP 2: MAKE ACCOUNTABILITY STICK

Determining who is accountable and "should" be taking action is all very well, but getting owners to take action is harder still. Most of the departments and executives who are accountable for customer service contacts and issues have never thought or felt that they were accountable or responsible for service—after all, isn't that why there's a customer service department? Why should they suddenly be obligated to take action?

It's quite likely that the reactions will follow the five-stage process we described earlier when talking about Amazon, including active denial and resistance rather than simple inactivity. For instance, a major bank started reporting customer contact drivers and asked different departments to take ownership, but many of the new owners fought against it. They claimed it wasn't their issue and then failed to attend the meetings and reviews that had been arranged to drive the necessary actions. Don't be surprised to see these common reactions:

Reaction	Articulation
Denial	It's not my issue. Your data [or process or allocation] are incorrect.
Anger	Don't be ridiculous! That's nothing to do with us.
Rational refusal	Even if it is our issue, we've got better things to do.
Pseudo-bargaining	Even if it is our issue, how are we to find time and resources to tackle it? It's not in our plan or budget. We have already allocated all our change resources for the next year.

How do you anticipate and overcome these kinds of reactions? There are three possible approaches that you can combine for even greater effect: (1) good old-fashioned sponsorship, (2) meaningful targets that matter, and (3) the glue of financial accountability.

Good Old-Fashioned Sponsorship

The first prerequisite to making accountability stick is sponsorship from the top down (as it is with every type of change management). If the CEO or managing director doesn't think ownership is important, then why those who report to him or her? At Amazon, Jeff Bezos championed accountability actively, participating in the weekly operations meetings where progress and actions on contact drivers were discussed and tracked. He made it clear from his actions that accountability was important: any executive owner of a contact category who could not explain why the rate (expressed as contacts per order, CPO) had gone up or down was challenged by Bezos, who repeated that this was an important part of the job of the contact owners. This steady pressure from the top drove the behavior he wanted: contact owners spent time with the customer service area in advance of the meetings so as to understand how their contacts were trending and why. They researched issues before each meeting and were determined to prove that their actions were working. Suddenly everyone was "in the boat pulling on the oars in the same direction," using the same language (CPO) and arguing how to improve customer experience over time.

Contrast this with the banking example we mentioned: the owners of key contact categories often failed to attend the contact reason action meetings—they either sent delegates or failed to be represented at all. On closer inspection, however, it turned out that these owners took their lead from the project sponsor. First off, he didn't have the authority to hold people accountable; he was a peer of some of the owners. Second, his own behavior demonstrated that the process wasn't important to him: he was twenty minutes late for the first meeting that he was supposed to chair and then, when he arrived, he spent fifteen minutes discussing other business before tackling the agenda at hand, leaving a mere twenty-five minutes to discuss customer contact strategy and results. Not surprisingly, actions were neither agreed to nor acted on, and the next meetings had an even lower level of attendance.

Meaningful Targets That Matter

"This isn't in our plan" is a common reaction of denial when accountabilities are first reallocated to the real owners of customer issues. What this really means is that the targets and measures that already exist don't include these new accountabilities, and the new owners are therefore being pulled in a different direction. Resetting targets that reflect and include the needs of customer service is often a critical part of the process; the simplest way to do this is to add a key performance indicator (KPI) or to measure the change required to improve customer service. For example, an executive responsible for billing might be given a target to reduce the number of contacts querying late bills.

Adding a target like this might appear unwieldy, but often the customer service impacts provide a way of measuring the effectiveness of back-office processes that previously lacked measurement or were too costly to measure. For example, checking outgoing billing accuracy through sampling and investigation is an expensive way to validate the process, whereas using the volume of customers who query bill accuracy is a cheaper and more accurate measurement technique. Of course some of the customers might be wrong, so the measurement process may need to make this distinction (representing two root causes: that the bill is wrong and that the customer thinks it is wrong), and some customers with inaccurate bills might not think to complain. In many processes, adding the customer service metrics contributes the VOC dimension to a previously unbalanced scorecard. In the utility example discussed earlier, the functions outside customer service, such as billing, credit and collections, and payment processing, had no mechanism to assess their customer impact. The billing manager was measured on the timeliness and accuracy of bills using the company's internal view of timeliness and accuracy. However, once the company started tracking contact drivers, they were able to set targets for the billing manager based on the volume of calls driven by late bills and the percentage of calls correctly querying the bill's accuracy; having these targets made the timeliness and accuracy issues more meaningful to everyone in the billing department. As a result, timeliness and accuracy targets were no longer just management objectives, because the billing area staff could see the correlation between their work and its impact on the customer. Once the process started, they initiated a set of projects to improve timeliness and accuracy.

The Glue of Financial Accountability

In some companies, having clear targets for those who are accountable may be enough. However, at Amazon it wasn't just the sponsorship that made accountability stick. The "contact demand" reports from the customer care area at Amazon (known as the Skyline report, introduced in Chapter Two) showed the volume and cost of each contact category in each period, each category having an owner among the executive team. When CFO Warren Jenson saw the Skyline report, he said, "Why don't we charge these costs back to their owners? Their costs shouldn't be in the customer service cost center; they belong in the groups causing the pain." So that's what Amazon did: each owner department had the cost reallocated to it, but that didn't mean adding to that department's budget. In the case of marketing, for example, the department still had to achieve its revenue targets using its allocated budget, but it also had to pay for the cost of any unnecessary contacts that it caused.

Cost reallocation is the "ultimate weapon" to drive account-ability and ownership, because if the issue is hitting an executive's budget, he or she has little choice but to take greater interest in it. Amazon's IT department, for example, had a far greater moti-vation to fix bugs and errors once it started shouldering the costs of the bugs and error problems on the Web site. For example, one of the four "Where's my stuff?" reasons showed that the root cause was customer confusion about when an item would be delivered; in essence, customers were contacting Amazon too soon. The Web site should have set this expectation more clearly, but initial discussions of solutions led to denial reactions:

"We can't fix that."
"Customers can't expect us to tell them exactly when they'll get the item."
"We can't predict when an item will be delivered to the customer."

Luckily, the customer service staff would not let the issue drop. "Why can't we predict it?" they asked. Because the IT department owned the budget for this contact category, the IT staff went away and had a harder look at it and worked out that they had all the information needed to inform the customer: they knew where the customer lived, the shipping mechanism, which distribution center would ship the item, and the agreed-on delivery times for that item using the customer-selected shipping method. All that IT and Web development needed to do was to connect the dots, and they would be able to predict when the item would arrive, at least within a two-day range. Armed with that information, the IT shop and Web development changed the customer's purchase experience: rather than tell the customer after purchase when the item would be delivered, the Amazon site informs the customer before he purchases. This now gives the customer a chance to cancel the purchase or change his shipping details, for example, by upgrading the shipping method. Once this was in place, the number of "Where's my stuff, false expectation" calls plummeted, meaning happier customers, fewer contacts per order—in other words, another example of Best Service.

We have seen that financial reallocation of the cost of calls, issues, or complaints can be a critical mechanism to ensure that responsibility for service and customer issues is allocated correctly, but top-level allocation may not be enough. A phenomenon called "management black holes" can still undermine effective ownership.[2] Black holes exist where middle or lower levels of management counteract or undermine the required changes, indicating that sponsorship and responsibility need to filter all the way down through the company. For example, reallocating costs to the departments that cause customer contacts will make the leaders of those departments want to act, but if that accountability isn't shared within their department and doesn't cascade to those who manage teams and processes, then black holes will undermine the changes needed.

Let's look at a major contact center change that illustrates the potential impact of management black holes. The company's contact center manager had recognized that handle time was an inappropriate measure for the frontline agents because it was driving the wrong behavior on calls—agents were more concerned with getting to the next call than resolving the customer's problem. The manager established a new system that measured agents based on the quality of their calls, attendance, and adherence to their schedules, but with few productivity measures. However, team leaders continued to impose a handle time goal across the teams, causing a management black hole; the team leaders knew that they weren't supposed to measure the frontline agents on their handle times, but old habits are hard to break. If an agent's handle times increased week by week versus his team average, team leaders mandated additional coaching sessions, so the agents continued to believe that speed was among the most important things for them to achieve. After all, it appeared important to their supervisors, so they continued to believe it was important to the company. A year after the change, when the issue of "speed-focused behaviors" among frontline agents was raised, the contact center manager couldn't understand why: "But we haven't measured the agents on handle time for a year." She failed to understand that the new measurement system had created a black hole at the team leader level, allowing team leaders to pull agent behavior in exactly the direction the contact center manager wanted to eradicate. To remove the black hole, she had to remove handle time from team leaders' reports; as a result, the team leaders could no longer "lean" on their teams to achieve the speed targets, finally bringing in line more customer-centric behaviors among the agents.

STEP 3: LIBERATE THE FRONT LINE

Most of the issues of accountability we have described so far have been about fixing misplaced accountability across company departments, identifying which groups or senior executives are accountable, and making that accountability stick. However, accountability can also cause issues if it is not assigned to the right level within the department where accountability is ultimately owned. Figure 6.2 presents both of these accountability dimensions.

FIGURE 6.2: ACCOUNTABILITY SCHEMATIC

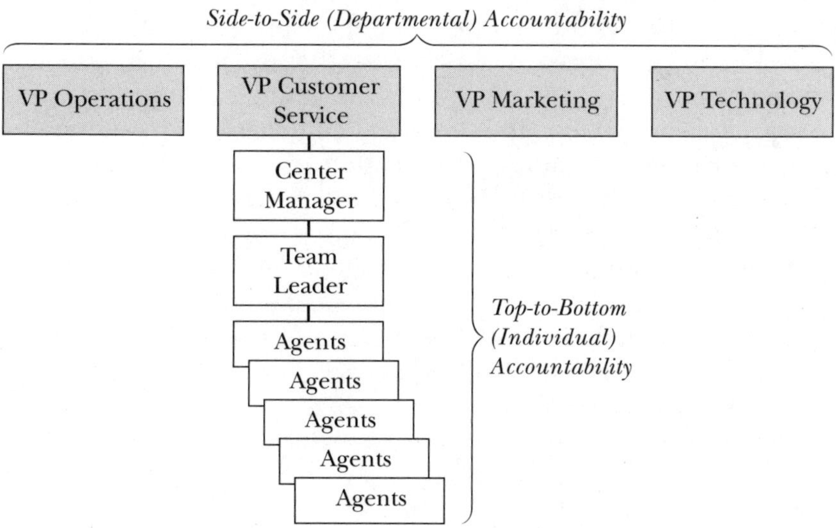

The top-to-bottom issues in accountability manifest themselves when staff are not able to deliver service in the way customers want because they do not feel empowered to do so. This lack of empowerment can take many forms: either the staff believe they are not empowered, or the rules, policies, and processes may dictate that staff cannot deliver the service the way customers want. We will consider each issue in turn.

A common problem of policies and procedures inhibiting individual accountability for the customer experience is what we call the policy shield. In these situations, the frontline staff "hides behind" what they believe to be the policies and guidelines for the process they use to deal with the customer. Privacy policies often produce policy shields. For example, a customer may call in on behalf of an elderly or sick relative. The frontline staff identify that this is not the customer, and therefore, according to the policy guidelines, she cannot be served.

Makes sense, right? In some cases, however, this policy shield can lead to some ludicrous customer experiences. A finance journalist in *The Age* newspaper wrote of just such an experience.[3] She called her husband's wealth management business to make a payment on her husband's behalf. The service agent identified that she was not the customer. When the journalist asked to make a payment, the agent refused the request. The customer asked for an explanation. "I just want to pay money into my husband's account. Where is the risk in that?" But the agent still refused to consider it. The journalist was so irate that she wrote an article in that week's finance section highlighting this experience. In the mind of the journalist, the staff was being lazy and incompetent. She was clearly not alone: that section of the paper the following week was filled with letters from customers sharing similar dumb experiences, including other cases of payments not being accepted, of relations calling on behalf of dead relatives and being turned away, of customers whose parents spoke little English being refused access on their parents' behalf, and so forth. All the stories appeared to show service experiences where common sense was lacking.

So why does the privacy policy shield prevent frontline staff from doing the right thing by the customer? There are three related causes that need to be addressed:

1. The risk-averse "blanket" policy
2. The penal measurement system
3. The lack of individual accountability

Risk-Averse "Blanket" Policy

The risk-averse blanket policy occurs when companies feel that exceptions or variations create unacceptably high risk. It's safer and easier to implement a system that says "Don't provide service to anyone who isn't the customer" than to train or trust frontline staff to adjust or adapt the policy to suit a range of circumstances. It's far easier for the department in charge of privacy issues (often the head of risk or internal audit) to administer a single blanket ruling. We've seen it across many industries: banking, insurance, investments, utilities, telecommunications, and others have adopted this privacy safety net.

Penal Measurement System

The penal measurement system then kicks in to enforce the policy. Most quality measurement systems enforce adherence to company policies in the form of supervisor or quality team reviews of calls, letters, or e-mails. Agents may get a "fail" or "needs improvement" quality score if they incorrectly give advice or information outside the strict privacy guidelines; they are encouraged *not* to step outside the policy shield and not to question it. The supervisors or quality checkers also believe it is their job to enforce the policy.

Lack of Individual Accountability

The third factor that causes this problem is that frontline staff don't feel empowered to do what they believe is right for the customer. Even if their policy shield does allow for some exceptions, unless individual accountability is encouraged, most staff will take the safe path rather than risk a measurement slap around the head. To remove the policy shield, companies need to fix accountability issues both across and up and down their organizations. First, managers who develop and create the policy shields need to understand their impact and the trade-offs. They need to do the following:

- Be shown that for every one case of potential fraud that a blanket policy may catch, many more customers are going to be denied service in a way that makes no sense to them.
- Consider the risks of poor publicity, frustration, and customer loss that occur from denying service to many customers (see again the financial journalist's cry that was answered by others the following week, and magnify that today with the power of customer blogs).
- Think through the exceptions that are reasonable.

However, the biggest change that is needed is for some accountability to be pushed down the organization to the front line. Imagine the difference in behaviors and attitudes in organizations that display some trust in their frontline staff. If staff are enabled to do what makes sense for the customer (some call this empowerment), they are usually able to get it right. Of course there is still the risk of extreme cases. There are instances of vengeful divorces where one of the former spouses cancels products and services on behalf of the other, but those are exceptions that can be managed: it's easy and simple to reinstate the service or product and possibly even compensate the "wronged" customer. But allowing fear of these exceptions to impact far more customers doesn't make sense to us. There is also a clear cost benefit.

At one company, 15 percent of the customers were turned away because of inadequate identification details at the start of a call. Nearly all these customers had to call back and repeat the process; by that stage, they were frustrated and angry. But in many cases they were calling to tell the company something rather than to gain access to private information. The calls were denied even though the nature of the call was unclear.

There are two solutions to this situation. First, staff could have been trusted to find out what the customer wanted before turning her away. Customers who want to pay, for example, represent little or no fraud risk. Second, the rule could have been relaxed for many exceptional circumstances, such as the customer being sick, abroad, and so forth. If the company had changed the process, it would have been able to refocus efforts on the very low percentage of true exceptions, and the returns would have been substantial.

The benefits from countering the policy shield are not just about reducing contact volumes or increasing customer satisfaction, although both are clearly positive results and adhere tightly to Best Service principles. The difference between an environment where staff fear doing the wrong thing and one in which they are rewarded and applauded for doing the right thing is palpable and also measurable. These latter companies have fewer repeat calls, fewer complaints, shorter calls, and more satisfied customers, and they also have happier and more motivated staff. They attract and retain frontline staff who gain personal satisfaction and fulfillment from satisfying customers' needs. Companies that operate "command-and-control environments" have high absenteeism and staff turnover, with all the associated costs. The consequences of blanket policies and policy shields extend to both customers and staff.

It is therefore critical to assess the extent to which accountability has been extended to frontline staff:

- Do they have the training to recognize exceptional issues and circumstances?
- Do they have the ability to handle and manage these exceptions?
- Is there a closed-loop process enabling staff to report these exceptions and how they were handled to the policy-producing departments?
- Can policy exceptions be posted quickly for all agents to see and use, instead of being closeted or handled differently across the organization?

A common "testing ground" for the extent of accountability at the front line is the ability of staff to waive fees, write off costs on behalf of the customer, or provide free replacements. Command-and-control environments see this as a great risk area where customer-facing staff cannot be trusted; the management fear that staff are "soft" and will always favor the customer at the expense of the company. Consequently, the company sets a policy that limits staff's financial discretion. However, these companies confuse the need for organizational control and the necessity for control of the front line. It is possible to give accountability to the front line and keep organizational control through remote measurement and exception management, as we'll illustrate.

One of Amazon's early "enablers" granted free replacements and other concessions when customers complained or simply commented about missed promises or damaged books or CDs. Amazon trusted its customers and empowered all agents to "do the right thing" whenever needed, at that moment and not after "research"; it followed the age-old proverb to "seek forgiveness, not permission." As Amazon grew, the informal rules had to tighten (you can't agree to replace a digital camera or generator as simply as a $12 book), and agents understood the difference, with minimal direction or reminders. But later, the company's CFO feared that frontline staff could not be given carte blanche to provide replacement items or refunds, fearing that the agents would be too generous and that these write-offs would impact the bottom line. The CFO's preference was to set limits per agent, report weekly actual results versus targets, and call out those who overstepped the norms. Fortunately, wiser heads prevailed. The customer service department collected data across the entire operation and per agent over time, revealing that the total "hit" to the bottom line was very low, that there were very few outliers, and that there had been considerable positive word of mouth and positive feedback thanks to the original practice. In the end, no individual financial limits were put in place—the frontline staff could issue refunds and replacements as they saw fit, the opposite of the policy that the CFO had sought. The customer service management team continued to monitor these concessions, running reports on the total cost of the policy and on each agent's levels, allowing them to manage quickly any agent who was overly generous (interventions were very rare).

Had the CFO's policy been implemented, you can imagine the results: upset customers, reduced sales, and frustrated agents. Relaxing this proposed policy demonstrated to staff that they were trusted to take responsible decisions; it made sense to them and to the customer. There was a financial benefit in that fewer cases were raised to supervisors for authorization, so there were fewer long contacts in this area. It was a win-win-win situation: simple and commonsense experiences for customers, efficiency gains for the company, and empowerment for staff. This is a clear demonstration of the value of liberating the front line.

Summary

Delivering improved service is rarely the responsibility of the customer service area alone. Companies need to work out who is accountable for service and related issues, have a range of mechanisms to make that accountability stick, and involve all the departments to deliver Best Service. As well as working across the company side to side (by department), companies need to examine and enable accountability top to bottom (within departments). They also need to find ways to create an environment where frontline staff can do the right thing for the customer and the organization. If accountability is in the wrong place, companies need to

- Knock down the accountability barriers by identifying and communicating the root causes of contacts and issues.
- Use sponsorship, measurement, and cost allocation to make accountability stick.
- Remove the policy and measurement constraints so that frontline staff can be made accountable for service delivery.

Survey Questions

Please score your company for these three key questions covering the idea of owning the actions across the organization, and refer to Appendix A to check your progress from Basic Service to Better Service to Best Service.

14. In our company, customer service is
    a. Solely the responsibility of the customer service department.
    b. Part and parcel of everyone's role, and a shared accountability across the whole company.
    c. Discussed at all levels, but managed solely by the customer service team.
    d. Part of marketing.

15. In our company, the CEO
    a. Reviews issues in service only when key targets aren't met
    b. Treats customer service as a cost center.
    c. Sees customer service as one of our most important departments, critical to our decisions and strategy.
    d. Takes a continuous interest in service and ensures that all parts of the company contribute to service outcomes.
    e. Says that customer service is important, but really has no interest in customer service.

16. Our frontline customer-facing staff
    a. Are empowered to make decisions that help the customer.
    b. Perform their role within broad policy guidelines.
    c. Are measured and monitored on process and policy adherence.
    d. Cannot be trusted without tight process controls.

CHAPTER SEVEN

LISTEN AND ACT
Instead of Letting Customer Insights Slip Away

We feel really close to our customers. When we want to know what's on their minds, we don't need to put them in a sterile room with a swinging bulb.
—AUDREY DUMPER, TRADER JOE'S, *FAST COMPANY*, OCTOBER 2004

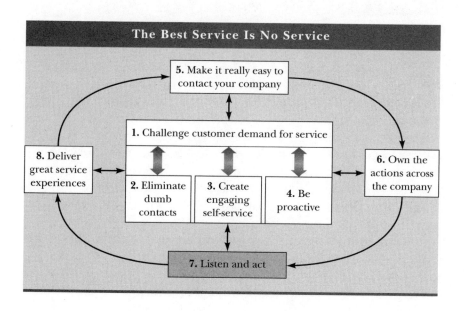

The Best Service Is No Service

5. Make it really easy to contact your company

1. Challenge customer demand for service

8. Deliver great service experiences

2. Eliminate dumb contacts
3. Create engaging self-service
4. Be proactive

6. Own the actions across the company

7. Listen and act

THE PRINCIPLE

It's amazing to us that so many organizations spend millions of dollars a year trying to understand their customers using market research companies to survey them, call them, or run focus groups to get answers to such questions as "Who are you?" "What do you want from us?" "What makes you tick?" "How happy are you with us?" and the like. This has become a standard way to get insight about the customer, but there is a better way: as we have described in the first six chapters, prospects and customers are constantly contacting your company. They are writing, calling, or visiting you and also spending millions of their hours in various forms of contact. Furthermore, through their behavior, customers are also telling companies what they think; they are buying more or less or even leaving, using self-service or not, and even sharing openly their experiences with your competitors and with companies that they admire (what we call "last contact benchmarking"). Why do we need to take up more of their time with surveys weeks after an interaction or pay them to come into a focus group to tell us what they're thinking?

The answer is that not many organizations have learned how to listen well to the interactions that exist today, or how to interpret the behaviors that are occurring naturally. Best Service companies that "listen and act" have

- Figured out that each contact is a chance to listen, each complaint a gift.
- Trained their staff to listen and not simply process.
- Given their staff the time, systems, and processes to help them listen.
- Developed ways to capture what customers are saying.
- Created continuous feedback mechanisms.
- Found new ways to engage their customers and get feedback quickly and cheaply.

These companies have also realized that they can cut back on some of the old-fashioned satisfaction research and scorekeeping, instead mining their customer interactions for incredible value and insights. They have figured out that customer interactions produce much more responsive reactions to their customers' "voice" and save themselves a small fortune on expensive research that all too often doesn't drive action. Moreover, they realize that there is a mountain of customer insight to be gleaned from the contacts and interactions they have with customers today, and have created processes to listen and act. This enables them to make more rapid improvements in service and ensure that their customer-facing staff are more focused on what customers care about most.

We'll explain how to listen and act along these three dimensions:

1. Learning to listen and when to do it.
2. Smart ways to listen that make it cheap and effective.
3. Turning listening into action.

EXAMPLES OUTSIDE CUSTOMER SERVICE

Let's first turn to examples of listening and acting found outside the world of customer service.

FORTY-ONE YEARS LATER

In 1953, Nelson Mandela was one of the leaders of the South African socialist movement known as the National Action Council (NAC), whose actions illustrate this Principle of learning to listen. As Mandela recounts in his autobiography, *Long Walk to Freedom*, the NAC invited all participating organizations and their followers to send suggestions for "A Charter of Freedom," a massive effort that included sending circulars to townships and villages across the country. The surveys asked simple and basic questions, such as "If you could make the laws . . . what would you do?" and "How would you set about making South Africa a happy place for all the people who live in it?" Mandela and the NAC encouraged everyone in South Africa, "BLACK AND WHITE—LET US SPEAK TOGETHER OF FREEDOM! . . . LET THE VOICES OF ALL THE PEOPLE BE HEARD. AND LET THE DEMANDS OF ALL THE PEOPLE FOR THE THINGS THAT WILL MAKE US FREE BE RECORDED. LET THE DEMANDS BE GATHERED TOGETHER IN A GREAT CHARTER OF FREEDOM [capital letters *sic*]."

This urgent request for the voice of the people generated tremendous response—"Suggestions came in from sports and cultural clubs, church groups, ratepayers' associations, women's organizations, schools, trade union branches. They came on serviettes, on paper torn from exercise books, on scraps of foolscap, on the backs of our own leaflets. It was humbling to see how the suggestions of ordinary people were often far ahead of the leaders!"[1] The most common request was for "one man, one vote," which the South Africans finally attained forty-one years later in 1994 in the resurgence after apartheid's end and Mandela's election as president.

This example illustrates that there are many ways to "tap into" the voice of the community—customers, citizens, or members—and that sooner or later they will take root. Never underestimate how powerfully this community wants and needs to be heard. Expressing one's opinion is one of the most basic freedoms and desires that we have.

GET YOUR READERS TO HELP WRITE YOUR BOOKS

Rowan of Rin, written by Emily Rodda, is a popular multibook adventure series. Rodda decided to tap the readers of the books for input to the series. The later books in the five-book series credit readers for their suggestions of the adventures with which Rowan should proceed. Not only did this approach make the writer's job easier, but naturally the series continues to be popular and remains on the children's best-seller list.

Tapping into the excitement surrounding wiki software that enables collaborative contributions and edits online (see also our description of wiki for knowledge sharing), Penguin, the book publishing company, asked the public to write, together, what has become known as *A Million Penguins*. As a result of overwhelming interest, this jointly compiled book grew to have twenty-one chapters, all building on initial suggestions by the publisher with details that built on earlier themes, truly a community effort—an emerging example of "listen and act."[2]

SHUTTLE *ENTERPRISE*

Many of us were, and still are, fans of the TV show *Star Trek*, along with its many movies, its colorful characters—Spock, Captain Kirk, the Klingons, Tribbles—and of course the starship *Enterprise*. In late 2006, the popular Web site Collect Space featured this article about how the public in 1976 successfully lobbied to change the name of the NASA spacecraft:

> September 17, 2006 / 9:30 A.M. CT (1430 GMT)
>
> These are the voyages of the space shuttle Enterprise. Its 30 year (old) mission (today) to explore strange new approaches, to seek out new landings and new facilities, to boldly go where no U.S. reusable winged orbiter had gone before. . . .
>
> Thirty years ago today, NASA rolled out its first shuttle orbiter, OV-101. Originally named Constitution, *Star Trek* fans staged a successful write-in campaign to re-christen it Enterprise. Though never to launch into orbit, Enterprise flew an important series of approach and landing tests as well as was used to configure

launch facilities at Kennedy Space Center in Florida and later at Vandenberg Air Force Base in California. In 1985, NASA delivered Enterprise to the Smithsonian, which in 2003 placed it on display at the National Air and Space Museum's Udvar-Hazy Center.

To celebrate the 30th anniversary, Exp. 11 badge artist Tim Gagnon and Bill Coukoulis, Jr. of Space Emblem Art partnered to design and produce a commemorative patch. The insignia depicts Enterprise's launch and landing tests.[3]

BAD CASES

Now let's turn to a review of six bad examples of "listen and act" in customer service: we refer to them as choking off the wells of invention (which has a silver lining, at least); the dangers of denial; something in the air(line); chained to the office; what our customers are saying if we could only hear them; and the craziness of customer notes.

CHOKING OFF THE WELLS OF INVENTION

Global professional services firms must maintain a delicate balance among local partnerships working under global brands and management. Thus being able to "listen" to local needs and demands is a critical competence. One such firm showed the dangers of having the head office lose the ability to listen. This firm had generated amazing growth of 20 percent per year for over twenty years, with much of this success coming from the ability to take ideas that were developed in one country or geography to other companies and economies all over the world. The model was described as being one of "invent locally, scale globally": the local practices acted as the eyes and ears tuned to customer needs and to trends and developments that would take off all over the world.

However, through the late 1990s, the global management team, based in North America, began to see the local practices as areas that needed to be controlled, as squandering investments on ideas that didn't go anywhere. The central management began to think that it was far better to channel increased budgets into central think tanks and R&D instead of harnessing local innovations, believing it to be better to standardize offers all over the world and focus efforts on a more limited set of offers that could be leveraged and scaled. The appeal of scale and central control were enticing to produce lower cost but also greater leverage of investments. The company went ahead with the change. Localized investment and R&D budgets were removed, and countries not executing one of the standard project types had to seek special approval. The company tried to focus on fewer offers and to control investments and research at the center of the company, but it didn't work: annual revenue growth slowed to below 10 percent for the first time in the company's history. Through this centralization model, the company lost its ability to listen and invent for the market. Furthermore, the central R&D and solution development practices were slow and cumbersome compared to the local diversified practices that had to respond quickly to client needs. The local partnerships became more and more frustrated at their inability to respond to local demands and needs. As growth slowed, the local partnerships rebelled, dumping the central management team. The new team quickly restored local investment budgets and local company autonomy, and the company started listening and responding to needs all over the world, rediscovering the engines of invention. From stagnation and retrenchments, the company started to grow again: a clear illustration, in our view, that every company needs to find ways to listen to its customers.

THE DANGERS OF DENIAL

A major IT-related company was struggling to maintain its growth and starting to lose market share. The American Customer Satisfaction Index (ACSI, mentioned in Chapter One) had traced the drop in customer enthusiasm toward this company. Customer satisfaction was increasingly negative, and people who had been longtime fans and customers were starting to vote with their feet and wallets. Blogs were emerging to complain about the company, particularly its technical support.

Internally, the feeling was different; the internal tracking of customer satisfaction told a different story. Customers appeared happy with the service, and the downward trends tracked externally were not apparent. The market research department's message to the rest of the company was "The ACSI is wrong—we're doing OK."

Meanwhile, revenue growth continued to stall. The disconnect between the internal and external measures of satisfaction became more and more marked. Furthermore, other business indicators, such as revenue, correlated with the worsening external measures of satisfaction. Eventually those responsible for the company's own customer research were asked to explain their results, and that's when the methodology issue emerged. Like many companies, this company surveyed customers a few weeks after an interaction. The market research department collected data about customers who had called and been given technical support. But therein lay the problem. The data logged to the systems only recorded customers who had been provided with some form of "successful" technical support. Customers who had given up while on hold weren't tracked; customers who had equipment that was broken or unfixable weren't tracked because these issues didn't need a service order and weren't logged to the system; customers who couldn't be helped were also, in many cases, not recorded. The net result was a biased survey sample: customers who had a problem "fixed" constituted a disproportionate volume of those surveyed and were far more likely to be satisfied than customers who had given up. In contrast, the ACSI had no such survey bias, as it includes all customers, including former customers.

Once the company recognized the problem, it began to take the ACSI data and revenue drops far more seriously and started probing the issues in service that were annoying customers. They found all kinds of problems, and the company mobilized a team to fix these issues; later in this chapter we'll describe the techniques the company put in place to ensure that it could listen and act more proactively in the future. This case proves the dangers of not being able, or willing, to listen; it doesn't take long for even the most successful companies to lose touch with their customer base.

SOMETHING IN THE AIR(LINE)

A major national airline carrier had for many years a very proud reputation for service. People in that country were proud to fly with their national carrier, it frequently polled well in international surveys, and the management team running the company at that time were passionate believers in service. Twice a year, the CEO took the leadership team of the company "away for the weekend" with a cross section of invited customers, who were asked to tell the company what they thought. The CEO made the leadership team listen to the feedback and act on it. The next CEO (the former CFO) did not maintain this process and other techniques; he was more concerned with financial returns and such macro strategies as establishing a "budget" airline and finding cheaper sources of labor. Over time, the level of dissatisfaction increased. A new competitor emerged and took significant market share from the incumbent; other overseas competitors started to challenge the company on lucrative international routes that it had previously dominated; private equity companies started to circle the airline like vultures. While the company maintained its focus on premium customers (first and business classes), its reputation began to slide in all other areas.

Two public studies indicated the extent of the demise. A major business school surveyed two thousand customers using what is known as net promoter methodology. Customers were asked to rate their likelihood of recommending various companies to their friends and colleagues on a scale from 0 (would never) to 10 (would strongly) recommend.[4] This airline not only earned an extremely low score (more people would advocate not using it) but also finished below all its overseas competitors and only marginally ahead of its "budget" airline rivals. Six month later, a consumer choice magazine conducted a survey of airlines and rated this company the worst in both the domestic and international sectors. The company's management went on television to protest that "they had the best crew and the best staff of any airline." Clearly the public disagreed. A major newspaper and a Web site started blogs asking for feedback on the airline. Within twelve hours there were 450 entries on one site and more than 200 on the other. Clearly the public was unhappy. The airline had lost the ability to listen.

CHAINED TO THE OFFICE

Why do so many senior managers and executives appear to be chained to their offices? A couple of mini-cases exhibit this malaise.

One of the leading specialty steel producers in Europe heard from one of its top customers that the customer really wanted to develop a strong relationship with the company's R&D labs. In essence, the customer wanted to create even better grades of alloyed steel that could withstand weather and other demands. The company said no, proud of its R&D prowess and focusing instead on becoming a lower-cost producer. Upshot? The steel company not only lost that customer but also lost the overall game—they were acquired by a smaller rival.

A fast-moving business services company got a call one afternoon from a disgruntled customer calling late (in his time zone) unable to process a simple transaction on the company's Web site. The agent tried a number of tricks, but never solved the customer's problem; he also failed to ask for enough information from the caller to find out that the caller was from the company's second-biggest account. The company's head of sales, marketing, and customer service (an unusual combination, but one that fits neatly with Jeanne Bliss's chief customer officer role) wasn't happy that the agent hadn't gone out of his way to service this important customer, but it turns out that this executive had never listened to a single customer phone call, and his office was only eight feet from the closest agent! Upshot? The big customer stayed with the company after the company's executive reached out to him, but that executive never did learn how to listen, and within a year he was working somewhere else.

WHAT OUR CUSTOMERS ARE SAYING IF WE COULD ONLY HEAR THEM

In Australia, each state has its own department and register of motor vehicles. Selling a car interstate means removing its registration in one state and then registering it in the new state. A customer needed to perform just such a transaction and went into his State Transport Authority Web site to record that the car had been sold. He found the appropriate page and filled out the details, such as the registration number, model, color, and the like. The last field he needed to complete asked for the last four digits of the vehicle's identification number, a unique identifier used to prevent theft and fraud. He entered this from his old documents (provided by the same authority), but a message appeared saying that the number was "invalid." He tried repeatedly and in different ways to enter the information, but each time received a message that it was invalid.

He called the authority's contact center. After a considerable wait (longer than ten minutes), he got through to a rep. He explained the issue, and the rep said, "Let's try that again with me on the phone." So he did and hit the same problem. The agent told him, "Yes, I've had quite a few customers tell me about that problem." Clearly the Web site was broken, but this agent had no way of reporting it or getting it fixed—a classic case of a company desperately needing a way of hearing from the front line what customers are experiencing. Meanwhile, how many customers were trying and failing and then needing help that should have been unnecessary?

THE CRAZINESS OF CUSTOMER NOTES

There are contact centers all over the world that ask their agents to record notes about customer calls. We have seen it in a wide range of industries—credit cards, utilities, insurance, health insurance, telecommunications, government, and single-line retailers. These notes are most often used as an audit trail of the discussions that were held with the customer. A typical example might be "The customer asked for a payment extension but didn't meet the criteria and was turned down" or, more rarely, "The customer called to find out what other features were available on the product. I advised him about features x and y, but he chose not to take up these options."

Often the agent will use a form of shorthand to prevent excessive typing. "Bad news" interactions, such as turning down a request, are the most commonly recorded in case the customer calls back and speaks to a different agent. Some centers even record the fact that they performed ID checks and provided balances. Quality-checking procedures will often include the criterion that adequate notes were taken.

There are four reasons why these practices do not make sense for the customer or for the agents supporting them:

1. Agents often record information that is of no value. Recording that a customer asked for a balance is of no use on any

subsequent call. Knowing she was ID-checked is even less valuable, given that most centers make this a standard part of the process. The fear of being checked and the blanket nature of policies (see Chapter Six) mean that agents are scared to differentiate between important and valueless information. They tend to think, "Far better to write it down than be slapped around the head for missing something." The blanket policies make no sense and waste time for the customer and agent (often the customer is held on the phone while all this recording activity takes place). In many cases, it is only the exceptions that need to be captured. For example, failing an ID check (the exception) might be valuable in fraud detection or as an audit trail, but all too often, agents aren't trusted to distinguish between valuable and valueless information. Out of fear of having an incomplete audit trail, agents are told to log every call. Since much of the information is of no value, this is a waste of time. Far better to define some simple rules and to empower agents to understand what is important.

2. Agents are often recording things that the system already knows, self-evident issues such as "The customer called to change his address." In this case, the address change has already been logged elsewhere, and there is a separate audit trail somewhere in the system (or had better be!). Companies also fail to adapt this process even when other technologies, such as call recordings, are providing complete audit trails. Note taking has become so entrenched that it continues anyway.

3. Little or no use is made of valuable information captured in agent notes. In most organizations, notes sit on the system and are only accessed by agents on later calls. Some of these notes contain hidden gems of insight—for example, knowing that a customer asked about a product feature could be valuable for product planning, supply chain, or marketing campaigns to this customer as a high-potential buyer. However, the information in these notes is sitting in free-format text that no one can access or mine. The questions asked by customers may be equally valuable for many purposes—for example, to suggest areas of self-service, new processes, and new product features. If a customer asks, "Does your product offer feature x?" it is probably because she believes a competitor does. The frequency of these questions is a key indicator of the level of interest in that product.

Instead of looking at this sort of information, the market research area may be busy running focus groups and surveys trying to find out if customers are interested in feature x, unaware that the data are already sitting in the notes hidden on the contact or CRM system. In one company we know, agents spend sixty seconds or more describing the call in considerable detail so that if the customer calls again, the next agent gets a running start, but usually the next agent is under so much time pressure that he skips the history and starts from scratch—this frustrates the customer to no end, yet what does the second agent do after that call? He goes ahead and spends another sixty seconds or more preserving for posterity the contents of that call. The circle continues.

4. Agents are rarely if ever told to capture other things that customers actually say. For example, an agent might record "Customer asked about feature x," but if the customer went on to say, "because Company Y offered me feature x at rate z," those other pieces of crucial information would not be recorded, for two reasons: (a) the agents typically have not been told that other information is valuable, (b) it isn't a useful audit trail for subsequent calls. Even if a customer said she was having a baby or getting engaged, no one has told the agents that those are key life events for other areas of the business to know. Even worse are cases where agents know that nobody in marketing or product design bothers to look at the notes, so even if the agents recognized this information as insightful, they see no point in recording product-, competitor-, or process-related issues.

Good Cases

It's time now to study good cases where companies have learned how to listen and act. We will review Mars, Cable & Wireless, ahm, NetBank, and Trader Joe's.

Sweet Success at Mars

M&M candies have been one of the world's most popular snacks for over fifty years, the flagship of the Mars Company. For many years, Mars marketed Plain M&Ms in various package sizes, but that was about it. But something fascinating happened at Mars that mirrored the explosion in varieties of Monopoly games (you can now buy over forty variations) and the auto industry—Mars started to listen to customers who wanted to buy and consume the tiny candies in a wider variety of colors, such as purple or blue. Mars decided to put this to a vote—one of the huge successes in customer-paid inbound calling in the United States, getting millions of customers to pay to tell the company which colors they wanted to see produced.

Today you can get all sorts of flavors, dark chocolate as well as original milk chocolate, and all the colors under the sun. You can also order designer M&Ms printed with your company's logo or even greetings to friends, another result of Mars's listening to its customers.[5]

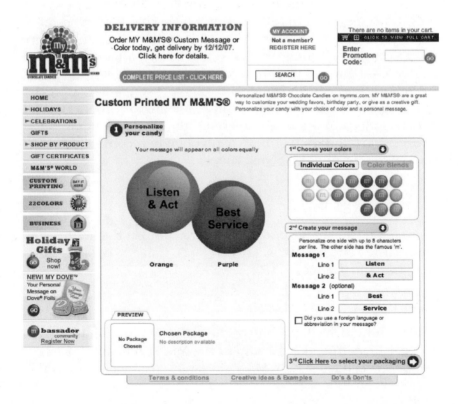

Teaching Engineers to Listen at Cable & Wireless

In the late 1990s, Cable & Wireless (C&W), a major telecommunications company, started to expand from its historic strength in landline infrastructure to services provided directly to corporate and retail customers, a brave new world for the company. The culture of the organization was one built around its history as an investor in infrastructure rather than as a direct service provider to customers, so it had few mechanisms for listening to or understanding its customers.

C&W needed ways to find out what its customers were thinking of these services and needed this information fast. Unfortunately, its in-house approaches for tracking customer loyalty were out-of-date, ineffective, and expensive. The legacy systems provided plenty of information about who C&W's customers were, but almost nothing about how these customers perceived the services that were being delivered, a classic "rearview mirror" syndrome. Only two of the six business units had any form of customer satisfaction tracking, but even they shared these major problems:

- The data took so long to gather and analyze that they were out-of-date by the time the company looked at them.
- The customer information was only circulated to a small group of specialists, not to the people who actually dealt with customers.
- The feedback ultimately produced no impact, as it was not linked to business processes, financial performance, or staff incentives.

In short, all these expensively collected data were not worth gathering because they did not drive any improvements.

C&W later established a customer advocacy team that created three processes they considered essential to managing customer loyalty:

1. A real-time customer feedback system providing immediate data on how customers felt about their experiences with the company
2. A network of "customer champions" who acted as customer advocates in each department
3. Staff incentives and recognition programs to motivate better service and enhance even more listening to customers

C&W then changed the processes to respond to customer feedback, using the automated system that captured customer feedback after each interaction, asking each customer only five short questions about his or her interaction. This quickly provided plenty of statistically accurate, immediate, and detailed data that were easy to understand; enabled analysis of processes, products, and individual staff member performance; and provoked intense discussion across the organization. The system dramatically shortened the cycle time of the customer feedback process and shifted the focus to action rather than the survey process itself.

This new accelerated feedback system created two levels of response: (1) tactical, handling customers who reported a bad experience or issues; and (2) systematic, learning from the feedback. The customer advocacy team made sure that executives across the business were accountable for the issues raised by customers (similar to our concept of owning the actions across the organization)—each department had to show how it was going to address systematic issues deduced from the customer feedback, and to set KPIs in every area that related to the customers' feedback.

The process was a great success. Within a year of setting up these mechanisms for listening and acting, the company reduced customer churn by 30 percent, an effective investment in listening.

THE HIDDEN VALUE IN CUSTOMER NOTES AT AHM

Despite our slam of customer notes earlier in this chapter, companies can obtain significant value from them if they manage the process correctly. ahm, the Australian-based medical insurance provider, asked agents to record free-format notes on each call, recording such details as customers asking, "Am I covered for x?" or making simpler requests, such as "When is my next payment due?" These notes sat in one of the systems until the customer called again.

However, this company wanted to find a way to tap into the value it suspected was in these notes. Could they provide insight into what the customers were thinking and doing? Could they provide warnings of impending customer defections or fraud risks? Unfortunately, the agents had been conditioned to use the notes as an audit trail and didn't think to record other forms of information, so if a customer asked if he were covered for a type of dental treatment, they might record "Customer asked if cvrd 4 major dental." The notes didn't record the response or the customer's reaction. If the customer mentioned competitors or even life events (such as having a baby), these weren't recorded.

To get value from these notes, ahm sought to reinvent how they were being used. The insurer

- Retrained their staff on what to put in the notes.
- Taught them to record key customer reactions, such as disappointment, anger, and concern.
- Asked staff to capture insights on competitors' products, life events, and the like.

After capturing these new data for several weeks, the health fund started analyzing them using text analysis tools to search for key words and key themes in the notes. When they identified themes related to customers who might leave, the data were linked back to the customer records to see how many had defected. Other themes, such as disappointment about a claim payment, were analyzed against the products held by customers to see if consistent issues emerged in product design. Further analysis looked at which types of customers, and in what state, mentioned specific competitors by name.

Using these and other insights, ahm recognized that certain questions and reactions were very likely to lead to customer defection, and took a series of preventive actions (see also Principle 3: Be proactive). The insurer trained agents to spot these critical questions and reactions and then channel the at-risk customers to a specialized retention team. This team, trained in appropriate responses that might help retain the customers, in some cases moved customers to a lower-level product and in other cases upgraded customers to policies that had the features customers were seeking. This team achieved retention rates of well in excess of 50 percent and, when tested against control groups (where no intervention occurred), were able to show the value of the process.

Insights into its competitors helped ahm reprice some of its products to match competitors' offerings more closely and, in other cases, refine pricing processes. The company also developed industry-leading Web capabilities, cut back on market research spending on focus groups and outbound surveys, and overall demonstrated that the interactions themselves could be a rich vein of insight if the right tools and methods were applied.

CHANGING "GETTING STUFF OUT REALLY FAST" AT NETBANK

U.S.-based online banking pioneer NetBank faced some serious challenges in late 2005 and early 2006: in their intensive monthly risk management meetings, executives were blaming customer service for high operating costs and occasional complaints to regulators; customer service was struggling to hit its objective for e-mail responses within twenty-four hours (peaking at ninety-two hours); and its largely outsourced agents were getting burned out. Daunting task? Former VP of customer service Art Hall knew what to do, and it was nothing short of a total turnaround in perceptions, metrics, and procedures.

First off, Hall knew that he needed support on his side, and what better place than from NetBank's customers? After implementing a short four-question post-call IVR customer satisfaction survey that captured customers' comments online, moving away from speed metrics like AHT in favor of revenues per call, and adopting a "VOC ROI formula," Hall's team was able to "level set our senior executives' pre-conceived notions, expose where our customers were most frustrated, and reveal that the bank's 'getting stuff out really fast' was, in fact, hurting our customer experience," says Hall. After reporting the VOC with the owners around the table, the risk management meetings started to take a very different tack; according to Hall, he began to hear "We crippled you [customer service] by doing this" apologies and "We need to partner more with you" commitments.

According to Hall, "In cases where our agents did not understand the company's policies or products, we provided to them the right tools and the right communications, and then broke down the skills silos that had caused four to five transfers. We really focused on empowering the agents, for example calling customers who had e-mailed us again on the same issue." As a result, NetBank's numbers soared: (1) e-mail was now being answered within eighteen hours, (2) customer satisfaction improved by 8 percentage points in the first six months, and (3) the customer service department cut its annual expenses by a whopping 40 percent. What's not to like with that scorecard?

Amazon's Tell Me What You Think

Amazon is renowned for its personalization programs that make customers believe that the company truly knows their wants and needs—for example, with the recommendations engine ("Customers who bought x also bought y and z," prompting many customers to acquire y and z as well). From the beginning, Jeff Bezos also sought a dialogue with Amazon customers, inviting "Help us build our store" initiatives and often sending e-mail messages to loyal customers thanking them for buying a lot of DVDs or to the entire customer base to announce new store launches.

One year, Amazon decided to launch two stores—Toys and Electronics—on the same day, a huge undertaking but well within the company's seasoned IT and Web teams' skills. As he had done for each of the earlier store launches, Bezos penned an e-mail message with help from managers from marketing, PR, and customer service (that, in itself, says a lot about including many heads to create better solutions). After they left his office, Bezos decided to add the fateful clause "and tell me what you think" about these two new stores. Always a fan of Amazon customer comments as "our best focus group," even Bezos didn't expect the avalanche of e-mails that poured into the customer service department over the next week. The messages broke down into three categories:

1. "Why the heck are you moving further away from books [or other existing stores]?" This type was viewed as an opportunity to shore up those core stores and communicate with those customers over time.
2. "Thanks, Jeff; I've been looking forward to buying toys online at Amazon." This type was seen as affirming the decision to launch that store.
3. "When will I also be able to buy x or y from Amazon?" This type reinforced the listening loop.

The listening loop based on the many, many customer requests for new stores and products led directly to Amazon's building and launching at least two new stores: (1) Kitchen & Dining and (2) Apparel & Accessories, and constructing on the Web site a more comprehensive form for Amazon prospects or customers to tell the company what more they wanted to see available on the Amazon sites.

With more than forty stores and well over $12 billion in annual revenues, Amazon continues to listen to its customers and act quickly.

Trader Joe's Leading Listener

Popular U.S. specialty grocery retailer Trader Joe's has learned to listen without the trappings of focus groups or expensive research and with a bare-bones Web site, garnering recognition as "Leading Listener Winner" by *Fast Company*'s panel of experts. According to the magazine, "In a sense, Trader Joe's entire inventory is a result of listening to customers—both their feedback and their dollars."[6] In response to customer requests or inquiries, the company has introduced allergy labels before they became federally required, has stocked products quickly after they are mentioned, and has provided considerable autonomy to store managers to stock to suit local needs. "Captains" and "crew members" adhere to an extremely generous return policy and cheerfully allow taste tests, another form of listening and of immediate feedback.

The Framework

The techniques an organization can use to listen and act vary from the simple to the complex. We've already shown that the risks of not listening include losing touch with customers, losing customers, or spending money on the wrong things. Above all, we are advocating finding ways to listen better to the contacts that already occur, rather than urging you to conduct more after-the-fact customer interviews or to run more focus groups. Nor are we pushing you to invest more in scorekeeping. Although we mentioned the net promoter score that some companies are embracing, it's important to note that it's just a score, a benchmark that can be useful as an indicator of progress or regression. Companies must understand that it isn't actionable. Knowing that your net promoter score moved from 0.25 to 0.27 is interesting, but it begs the questions "Why?" and "What did our competitors' score do, and why?"

Rather than spending more on research and measurement, you will find that applying many of these techniques should enable you to spend less on market research companies—which may be a threat for some marketing departments that think they are providing your company with the voice of the customer today. If your company creates and circulates every month or quarter some form of "customer contact tracker" but no one ever acts on it, then you need to apply the thinking we advocate. Pushing back on multimillion-dollar research budgets will help teach the marketing departments that there is a better way: listening to customers who are eager to share and are doing so constantly today with each of your customer-facing channels.

We'll explain first how an organization can learn to listen. We'll explain when to do it and some of the easiest techniques that can get you started. Then we'll dig a bit deeper and cover a range of smart ways to listen that make listening cheap and effective or that expose different insights. Last we'll look at the mechanisms and processes that turn listening into action.

LEARN TO LISTEN

In your organization, you probably have thousands of people who are already listening:

- Your frontline staff listen and respond to customer issues and needs thousands of times a day.
- Your supervisors and quality checkers listen in to calls or listen to the dialogue between customers and branch staff.
- Your e-mail and correspondence answering teams "listen" and respond to the queries posed by customers.
- Your complaints handling and retention teams (if you have them) are probably very good at listening.

So why do we think your company needs to learn to listen? It's because of what your company isn't hearing and what it isn't acting on. Even companies that spend large sums on formal customer surveying can often miss the insight that is trapped within the existing contact mechanisms.

Before an organization can listen effectively, the CEO and his or her direct reports need to be convinced that listening is valuable. To do that, *they* need to be made to listen directly and listen often to customers: there is nothing better than direct exposure to customer contact and real experiences to get executives focused on change. There are a whole range of simple mechanisms that any company can use to start to get the executive team to listen. We call them free listening posts.

Free Listening Post	How It Works
Hand out call recordings to senior executives ("listen to this")	Calls are recorded onto CDs or MP3 players so that while in their car on the way home or on their next flight, executives can hear what customers are saying. This can be biased with bad experiences as selected by the quality team, but should also include positive feedback, suggestions, and statements related to competitors.
Spend time observing and also answering customer contacts ("back to the floor")	Senior management spends time listening in, taking contacts, or both. Jeff Bezos at Amazon would regularly perform the work of an agent. One supermarket chain makes every executive spend one day a month in a store. IKEA requires one month per year working in a store. Craig of Craigslist calls himself chief customer service agent, and loves his job!

Circulate and share e-mails ("bombardment technique")	Send e-mails or complaint data to the owner department so that it has to listen!
Mystery-contact your own business ("experience the experience")	Ask senior executives to experience what is inflicted on customers. Have them call your company's toll-free number and navigate the menus and shop in your stores. Michael Dell and his top team place mystery tech support calls each month and score them the same way that a quality team scores—from the customers' point of view.
Go listen to the help desk ("hear the pain")	Find out which issues and problems the staff aren't handling. Manage by wandering around, the old Hewlett-Packard process promoted in *In Search of Excellence*.

All these free listening posts will start to expose a company to the issues it puts customers through and teach the executives to listen. Once that process is started, the company is ready to tap into other techniques and learn to listen for free, listen to the systemic pain, and ask the front line.

Listen for Free

Listening for free means tapping into what is already going on and isn't being used, including customer notes, which we've already described, but also many other sources of listening that you may not have considered: call quality or other checking teams, a complaints database, the contacts themselves, and customer behavior.

As we have already mentioned, your quality or checking teams are a great source of insight about the customer. A thousand agents in a contact center may be monitoring as many as ten thousand calls or e-mails a month and can provide you an opportunity to tap into the reaction of as many as ten thousand customers. If you were to ask a customer research firm to interview those customers (at $50 each), it could cost $500,000, but your quality team can do it for almost nothing today.

The best quality-checking processes recognize that the complete range of information that they have gathered (rather than the individual sample for each agent or staff member) is the real source of insight, and can be used to assess which types of contacts are frustrating for customers. They can tell you whether certain processes always get certain reactions, which you can discover quickly if certain types of customers always call for the same situations. To achieve this level of insight, the checkers need to move beyond "Did we execute the process as expected?" box ticking and view themselves as purveyors of insight about the customer; in other words, the checkers may also have to learn how to listen: (1) they need to listen to the customer as well as the agent response; (2) they need to assess the customer input, emotion, and response; (3) they need to assess the process involved, and the outcome for the company and for the customer, and consider why the original customer contact occurred; and (4) the data need to be aggregated and analyzed for themes and trends.

Some companies are beginning to follow this process, and it's producing terrific results. In India one of the leading mobile telecommunication companies outsources monitoring its customer calls, looking for those types of insights. The analysis team assesses whether certain processes are broken, compares different contact centers and asks why they are performing differently, and examines how customers are reacting to certain products. The company is learning a lot, reducing customer churn and growing by leaps and bounds.

As mentioned in Chapter One, Yarra Valley Water has learned to listen to complaints; they were already good at responding to complaints, but listening was different. Listening meant working out if the complaint represented a one-off incident or something more systemic, likely to reoccur; listening also meant asking senior executives to analyze the root cause of that complaint. We'll talk more about this in the section on listening for systemic pain.

Dell has launched a brand-new small business line of computer products after listening to its customers. The Vostro (*vostro* means "yours" or "belonging to you") line combines systems and services, including dedicated technicians who can help small business owners set up and get maximum use from their systems.

Urging you to listen to the contacts themselves is our way of saying, "Go analyze what the mix, timing, types, and trends of contacts are telling you." In Chapters One and Two, we described how to look at individual contact categories, but sometimes there are bigger-picture insights that come from looking at all the contacts in one channel or even the mix and trends across the contact channels. This mix may be changing because one of the contact channels is broken, or it could be that calls increase because there are bugs on the Web site or that e-mails go up because your contact center is too hard to reach.

Even something as simple as the AHTs for phone calls can tell you about the customers: if customers are becoming frustrated and dissatisfied with any part of the process, handle times increase because they vent at the beginning of the call, and they argue more and insist on escalation of issues.

Listening by analysis can also be applied to more complex customer behaviors. Let's consider one as an example. Some companies fail to look at the data regarding how many customers are abandoning a contact before they get queued to talk to someone. The speed of answer (or wait in queue) is a common measure, but what about those customers who abandon before they even get in the queue? What are they telling you? Could your menu structure be too complex or confusing or even broken? Are customers getting stuck in the IVR?

Listen to the Systemic Pain

Some companies confuse listening and responding to individual issues with learning to listen for themes and systemic trends. They conflate the ability of their staff to listen and solve an individual problem with the need to assess whether the problem is already occurring multiple times or could reoccur. Here we are not talking about how well each agent handles each query or issue—that level of response is shown on the left-hand side of Figure 7.1 (steps

FIGURE 7.1: TWO LEVELS OF LISTENING AND RESPONSE

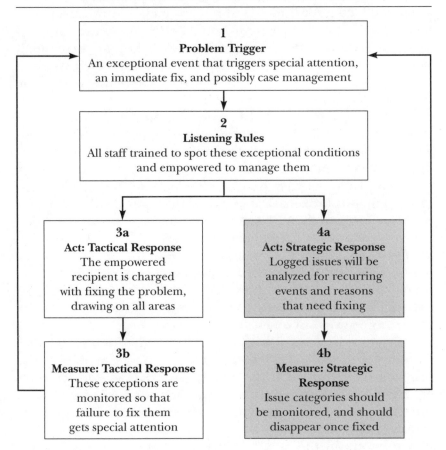

3a and 3b). Listening to the systemic pain is all about how a company acts to prevent the issue from occurring in the future, as shown on the right-hand side of the figure (steps 4a and 4b).

To listen to the systemic pain, a company needs to

- Spot the pain or recurring issue; this could be a contact type that shouldn't be happening, a type of repeat contact that is getting worse, or a collection of similar issues.
- Get to the root cause and determine who owns the issue, as we described in Chapter Six.

Sometimes companies can find mechanisms for spotting the systemic issues almost by accident. Amazon, like many retailers, has a huge spike in workload leading up to the holidays. The customer care area is so busy that alumni staff get seconded back as "elves" (as mentioned in Chapter Six). These elves often act as well-qualified listeners for systemic pain; because they had come from other parts of the company, they would often spot the root cause of issues in the areas where they had worked. They were sometimes able to go back to their departments and fix the issues. A great example was when Amazon marketing managers handled "tier 1" e-mail or phone calls during the holidays and suddenly realized that a number of customers' questions were caused by their confusion over the duplicate or confusing promotional offers they were sent. As a result, the marketing managers banded together with customer service after the holidays to create the "Promotion Council" to make sure that the stores' promotions didn't conflict with each other, dovetailed as much as possible (kids books and toys, for example), and were made available online in real time for agents to access when customers did call or e-mail with questions.

Ask the Front Line

Among the simplest ways to learn to listen is to ask the front line. Amazon established the process of asking agents to act as its listening post in many venues, including the weekly team meetings, where supervisors ask the agents to share stories about what customers were saying to them.

Other companies, such as CheckFree and Dell, have now applied a WOCAS-like process to tap into their agents' incredibly smart insights, often suggesting improvements as well. In most cases, the agents send their observations and ideas to a central database, often engaging local experts. The whole company gets engaged, with "owners" similar to what we described in Chapter Six. The WOCAS process provides a cheap and quick way to start listening. It's particularly good for spotting new trends and emerging issues as frontline staff identify the exceptions among the more routine inquiries. If staff know they will be asked for these insights, they become more attentive to customer needs and are better listeners. At some companies, implementing the

WOCAS process has correlated with improved quality and customer satisfaction scores.

Another quick example underscores this point and relates also to Principle 2, Create engaging self-service (Chapter Three). At one high-tech firm we visited, we sat next to agents to observe calls. Every so often, a customer opened the call saying, "I've been looking everywhere for the answer, so maybe you can help me!" to which the agent dutifully responded, "Sure, can I have your seventeen-digit product ID number?" thus completely bypassing what the customer could have said. These "golden thirty seconds" at the start of almost every call are full of incredible insight that the customer is eager to share but that is often ignored.

If the agent had instead slowed down to say, "I'm sorry that you had so much trouble getting your answer. Where did you try?" then the customer could proceed with "I looked on your Web site to download that silly ring tone my daughter wants, and boy, you sure have a lot on your site, but I couldn't find it!"

To which the agent can say, "If you're online now, I can show you where."

In almost no time, the customer would have found what she wanted in the first place, and the agent would have "educated" the customer; the agent could (should!) then forward comments to the Web development team to simplify the ring tone ordering button and prevent future contacts—Best Service in a nutshell.

In summary, learning to listen is about adopting techniques to do so. But it is also about a mind-set shift within the company. The company has to want to listen and want to act before any of these techniques will start to be effective.

SMART WAYS TO LISTEN

In addition to the simple "getting started" techniques that we've just described, there are a plethora of effective listening techniques to test and employ (at least twenty-five of them, in fact). Here are possibilities for some of the most common contact channels:

Contact Channel	Examples of Listening Posts
Branch	In-store instant survey, kiosk, or handheld device
	Web site survey in store
	Comment cards
Letters, e-mails, administration	Text mining e-mails
	Opt-in e-mail surveys
Web site	Contact Us entries
	Structured feedback—"Tell us what you think"
	Panel of site users
	"No match" searches (tells you what customers want that you don't have available on the site)
Contact center	Post-call IVR surveys
	Recorded call speech analysis
	Real-time call observation
All channels	Complaint analysis
	Customer behavior analysis
	Customer advisory council (that is, a group established to give regular feedback)
	Weekend with the customer: leadership meets with customers and receives and responds to feedback

Let's now explore three other techniques that can be used to listen more effectively: text and speech analysis, automated feedback tools, and blogs.

Text and Speech Analysis

Because every contact center collects agent notes, stores e-mail or Web chat threads, and records phone calls, there is a huge potential gold mine of "listening data" already available. A range of text and speech analysis tools (many of which were developed in response to security agencies' need to tap phone calls and monitor huge quantities of data) exist to enable the capture of valuable information. Text analysis tools enable large volumes of free-format text to be searched for themes and trends around key words, or producing from scratch these themes and trends—for example, for such sensitive topics as "I am going to cancel my service" or contact coding, covered in Chapters One and Two. Speech analysis does the same to voice recordings, but in this case the customer's sentiments and intentions are much more clear than through merely reading and scoring text.

Before text analysis can be effective, agents need to capture "the right stuff" in the text. Analyzing millions of megabytes of data where agents have recorded that they have completed ID checks won't deliver much insight. Agents may need retraining on what they should put in the notes so as to capture valuable information. The following list shows some examples of the kinds of notes that yield insights.

Notes Area	Source of Value
Competitor information—for example, "Company B offered me x"	Product and value proposition research
"Do you have x?" "Can you make me y?" "Can my product do z?"	Product design, campaign design, sales process redesign
	Retention campaigns
Process comments—for example, "It would be easier if I could do b instead of c"	Process redesign
Channel comments—for example, "I tried to do this on the Web, but it wasn't available"	Channel design and growth
Customer emotions, including "This really annoyed me"	Retention and follow-ups
	Correlation between process and reaction

With these insights in the text, the tools can be used to search for themes and correlate these themes with associated customer behavior. Text mining can show, for example, that a certain type of inquiry is more prevalent among customers who are preparing to take their business elsewhere. One company identified that the apparently innocuous "When's my next payment due?" inquiry was in many cases a warning signal that customers were considering offers from competitors. Prior to changing their notes strategy, the company had grouped all inquiries together as one type of note and could not glean this insight.

One of the major manufacturers of DVD players used text mining to discover that one of its players could not play a popular kids' title from one of the big studios, after they had steadily told customers, "Sorry, your DVD is bad, so you'd better return it to the store," and the store had to send them back to the studio. This manufacturer went to the studio with its tail between its legs apologizing for its error. (Despite this problem, the company in the end won considerable goodwill from the studio.)

Speech analytics can perform the same type of thematic correlation analysis on recordings of calls, highlighting emerging trends and themes and determining how important they are. Imagine being able to analyze how many times customers mention a specific competitor. Some of these tools are now being used in real time to spot a key word or pattern during a call and prompt the agent to ask for something he may have missed—in effect, these tools are acting as additional ears for the company during the calls.

Automated Feedback Tools

Automated feedback tools allow a company to poll or survey customers without going through the expense of hiring a research company. They offer a range of benefits over conventional customer feedback techniques:

- Speed—can be conducted immediately after a call, e-mail, or branch visit, enabling rapid recovery if needed.
- Accuracy—can reflect what really happened instead of stale recollections weeks later.
- Anonymity—can ensure confidentiality and increase response rates.
- Volume—can capture significantly more data that are easier to act on than by placing calls.
- Qualitative as well as quantitative capture—many of the feedback tools allow customers to record messages or write text; using these mechanisms, companies can also capture a large

volume of comments that can be analyzed using the text and
speech analysis tools mentioned earlier.

- Triggers and closed loops—they enable fast one-on-one
  customer actions; some of the tools allow a company to set
  "alerts" if certain conditions are met so that if a customer gives
  really low scores in a survey following a contact, someone can
  be assigned to contact that customer. Others allow a flag to be
  set if a customer leaves a comment, and therefore ensure that
  all comments are listened to. Thus the tools can trigger retention or customer recovery actions.

Because these techniques use automated capture, they cost very
little per "survey." Whereas conventional customer research involves
sampling techniques, these mechanisms can gather feedback on
almost every interaction, although few companies use them that
way today. These techniques gather much larger quantities of data
and therefore the data can be used for more detailed analysis; can
be linked to individual processes, to products, and even to the team
or agent that handled the customer; and are therefore much more
effective at getting to the root causes of the issue.

These immediate customer feedback tools offer significant
potential to increase a company's ability to listen. One cable TV
company had been tracking that its service-related churn was
running at 10 percent of all customers, and its service reputation
was among the worst of all companies in that country, not just of
the cable TV industry. It started using these immediate customer
feedback tools to tap into the sources of dissatisfaction. Issues
and problems were allocated to specific departments, which were
required to respond. The whole listening and acting program was
sponsored by the company's managing director, so everyone recognized it as important. Even field service engineers, who installed
equipment, left cards that invited customers to give feedback.

The new feedback program produced many improvements.
The company was then able to identify and change the processes that were broken and apply more resources in areas that
customers requested. The program was such as success that within
twelve months, service-related churn dropped to less than 1 percent
of customers, paying for the investment many times over and
reinforcing the huge gains from Best Service.

Company Blogs

We have already described the explosion of company blog sites and wiki tools. Blogs and wikis both offer an unprecedented level of transparency into companies and organizations. In turn, companies are receiving unprecedented amounts of useful and articulate feedback from the blogosphere. But the blogosphere can also wreak havoc on a company's image: some companies are so unpopular that customers have started their own blog sites to complain about the service or products.

Smart companies, such as Southwest Airlines (blogsouthwest .com), have dedicated blogs that regularly receive positive buzz and input. Started in early 2006 and maintained by its employees, the blog has entries that are honest and straightforward, offering the public a peek into the back end of the business. "There was a growing online community having conversations about travel and Southwest," said company spokeswoman Linda Rutherford. "We could watch that conversation, or become part of it."[7] Cass Nevada, a blogger and consultant on Web 2.0 applications, notes that "the Southwest blog is everything you want a company blog to be: fun, interesting, helpful and as a result, has a high page rank and an enviable following of commentators and readers. They even recognize their most loyal commentators with happy birthday wishes posted *in the blog itself*—talk about community building!"

Starting a company blog can be a risky undertaking, but is well worth the careful investment of time and focus. However, if a company does want feedback in this way, it must be willing to respond with both comments and actions. Ignoring customer feedback on blogs is even worse than not getting it in the first place—if a company is unresponsive to a blog site, the nature of this response is very public. Companies who have ignored blog sites or tried to suppress them have angered customers even more. Far better to see blogs as free feedback that can help, rather than as something to be fought against.

One of the better-known company blogs is Direct2Dell (www .direct2dell.com), launched by the company in late 2006. Customers flocked to this blog, not only submitting product criticisms—which Dell took pains to answer in detail, often apologizing and winning kudos—but also asking for new or different features. Dell has prided itself on its customer intimacy, until recently selling its computers and related systems only online or through its network of contact centers. However, the company was taken aback when it got more than ten thousand votes on the company's IdeaStorm Web site from customers pleading to be able to have the older Microsoft XP operating system installed, rather than an automatic installation of Microsoft Vista, which in its early months was not totally compatible with some printers or supported by IT departments. Dell responded quickly by offering XP or Vista on a large number of machines, landing headlines and legions of loyal customers.

LEARNING TO ACT

All this newfound listening to one's customers is all well and good, but it needs to be backed up with action, or it runs the risk of measurement or feedback for no purpose. We have already commented that calculations such as net promoter scores are useful scorekeeping but not much else without more analysis. Some mechanisms, such as blogs or immediate feedback mechanisms, create a customer expectation that action will be taken if problems are raised.

Companies that are service leaders use these sources of feedback to drive continuous improvement. They build it into the fabric of how the business runs, setting up a process like that illustrated in Figure 7.2.

What is critical to make this improvement cycle work is not just the listening part but also allocating the resources to discover what it's telling the company and how to fix it. As we discussed in Chapter Six, finding the real owners of the issues is critical, as only they have the authority to make the change happen.

One major software company demonstrated the degree of effort and sponsorship needed to design and implement issue-driven improvement. This company

- Set up a wide range of listening posts, including asking the front line to raise issues and log "what customers were saying" (or WOCAS), as well as running focus groups and inviting customers to give feedback using many mechanisms.

FIGURE 7.2: FEEDBACK-DRIVEN IMPROVEMENT CYCLE

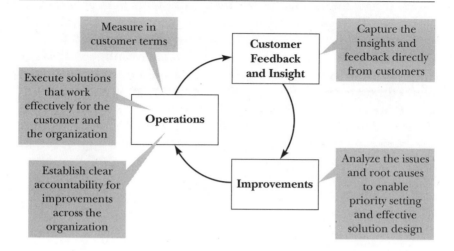

- Merged the data and mined key themes and issues.
- Reviewed these trends in an "improvement council" that set priorities for improvements based on their value to the customer and the company.
- Forwarded these investment recommendations to senior management for approval.

There you have it: a complete system incorporating mechanisms for listening and for acting on what the organization was hearing. The system as a whole was designed to escalate issues up the organization so that those who were accountable could take action. This company demonstrated the effort and processes required to take action, tackling successfully more than three hundred issues in the first year of operation, so both the company and the customers saw the benefits.

TURNING THE SHIP

The computer company described in "Bad Cases" also learned to act as well as listen. It has implemented additional ways to listen using immediate customer feedback tools, attaching them to their technical support center so that customers can report what the experience was like. The company has also started acting on the issues. It recognized that far too many customers were abandoning calls in its IVR, which was much too cumbersome and complex, so it stripped the IVR back to fewer layers and made it a lot simpler. The company also sought ways to enable frontline staff to get faster answers to customer problems and questions. It has implemented new tools to capture and disseminate knowledge to frontline support staff, enabling agents to resolve more calls and do so faster. Already customers are noticing these improvements, and satisfaction is starting to climb once again. The new approach has also been cheaper: fewer repeat calls, less cost on toll-free numbers, happier staff who are less likely to quit—all in all, the hallmarks of Best Service, benefits derived from learning how to listen to their customers.

SUMMARY

This chapter has shown that there is no excuse for companies not to listen. No additional investment in customer research is required; companies will obtain huge insight from the contacts they are getting today. They need, first, to be prepared to listen. Then they need to apply the techniques that allow them to tap into all the free or cheap forms of feedback that their customers and staff can provide. Listening is not the end game, however. The whole purpose of listening in this way is to take action and drive improvements for the customer and company. Many companies are stuck today in a cycle of measurement that doesn't drive action. The alternative techniques we described in this chapter have the detail and immediacy to drive the actions customers require.

Survey Questions

Here is the final set of questions to test whether your company is on the road toward Best Service. As before, select the most appropriate response and check your score in Appendix A.

17. In our company,
    a. Customers are surveyed monthly or quarterly by marketing for their satisfaction with our service delivery, using a limited sample.

b. We follow a single index as the key measure of customer satisfaction.

c. Customer satisfaction is gathered from multiple touch points and is used all over the organization.

d. There is no mechanism to gather data on customer satisfaction.

18. In our company, the CEO

a. Takes time at least once per month to listen to customers at the front line.

b. Has never spent time listening to customers at the front line.

c. Views marketing as the department to find out about what our customers want and need.

d. Visits the front line briefly once or twice a year to meet the teams.

e. Reads verbatim comments from customers that we capture.

19. In our company,

a. Customer focus groups are convened periodically to gain insights about customers and to develop action programs.

b. There is a clearly defined process to listen to customer suggestions through multiple listening posts in a closed loop.

c. There is no process for gaining insight into what our customers are saying.

d. Our frontline staff submit suggestions to improve our customers' experience, but rarely, if ever, hear what happened afterwards.

e. Other departments ask our customer service team for information about our customers.

20. In our company,

a. Customer-facing employees record notes about each customer interaction as an audit trail of what has been said.

b. Our customer interaction system logs each interaction with the customer, but no one ever reads or uses the logs.

c. The frontline staff see it as their role to capture key insights from customers and forward them for action.

d. We use a contact recording system as an audit trail of customer contacts, often mining it for insights.

CHAPTER EIGHT

DELIVER GREAT SERVICE EXPERIENCES

How to Delight Customers with Awesome Support When They Need It

When the concierge [cleaner] told him that . . . she couldn't finish the cleaning today, that Monsieur didn't realize how much work there was to do, Charlie replied sweetly but firmly, "You'll manage somehow, Madame Logre. You'll just have to work a bit faster, that's all."
"Fast and good don't always go together, Monsieur!"
—IRÈNE NÉMIROVSKY, *SUITE FRANÇAISE*

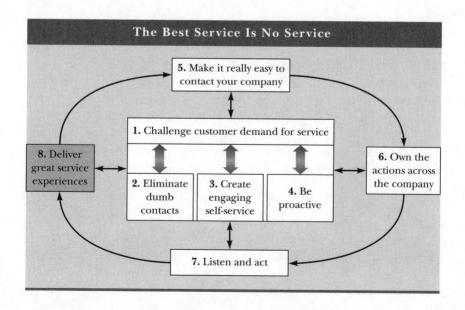

THE PRINCIPLE

We have set out a challenging agenda. Many of the Principles and other concepts that we have covered earlier, such as eliminating dumb contacts (Chapter Two), constructing proactive alerts (Chapter Four), opening the floodgates (Chapter Five), or learning from consumer blogs (Chapter Seven), might seem difficult to implement. We realize that changing the behaviors and attitudes in companies that are stuck isn't easy. This final chapter covers overcoming the challenges in delivering service in the way we have proposed. We will arm you with the ammunition to overcome the problems you might face in pursuing and achieving Best Service.

The first challenge in trying to achieve Best Service is convincing the company that it's possible and worthwhile. In the first section, "It Works and It's Worth It," we provide cases of companies that are achieving Best Service and describe the benefits they are reaping. If everyone in a company is on board, that's a great start, but we also recognize the challenges that some of these ideas and processes pose. In the section "Roadblock Removal," we'll describe five of the most common obstacles and suggest ways to overcome them.

Unfortunately, that isn't the end of the story. We acknowledge that despite all our efforts to achieve the nirvana of Best Service, no company will ever get there. As we described in Chapter Two, when the contact is valuable to the company and valuable to the customer, companies will want to increase the volume and intensity of customer interactions. For the other three quadrants of the Value-Irritant Matrix, even after removing the need for service, creating and providing consistently engaging self-service, and being proactive, customers will still call our contact centers, write letters and e-mails, and walk into branches for help—it's an imperfect world, and companies will never eliminate the need for service entirely. Customers will still need to, and want to, interact with companies, and when they do (which will be a lot less often), their experiences need to be very, very good. In the section "Awesome Service Delivery," we describe how to deliver the type of experiences that customers want and how to overcome the "stuck conditions" that we described in Chapter One. We will also discuss measuring what matters, creating customer-focused processes, matching the service experience to the customer, and meeting the challenge to deliver "virtual" Best Service in your own operations or ones provided by third-party outsourcing firms.

Finally, we recognize that this is not a one-off exercise. The challenges to designing and delivering Best Service or even No Service are constantly changing as customer expectations change, technology develops, and workforces evolve.

IT WORKS AND IT'S WORTH IT

We have seen significant benefits to adopting the Best Service Is No Service mantra. We've cited many cases throughout the book and have seen it in person, starting with MCI in the 1990s and Amazon in the late 1990s, the companies we have worked with since late 2001, and many others who are beginning to "get it." Among the benefits that companies have obtained are

- More satisfied customers who will buy more, tell their friends positive stories, and become loyal, rising 5 to 15 percentage points per year.
- Lower overall support operating costs. The changes have generated greater than 20 percent annual reductions in such key cost measures as CPX (contacts per order or contacts per customer). However, be ready for higher costs per contact as self-service success moves many of the shorter, simpler contacts from companies' most expensive and increasingly scarce assets, namely, frontline staff. The calls and e-mail responses will get longer and more complex, but there will be a lot less of them in the staffed channels.
- Happier agents who no longer have to apologize for chronic mistakes or broken products and processes. Resolving issues and responding to meaningful, or new, problems are a lot more interesting for agents than the endless repetition of routine transactions, such as reciting a balance or processing a payment. Because the staff are happier in these more fulfilling roles, they also stick with the company for longer periods, so recruitment and training costs are going to be much lower. But again there is a flip side, in that on average, staff may have to address a tougher set of interactions once those simpler contacts are being handled through automation or proactive messaging; this will require more tailored hiring, training (online instead of classroom based), and knowledge bases.
- More consistent support experiences across multiple channels and multiple enterprises, once third-party outsourcing firms are brought into the same routines and under the same metrics, including reducing contacts per transaction or member (CPX).
- Lower legal and complaint handling costs, as fewer contacts escalate into repeats or the use of formal complaint mechanisms (for example, ombudsman or state attorney general or Better Business Bureau cases).

The raw ingredients to build the case for becoming a Best Service company are

- Reduced contact rates in staffed channels and associated costs
- Increased revenue from repeat or cross purchases, and reduced marketing costs to attract new customers (as customer churn reduces)
- Reduced staff turnover
- Reduced costs of escalations and complaints
- Reduced costs of third-party providers (in some cases no longer needing to use them)
- Improved consistency of service delivery when the causes of spikes and changes in volumes are understood and eliminated

There should be plenty here to make CFOs or CEOs salivate at the prospect of pursuing Best Service!

This is not theory. Companies have put Best Service processes in place and are reaping these rewards. Here's how the Best Service Is No Service idea is becoming better known: (1) the critical reviewer, channeling the voice of the customer in articles or blogs; (2) the annual report, sharing directly with shareholders how seriously the company studies customer contacts and is committed to make its business fast and simple for all customers and thus returning greater value for its owners; and (3) the appreciative customer, instead of the ranting one, as the true and lasting voice that will pay dividends over time to the company and its shareholders.

The Critical Reviewer

We have already cited the emotional and positive reaction to No Service as a concept, expressed succinctly in this quotation in an article whose other examples demonstrated bad cases with many, many contacts per transaction: "I've never had to contact Amazon about any matter. I have had, in essence, no customer service from Amazon. Put another way, I have had such perfect customer service, the service itself has been transparent. That is exactly what Amazon wants. The goal is perfect customer service through no customer service."[1]

The Annual Report

A company does not need to be a multinational or in a new-wave industry to get value from Best Service. Take ahm, the Australian health insurance provider and only the eighth biggest in a relatively small market. Insurance products are tightly regulated, such that products and services are hard for customers to understand, but they are intensely personal for the customers who need the care. In its 2006 annual report (www.ahm.com.au/4395/Annual-Report), having adopted a similar philosophy to Amazon, ahm dedicated two pages to a section titled "Looking After Our Members: Excellent Service." In these pages, the company very clearly states to its customers (members) that it is aiming for superior service: "ahm prides itself on delivering a superior level of service to its members whether that is via the telephone, within our Dental & Eyecare Practices or more recently, over the web. In market research studies conducted amongst members during 2006, service was the most highly rated aspect of the Company, with nearly one in four members giving ahm a score of 10 out of 10 for satisfaction."

The company reveals the top five reasons "why members called," starting with 82,100 calls (21.2 percent) for "Teleclaim—a quick and easy way to claim ancillary benefits over the phone," through 22,515 calls (5.8 percent) for "Payments—contacting ahm to make a payment, check payment details or change payment method." The report goes on to describe the numerous improvements in Web-based services and initiatives, showing earlier in the report a 6.9 percent increase in online transactions. This shows that the company understands why customers called, and how it tackles the demand for service; it exemplifies attempts to become simpler for the customer and is prepared to share publicly the efforts it was going to establish and follow in order to improve service.

THE APPRECIATIVE CUSTOMER

Here is a small sampling of Web postings that are worth their weight in gold:

• For Zappos.com: "Great Great service! Best online shopping experience I had. I was really skeptical about ordering shoes online. But they really stand up to their guarantee with safe shopping protection. I guess they are the only company who allows you to call in to get a direct discounted price after price match, without waiting to email them after ordering (with the chance of the deal being dead). And I really like that."

- "They answer calls and process orders on Sunday. They offer free over night shipping (delivery and return), 110% price matching and excellent customer service. What's not to love?"[2]

- For Logitech and Good Technology: "I've had extremely good experiences with (warning: advertisement ahead) Logitech when they replaced a defective product for free (that I hadn't even purchased direct!) and with Good Technology who bends over backwards to help customize their product for our deployment. I mention these two companies often, because they provided me with a good experience."[3]

- For Egg: "I would recommend Egg banking anyday because their rates are great and the service received is worldclass. . . . If you are thinking about getting any form of credit I recommend Egg without a shadow of a doubt. With a quick turn around on their approvals of accounts and with easy 24 hour access to your accounts why use anyone else."[4]

ROADBLOCK REMOVAL

Given the revenue, cost, and brand benefits we've summarized, there should be few obstacles to embark on the Best Service track, leading to No Service. However, the path to success is not an easy one, and there are likely to be a number of challenges along the way. The most common obstacles include the following:

- The "What problem?" problem, better known as lack of evidence for the problem or, rather, that the company really doesn't understand the drivers of service interactions today
- The "Someone else's problem" problem—resistance or denial from the departments that need to make the changes
- The "Can't fix it" problem—the difficulties in identifying root causes and their solutions
- The "Can't afford it" problem—everyone is so busy that no one has the time or budget to address the issues or solutions

- The "But our customers are happy" problem—satisfaction data appearing to paint a positive picture of service today

Let's look at each of these five roadblocks in turn, and identify ways to overcome them.

WHAT PROBLEM?

When companies can't identify that they are a long way from the No Service ideal, the most common issue is lack of data or evidence. As we described in Chapter Two, many companies don't have a good handle on the reasons customers seek service and support; to overcome this roadblock you need data. In Chapter One we described mechanisms to capture and report on data continuously, but that isn't always what is needed to get started or to focus attention on the issues. The most common approach here is to collect a sample or snapshot of contacts occurring today; this will provide a lot of evidence of the issues that need to be fixed and that build the business case for further action. If your company is in denial, go get the data to break down that denial, even if you just do it once to get things started.

SOMEONE ELSE'S PROBLEM

Once you have data, the second obstacle tends to be denial of ownership, as we discussed in Chapter Six. The departments whose processes and issues need to change to help customer service may well resist becoming involved—they may see it as customer service trying to pass the buck, or they might not know how to approach customer service because it's "not their problem." As we described in Chapter Six, having sponsorship and financial skin in the game helps a great deal. However, the first roadblock is typically denial by other departments that there is an issue of their making. If that is the case, then some "shame and blame" may be needed—get the other department heads into the contact center to listen to the calls; share e-mail threads, chat sessions, and customer satisfaction survey verbatim remarks; show them the data behind the problem; and send them (and others if needed) the e-mails that relate to their issues or recordings of the calls related to the mistakes that their departments have caused. All these forms of guerilla publicity will, one hopes, get their attention, but the ultimate weapon is to make them pay for the issues and problems they have caused.

CAN'T FIX IT

This roadblock can take two forms. First off, the root causes of contacts or issues aren't well understood; second, even when they are understood, the solutions are not obvious. Let's face it: if the solutions were obvious, they would already have been applied. The most radical and far-reaching solutions often need rethinking of processes and deep questioning of the status quo—and these are hard. There are many techniques for root-cause analysis, but the first place we turn is to the customer service staff.

Asking your staff, "Why do customers call or write about *x*?" and probing about WOCAS will uncover a truckload of reasons that you can then investigate. There may be many symptoms as well as root causes, but at least you've gotten off to a great start. If you're lucky, some of your creative staff may also come up with solutions, but we'd recommend involving people who aren't too close to the problem, as they tend to miss the forest for the trees. People from other departments, internal consultants, or outsiders may identify more fundamental solutions. This stuff isn't easy. Such companies as Amazon, British Telecom, and CheckFree that have significantly reduced contact rates and volumes have looked at processes in very different ways in order to find solutions. Sometimes it means turning the problems upside down. For example, one bank that assumed that customers would want to grant permission to link accounts to their Internet banking profiles flipped the equation and moved to a model where customers had to ask *not* to have their accounts linked. That approach needed some IT, literature, and other changes, but it wiped out 20 percent of all customer contacts.

CAN'T AFFORD IT

This roadblock is typically about being too busy to tackle these issues. Many service departments are so busy fighting fires—trying to hire enough people to get the work done or dealing with next product or system launch—that there appears to be no time to stand back and ask why this activity exists today. The answer to that problem is that you need to make time. Any substantive change takes time and effort, but the payback here is significant. Few investments in faster processing or better planning or improved management information can deliver the scale of benefits possible from eliminating bad or dumb contacts. If organizations start getting a handle on the nature of demand for service, they will also enjoy more control and greater predictability. Instead of merely watching as contact volumes rise or processing times increase, organizations can now track why that happens and react immediately. We've seen companies that have only two people in customer service reap benefits from this, and it scales to those with tens of thousands in the support operations. Rather than ask "Can we afford to do it?" we suggest asking "How can we afford *not* to do it?"

BUT OUR CUSTOMERS ARE HAPPY

Another roadblock to Best Service that we have seen is a form of denial driven by customer feedback surveys or other data suggesting that the company's customers are happy. As we described in Chapter Seven, you had better make sure that you are surveying the right customers and asking them the right questions. Many companies are so busy asking "How was that for you?" that they forget to ask "Why did we make you call or e-mail us?" or "Would you have preferred not to have had to contact us about this issue?"

Companies might need to suffer significant customer defection or revenue loss before they will turn their attention to service problems. To this we say, unless your rate of repeat contacts is less than 2 to 3 percent or you have almost no complaints or you have less than 10 percent of contacts in the "irritating for customer and company" quadrant (see Chapter Two), you have plenty of reason to act. Customers may not be leaving in droves—perhaps you have great product features or an attractive price, or the competition is poor or the market is "sticky"—but the cost and efficiency benefits alone make it worthwhile to challenge demand. Doing so will also prevent someone else from stealing a march on your company and offering a superior service proposition or a cheaper one that your company cannot match.

AWESOME SERVICE DELIVERY

As we've stated earlier, no company will get rid of all staffed channel contacts, nor should it plan any time soon to go "light's out," as appealing as that may be. Things will go wrong, or some customers will obstinately refuse to use your Web site, or they will call up despite big messages on the bill saying "You do not need to call us—here's the answer." Some interaction with your company's contact centers is inevitable, so you had better get it right. This is the kind of reaction you can get when that happens, in a posting appropriately enough called "Customer service gone shockingly right":

> I bought a Nintendo Wii on launch day (11/19/06). Every day since then, excepting the two weeks I was on vacation, it has been lovingly used in our house. It has traveled to spread the gospel of Nintendo-style gaming in the homes of friends and relatives. It has been lent out as the star of children's birthday parties. And all this time, its optical drive was a little louder than I liked, but I thought maybe they were all that way.
>
> Over the past few weeks it started getting louder. I knew I should get it looked at. It wasn't damaging game discs, but it was really annoying when the vibration noise was louder than the game sounds. I just hated the idea of explaining to my 6 year old that when he does want to play—because he does a lot of things that are not playing video games, but it's a tradition for us to have a quick round of Monkey Ball or Mario Party in the evenings, and I traded in the GameCube for the Wii since the Wii plays all the GCN games—that it would be out for a few weeks getting repaired. I finally resolved to send it in over this coming weekend, when we had lots of outdoor outings planned.

So I called the Nintendo customer service telephone number, located right there on their web site (you would be surprised how many companies, and especially repair departments, don't list their phone number on the web). The message telling me I had to wait for a CSR didn't even finish playing before a rep was on the line. I explained my problem and she said she'd get me an RMA [return merchandise authorization] right away to get it fixed.

She asked for my phone number. I gave it to her. She did a bit of a verbal double-take and said, "Are you here in Washington?"

"I'm in Redmond, as a matter of fact [location of Nintendo of America's campus]," I replied.

"Well then, let's not bother with the RMA and the shipping labels and all of that. Just bring it on in to Nintendo," she said.

Wh-what . . . ?

She assured me she was not kidding. She gave me directions to the Nintendo campus building where the Customer Service Center was located, and five minutes later I was looking at an unassuming door. I took a deep breath, told my son to hold on to the Wii with both hands, for goodness' sake, and opened the door.

A life-size Mario and a larger-than-life Pikachu greeted us. So did a really nice, cheerful woman behind the sales counter. I related my telephone conversation to her, still certain that I'd been had.

"Oh, yeah!" she said. "We do that!"

"Awesome," I blurted. I really did say "Awesome." I'm embarrassed about that now.

"It's going to be about 30 minutes, though," she went on. "I'm really sorry."

She wasn't Japanese, but clearly Nintendo is a Japanese company. Only a Japanese service center would apologize for taking 30 minutes to repair a piece of electronics when my expectation going in was that I'd be without it for two weeks.

The boy played games in the waiting area while I sat under the watchful eye of Mario. 25 minutes later I saw her emerge from the back room out of the corner of my eye, but I was watching the boy playing a particularly suspenseful level of Wario Ware Twist [*sic*]. She waited until she heard the "level complete" sound to get my attention.

In those 25 minutes, they'd transferred all of my Miis, friends, and saved games from the old console to a new one. She logged on to make sure my 500 points transferred to the shopping channel. She sent me out with a $0.00 invoice showing a warranty replacement of my Wii and a reset of the warranty clock, meaning the Wii I took home has 15 months of coverage from today, even though I bought my original one almost 3 months ago.

So this is my Valentine to Nintendo. That was the most awesome customer service experience I ever, ever had.[5]

The rest of this section describes how companies can strive to deliver equally awesome levels of service. To do that, we will explore how to overcome the "stuck conditions" we described in Chapter One, including finding a way to break from the tired metrics that are in place today, hampering and restricting the agents. We will describe how to rethink service processes from the customer's point of view rather than from the company perspective. As the Nintendo example illustrates, the company thought of the customer first and itself second, and in doing so saved a lot of money in shipping fees, follow-up calls, and additional customer frustration.

Then we will describe the awkward issue that not all customers are "created equal": some customers are more valuable to a company than others, so it makes sense that service may need to reflect these differences. Although we would like to deliver awesome service to all customers on all interactions, the reality of business today is that service needs to be consistently more awesome for more valuable customers. Last, we will tackle the challenges of harnessing other units that are part of the service delivery chain to deliver Best Service in the same way.

Measure What Really Matters

Most of the metrics that the customer service industry has captured and tracked over the past twenty years are rubbish. Some are overly focused on speed (speed of answer or AHT and its flip side, contacts per hour [CPH]); others are applied too broadly across all staff instead of factoring in differences among customers, issues, and agent skills (AHT or CPH); and still others

254 THE BEST SERVICE IS NO SERVICE

are simply incomplete or hard to calculate and therefore easy to "fix" or game (first contact resolution).

Measurement Mayhem

All too often we see these symptoms of measurement-inspired mayhem:

Symptom	Symptom Description
There's no measure of complexity for the customer.	There's no focus on how often customers need to make contact.
Customer satisfaction and quality scores don't match.	Happy compliance department, unhappy customers!
The company is drowning in data.	Management and team leaders spend a great deal of time gathering and analyzing the information instead of acting on it.
Speed is king.	There's too much focus on how quickly things are done rather than how well they are done or why the calls occur.
Everyone hates the quality team.	Frontline staff are "wrapped on the knuckles" for poor quality, even though the complex compliance rules and processes are not their fault.
Measures are internally focused.	There's no measurement of the customer experience.
Executives shoot the messenger.	Executives beat up on the customer service area for issues caused elsewhere.
Staff are confused.	Staff don't know what is important.

As these examples illustrate, measures often are misaligned with what matters to customers. A recent U.K. National Consumer Council report (cited in Chapter One) that customers really disliked organizations that

- Overpromise and underdeliver
- Deliver impersonal and robotic service
- Are sneaky and dishonest
- Are incompetent and ineffectual

Speed didn't get a single mention, yet it is the dominant metric in customer service operations today, and the most commonly reported measure of service performance. You'll note that what is delivered and how is more critical to customers than how fast, yet few companies report and track the "what" and the "how."

The U.S. Internal Revenue Service (IRS) Employee Resource Center (ERC) supports its 109,000 IRS employees using its CARE program. (CARE is an acronym for both "communicate, answer, research, engage" and "customers are really essential.") According to Yolunda Davis, the ERC program analyst, "Our customer service representatives focus on delighting the customer with each individual interaction. They are concerned with the delivery of service metrics, like quality. Metrics are posted on the wall to increase the employees' awareness of how the organization measures success. It's management's responsibility to manage the numbers. We want our employees to put a smile on [the customer's] face." The IRS also uses employee engagement as a tool to drive success in an innovative example of an "outside best practice." For example, employees are sent on customer service scavenger hunts. According to Davis, "The purpose of the scavenger hunt is to have employees really think about their role in the delivery of service by having them become the customer. They identify exceptional customer service in a variety of businesses, including retail stores, hospitals, and other organizations in their community." In addition, as Davis describes, "We want our employees to think outside the box, since you can't plan for everything. We then capitalize on something unusual that happens and make it part of the process going forward." As we noted earlier, Best Service is not simply a business-to-consumer concept; as the IRS proves, it's also part and parcel of government contact centers and of internal employee help desks.

Customer-Centric Measures

As we've already mentioned, contact centers and customer service organizations are awash with metrics, many of which are contradictory and most of which are geared toward easy-to-capture speed or productivity. Measurements need to focus on what matters to customers, as illustrated in the following list:

What Customers Care About	How to Measure It
Did the problem get fixed?	Resolution rates sampled by a quality team or measured implicitly by measuring repeat contact rates
	Combination of snowballs ratio and immediate post-contact feedback from the customer
How was I treated?	Behavior monitoring in quality sampling of calls, letters, or e-mails
	Immediate post-contact feedback from the customer
Did I get the right answer?	Process adherence checking in quality monitoring
Did this get fixed in the manner and time that I expected?	Immediate post-contact feedback from the customer
	Delivery of all long-running processes in accordance with the standards already communicated to customers

These Best Service measures involve asking the customer, as close in time as possible to the interaction, what she thought of the experience. Technologies exist to enable this to happen quickly, as described in Chapter Seven. Note that speed of answer is not prominent among these measures—to us it is a "hygiene factor" or "table stakes" (a basic minimum requirement) usually bogged down in averages instead of tails. Of course customers cannot wait long for calls to be answered and will be annoyed if branch or supermarket queues stretch out the door, but the answer to queues and wait times rarely lies with the staff dealing with the impatient customers at the end of the queue. Fixing long queues depends on

- How well management matched the available staff or work-force to the demand.
- The effectiveness of processes and systems, especially easy access to customer history and knowledge articles, so that interactions can be handled quickly and efficiently.
- How customer care staff are trained and coached to be effective rather than to be fast.
- How well the work is organized to meet the demand—for example, can staff be switched from other tasks into queues during periods of peak demand?

Please note that pressuring staff to reduce handle times does not appear on our list. An example at Egg Plc, a U.K. online financial services company, illustrates this point. Egg never liked the traditional contact center metrics and "coped" with the pressure on agents by creating quiet rooms in the middle of their centers where agents could go and let off steam. As an experiment, Egg removed all the speed metrics in its main center near Reading, England, and was surprised that AHTs went down, customer satisfaction scores went up, and agent satisfaction comments also went up—everything actually ran more smoothly without the added pressures.

Wacky Behaviors

Getting measurement right is not just about what gets measured; it is also about measuring the right people on the right measures for the right reasons. If you measure people on the wrong things or in the wrong way, you get these kinds of wacky behaviors:

The Measure	The Wacky Behavior
Branch queue times measured using queue tickets and dockets	Branch staff go up to the machine in quiet times and print off fake dockets that they serve quickly using fake transactions (inquiries).
Grade of service (GoS) in contact centers	Organizing the technology so that the most recent callers get answered first (last in, first out). That way, more people get "fast service," and the center hits the

	required 80 percent in twenty seconds or other measure. Some customers get excessively slow service, of course—but it isn't measured.
Speed of answer (but not accounting for busy signals)	One contact center simply "choked" the queues into their phone system. The board only measured people who got through to the switch, so by having fewer lines in, there were fewer calls to be answered. The rest of the customers got a busy signal—but that wasn't measured.
Handle times in contact centers	Agents hanging up on customers before the call has begun to exceed their AHT. Ignoring cross- and up-sell opportunities to keep handle times low. Transferring difficult cases to somebody else.
Cross-sales statistics	Recording attempts that never took place or transferring customers to sales specialists when the customers just aren't interested.
Sales conversion percentage on inbound sales calls	Transferring customers who have turned down a sale to the service queue as though they were lost callers and therefore outside the stats.
First contact resolution (FCR) reported by the person handling the call	Uniformly produces resolution measures over 90 percent (highest we saw was 99 percent). The reality is often 60 to 70 percent.

Retention percentage only examined with the retention specialists

Agents claimed that the only agent who was hitting the target was leaving accounts "open" even when the customers expected them to be closed.

Five Things to Get Right

Once you have decided what matters to customers, you need to develop and roll out measurements in a way that helps the business. These five tests will help ensure that all the elements fall into place.

Things to Get Right
1. **Strategic alignment test.** Can you link all your measures back to the organizational strategy? If not, why are they there?
2. **Wasted effort test.** Are there data being measured and reported that aren't used to drive action? Why do you need to keep score but not act on it?
3. **Customer impact test.** Are you measuring the things that are key for the customer? If not, how do you know how to improve the experience?
4. **Control test.** Can the people being measured influence their results? If not, how does this demotivate them?
5. **Action test.** Do you have the processes in place to act on the measures you are obtaining? If not, why bother?

If you apply these five tests, you are likely to end up with a very different set of service measures:

- Improved measures of outcomes for the customer, such as repeat rates (interpreted as errors that need to be eliminated entirely, as at Fluke or Dell)
- Measures of complexity of the experience, such as contacts per order as described earlier (looking at the rates, not the total number of contacts)
- Measures of interaction quality, used for coaching and process improvement, again couched in customer language and not company-speak
- Speed measures used by management to assess overall effectiveness and consistency of the process and to monitor staff, but not used to bully staff into taking shortcuts

New Metrics to Consider

We have endorsed creating unique owners for each customer-speak contact code so that they can address underlying root causes to eliminate dumb contacts, deflect others to self-service or proactive alerts, simplify the operations, or exploit what the company learns (as we presented with the Value-Irritant Matrix). There are now tools to collect and disseminate reports on these contact-to-owner closed loops, such as Skyline and WOCAS, so in addition to proliferating their use, companies also need to work to standardize the contact codes by industry so that companies can share best practices.

We have also encouraged using last contact benchmarking, outside best practices (OBPs), and internal best practices (IBPs) instead of foolish same-industry comparisons that drive everyone to an artificial mean. However, much work still needs to be done within companies to understand where their customers are doing business and interacting with companies outside their direct competition to create superior experiences, and to find new, rigorous, and scalable ways to collect IBPs and circulate them to the rest of the enterprise.

We have also differentiated first point resolution (FPR) from first contact resolution (FCR), and introduced the concept of their complement, snowballs. Work needs to be done to standardize these definitions so that everyone is talking about the same metrics and interpreting their results the same ways.

We have promoted defining, measuring, and reporting customer self-service success rates to overcome the three deadly sins of self-service, but work needs to be done here by IVR and Web providers to be able to calculate predictably those success rates, and companies need to set standards for what represents acceptable levels (60 percent? 80 percent? more?). Companies will also have to determine how to capture customers' frustration if they need to contact customer service again; in other words, they will need to find a way to keep track of what we have called snowballs.

Over the last several years, we have introduced new metrics, such as dynamic individual handle time (DIHT), that cannot currently be reduced to the packaged software used today for workforce scheduling and management; we challenge that part of the industry to move away from "averages" like AHT to embrace tailored scheduling. The "intelligent call routing" providers are partway there, enabling companies to connect specific customers one to one with agents possessing skills to suit their needs, but then companies need to work on relieving those agents from universal metrics and reporting that fail to measure the value that they are providing.

Outsourcer Measures

As discussed earlier, many companies are relying on third-party outsourcers to handle customer contacts for them, in some cases 100 percent of all contacts or perhaps all the e-mail and chat if the company lacks skills and technologies in those channels. The trouble is that most outsourcing firms' strategies are to increase the number of agents that they can assign to each customer, not to find opportunities to reduce contact demand. We discussed the opposite example: MCI Contact Center Services in the 1990s, which suggested engineering change orders (ECOs) to Hewlett-Packard based on MCI's handling of technical support contacts for HP. There are few other positive examples out there, because unfortunately the outsourcing industry focuses on shorter handle times instead of eliminating contacts for their customers.

Therefore, to bring the company and the outsourcing firm "in synch," another key measure that Best Service aspirants need to test is the price that they pay for the outsourcers' service. In order to eliminate dumb contacts (Chapter Two), find the best candidates for self-service (Chapter Three) and proactive alerts (Chapter Four), and challenge customer demand for service (Chapter One), companies should consider carefully which pricing method to use. The following is a list of the advantages and problems associated with various outsourcing pricing alternatives:

Pricing Method	Advantages	Problems
Per agent	None	Outsourcer has incentive to add staff, not challenge demand.
Per hour or per minute	None	Outsourcer has incentive to add staff, not challenge demand.

Per contact	Could work with higher per-contact prices as contact rates drop	As discussed elsewhere in this book, moving (generally) short contacts to self-service means that AHT will increase over time, and might force outsourcers to sacrifice quality for speed.
Per first contact resolution (FCR)	Helps reduce snowballs	It is difficult to measure FCR accurately.
Per customer or subscriber	Company and outsourcer both have incentive to spot opportunities for eliminating contacts and moving to self-service and proactive alerts	This method is difficult to apply across multiple outsourcing partners handling the same types of contacts.

Based on the pros and cons of these five outsourcer pricing methods (the first three commonly used, the last two emerging), our overall recommendation is to pay outsourcers on a per customer or subscriber basis, with contractual obligations to reduce the rate over time consistent with obtaining lower CPX (contact per driver X). Short of that ideal pricing method, you will need to implement complicated bonus schemes to provide the right incentives to reduce customer demand for support. If you don't do this, what incentive do outsourcers have to get it right? If you pay them for each minute, why should they try to have fewer minutes or fewer calls? Even with balancing quality measures, there is still no incentive to drive down contact volumes.

In addition to addressing outsourcer contact pricing, companies pursuing Best Service should ensure that its third-party partners adhere to the listen and act practices (Chapter Seven) with clearly defined closed-loop processes, such as WOCAS, text and speech analytics, and frequent contact monitoring to obtain voice of the customer (VOC). If your outsourcer is the front line to your customers, then you will need to train its staff to listen for you.

CREATE CUSTOMER-FOCUSED PROCESSES

The second component of awesome service delivery is ensuring that processes work for the customer's benefit and not simply to make it easier for the company. The Nintendo case shows how a service agent put herself in the customer's shoes and found an alternative solution that worked for the customer and the company. Egg also uses the shoes analogy, almost literally. One of Egg's core principles for its agents is the "brown shoes" process—if the customer starts to talk about her new brown shoes, stop what you're doing and ask about her shoes. This is just one of the reasons why Egg has achieved such a great reputation for customer service.

Processes that focus on customers' needs have four critical attributes. Companies need to

1. Know the customer
2. Make it fast + simple for the customer
3. Enable choice and flexibility
4. Set and deliver to expectations

This sure sounds easy, but of course it isn't—otherwise, every company would be doing it by now. Many issues get in the way, so let's look at the barriers to customer-focused processes before we describe how to create customer-facing processes with those four attributes.

Barrier: Identity and privacy checks.

Description: Privacy or identity legislation requires that staff have to perform multiple identity checks at the start of many contacts.

Example: The worst example we saw was of an older customer in an early stage of Alzheimer's who knew her account number, date of birth, and address, and then was asked to remember details of her most recent transaction. The agent followed the prescribed process, but three minutes into the call, the guessing games continued. The customer eventually hung up, humiliated by the whole experience.

Solutions:
- Only check ID when it's really needed.
- Use caller line ID to partially verify the customer.
- Use voice or other biometric identification.

Barrier: The organization and its processes do not reflect customer demand.

Description: The work cannot be performed directly by those dealing with the customer.

Example: The Teleclaims department that took calls but could not process claims (described in Chapter Five) is a classic example of a process not matched to demand.

Solution: Reorganize the process so that those who receive demand can handle that demand without transferring the customer or adding unnecessary steps.

Barrier: System spaghetti.

Description: Legacy systems force cumbersome processes, such as rekeying of data, complex navigation, or manual calculations.

Example: At one company, a simple change of direct debit (automated payment) date took more than ten minutes of rekeying, as that function didn't exist; the customer needed to be "cancelled" and re-created to allow the transaction to be processed.

Solutions:
- Replace or hide front-end legacy systems with simpler browser-based solutions.
- Show the IT folks what system problems actually cost at the front line (or, better yet, charge back to IT for all customer service system outages or slowness).
- Use new solutions with a simple user interface to "link" older applications together at the agent desktop or on the Web site, also called "enterprise mash-up systems".
- Key the data later, when the customer isn't on the phone (or, better yet, strive for no "after-call work" by enabling simple notes during the call).

Barrier: No contact history or view of the customer.

Description: Staff have no means of viewing previous contacts or interactions.

Example: The worst instance we have seen of this was a combined gas and electricity utility where staff in the electricity or gas contact centers had to ask customers if they had the other product as well. A strong runner-up is the established long-distance telephone provider that instructed the new customer to call the sales office to tell the service office what the customer ordered so that it could help him.

Solution: Centralize all customer data so that marketing and analysts as well as customer support can access the information.

Barrier: One-rule mania.

Description: This is the policy shield we described in Chapter Six: staff feel they have no choice but to follow the rules.

Example: At a pension company, staff would not take payments from anyone who wasn't the customer. Where is the fraud risk? Who fraudulently pays bills for others?

Solutions:

- Question every rule and whether it has to be applied uniformly.
- Trust staff to take sensible decisions, and monitor only for outliers.
- Have a mechanism and process that enable every rule to be broken.

Know the Customer

Organizations need to know the customer to avoid wasting the customer's time and be able to listen and learn. The frontline staff need to have access to the customer's product and contact history (that is, with whom she interacted about what issues, when, and where). To the customer, it shouldn't matter whom she deals with in the organization—any service agent should be able to pick up where others have left off without asking the customer to repeat the story. This also means that the customer shouldn't have to repeat information or say who she is after she has already keyed in an account number or performed other automated tasks. Ideally the staff member also knows what the customer has just been doing or trying to do in the IVR or over the Internet.

Organizations who know the customer can cut the AHT (there's the payback). Agents do not have to ask for data the company already knows or ask the customer to explain the history of a problem when it has already been well recorded in a system or is evident from an audit trail. Companies can go one step farther in knowing the customer: they can now record and use customer preferences, such as wanting to get an e-mail rather than a phone call, for particular times to be contacted, or for a specific term of address—is it Mr. Price or Bill or William when the customer calls? Is it "Dear Mr. Jaffe" or "Dear David" or "Hello, Dave" in an e-mail opening?

Unfortunately, many companies still don't know their customers even at the most basic level. Some cannot show their staff a customer's interaction history across different contact mediums (contact centers, branches, Web sites), and others still have departmental silos between products so that a mobile phone customer is invisible to the broadband department. Others ask customers for details in self-serve IVRs and then lose those details once an agent speaks to them. Despite all the investment in CRM solutions that were supposed to fix problems like these, many companies have a long way to go.

An example of this disconnect was described to us during a meeting: "My credit card company called me three times a week chasing a payment, and each time they dialed my number, I answered "Cheryl X." And then they run a series of checks and a disclaimer to see if I am who they think I am—do they seriously think someone else wants to answer my phone and pay my outstanding account? This is time consuming—and an irrational interpretation of the consumer law."

Make It Fast + Simple for the Customer

"That's all done for you now" are blissful words for a customer; unfortunately, they often occur far too late in a process. Our colleague Peter Massey (Budd UK) researched customer needs and boiled them down to customers' desire for processes to be "*fast + simple.*" Instead of using reengineering methodologies, as Six Sigma or Business Process Reengineering principles proposed by Hammer and Champy, which do not work well with customer service operations, we look at each process and ask a series of questions:

The Question	Why We Ask It
What does the customer want?	This helps us define the outcomes that the process must produce.
What does the customer expect?	This brings in such concepts as how long the process should take and what level of involvement the customer would expect along the way.
Why are the current steps as they are?	Root-cause analysis of subprocesses helps us understand whether the causes are necessary or imposed by systems, organization structures, and the like.
Why is the process necessary?	This helps us identify opportunities to eliminate dumb processes.
Why do handoffs occur?	This questions who should be performing the process and why.
Is further automation possible?	This questions how effective the technology is at present.
Would the customer prefer it done another way?	This questions the extent to which the process has been designed from the inside (company view) out rather than from the outside (customer view) in.

Each of these questions enables a company to pull apart its processes to make them fast + simple for the customer. Removing handoffs, taking out steps, and removing the customer from certain steps create faster and simpler processes for the customer. Sometimes these modifications add complexity for the organization, but that's not usually the case. Simpler processes for the customer are often faster and more reliable for the company.

Enable Choice and Flexibility

Creating fast + simple processes can be a great leap forward for many companies, but a lot of the problems and issues we see stem from creating a one-size-fits-all process or not trusting staff to take rational decisions about exceptions. We hear many stories about inflexibility; some, such as this one provided to us at an executive forum that we run, are horrendous. A husband and wife were joint policyholders of some insurance company. The husband died, and the wife wanted to continue the membership. The wife advised the insurer of the death of her husband. At the next membership renewal time, she received a letter addressed to "The estate of the late . . ." The wife called the insurer and explained that the joint membership should now have reverted to her—as she had advised previously. She was told that she had not been covered for the previous period and must complete a form. Instead she went to an office with evidence of her husband's death in order to prove that the membership should now pass to her.

Death is inevitable and a stressful time, yet broken processes often place bereaved relatives in difficult situations. There is no excuse for this, and it is just one example of where flexibility is needed. Other obvious situations abound, such as when working with customers who speak a different language or when life circumstances (illness, handicaps, unemployment) dictate that some kind of empathy is needed and that the situation should be handled differently. The best-designed processes allow flexibility for these situations or at least give the frontline staff the freedom to handle them in different ways. No process or system designer can think up all the scenarios that will occur in real life, but enabling staff to vary their response or recover from problems is one of the approaches that have been proven to create loyal customers.

Even day-to-day contacts can have flexibility and choice built into them. At the crudest level, this can be telling customers that wait times are long and referring them to other contact channels or times of the day when the contact will be handled more quickly. Other companies have provided callback solutions that let a customer hold his place in a queue and then the company calls him once staff is available, or have implemented a "click to chat" function that opens a Web-based interaction tool immediately. All these solutions create flexibility and choice for the customer.

Set and Deliver to Expectations

Our last process tip seems the most obvious of all. In many situations, customers are looking for control of the situation and therefore certainty. A mortgage applicant wants to know when the application will be approved or rejected; a customer ordering a book or other gift wants to know when it will be delivered; a customer registering a complaint or engaging in a dispute wants to know when it will be resolved. These are natural reactions and often the simplest to accommodate. A client of ours expressed his frustration with customers' expectations, saying, "We tell them ten days, and they ring us after eight." We thought the answer was obvious: "Tell them ten days and deliver in eight or, better still, tell them eight and deliver in six." Nearly all "Where is my . . . ?" contacts relate to this problem.

Of course it's not as easy as just setting an expectation. There are times when customers don't understand why a process will take a certain amount of time, or times when they need it done faster than the standard, but those situations are addressable. The frontline staff need to sense surprise or concern when the duration of a process is mentioned; then they need to explain why it takes that long or, in some situations, see whether a form of prioritization is needed. That isn't always possible, but the first step is to understand the customer's expectation, part of the golden thirty seconds we mentioned in Chapter Seven. Listening to customer expectations will yield insight into processes that need to change. If many customers ask, "Why can't you tell me when the repairman will arrive?" they are really giving the company feedback that it needs a better system to manage and plan for repairman bookings so that they are predictable.

It's hard to provide customers with the certainty that they think they need: processes must be predictable and managed, and the frontline staff need to have access to information about backlogs, service levels, and expected turnaround times. Some companies do this exceptionally well. Amazon reached the point that it could predict within two days when an item would be delivered by a third-party contractor anywhere in the United States. If Amazon can do it, any company can do it.

If companies know their customers, make their processes fast + simple but also flexible, and manage and deliver to expectations, they are well on their way to delivering awesome service experiences. In these companies, customer expectations are set accurately early on and then met consistently, so that customers make fewer contacts because their needs are met the first time or in a manner they expect or, as we've frequently cited, in a way that prevents them from having to make the contact at all.

Kingfisher Airlines in India demonstrates clearly setting and delivering to customer expectations and knowing its customers or, as the company says, "our guests." Since its launch in April 2005, Kingfisher's chairman and CEO, Vijay Mallya, has consistently shared his vision for the company and his "passion to deliver the best of good times," as he states in his "Chairman's Message" on the Kingfisher Airlines Web site (www.flykingfisher.com/message.asp). How many CEOs dare to say, "I have instructed my crew to treat every guest in the same way as if they visited my home," and then invite comments and respond to those comments personally?

On this Web page and on the airplanes' in-flight entertainment system, Mallya shares his e-mail address and says, "If I have missed something or fall short of your expectations, please feel free to mail me directly." The company listens closely to its guests. It has converted unhappy travelers to big fans who now gush, "I much appreciate your excellent responsiveness to the slightest complaint" and "I am prompted to write this to you, as I have noticed action taken on some of the feedback I had shared"; it has also taken major new initiatives as a result of suggestions pouring into the company's many touch points, such as adding Kingfisher First, which is even better than its Kingfisher Class (coach), and deploying "roving agents" ("guests do not need to stand in a queue for check-in as the mobile agent can check them in").

A public Web site devoted to scoring the world's airlines has also included numerous positive testimonials supporting Mallya's desire to deliver the best of good times. The first one also appreciates the company's proactive alerts:

- "I found the experience best among domestic airlines in India. Will fly them again. I had purchased the ticket online while I was in US. On my first attempt to purchase, my CC [credit card] transaction failed for some reason, but I was not aware of this. I got a call from their call center in Mumbai on my cell phone to inform me of this and so I was able to correct this error and re-book. I found this personal touch refreshing."

- "I was very impressed with everything from the boarding to the in-flight service and Crew attitude. Nothing was a problem, the meals were wonderful (there were two for a 4 hour flight) and they gave out these brilliant little pouches with a pen, menu, free earphones (to take home!) and some boiled sweets to chomp on. I can't recommend Kingfisher enough— on time, pleasant Crew, the airplane was immaculate and the seating very comfortable—better than some Internationl [*sic*] airlines I have flown! They get five stars from me!"[6]

MATCH THE SERVICE TO THE CUSTOMER

The reality is that not all customers are created equal, and at different times in their relationship with your company, they need to be handled differently. For example, new customers and experienced customers need to be treated differently both in CPX calculations and in routing to agents skilled to handle their needs. New customers for DVR and cable services contact companies three to five times more frequently than customers who have "been around" for four months or more. This higher new-customer CPX drives higher demand and argues for the use of the Value-Irritant Matrix; it will disrupt workforce planning if all customers' propensities to contact are treated the same. New customers need different treatment because first experiences are so incredibly critical—they set expectations about the relationship and are key to retaining the customer. Some companies completely toss out handle time limits for new customers, arguing that the more they learn, the less their customers need to contact the company in the future.

Companies also need to dust off and re-apply customer segmentation marketing, including the now widely cited "one-to-one marketing."[7] The world is not a level playing field. Some customers are worth far more to a company and therefore need to be handled differently. Unfortunately, we've seen examples where more valuable customers were more likely to get poor treatment. In these situations, processes became more complex as the number of products increased, or the company didn't recognize obvious expectations, such as "If I change my address on product y, I'll need to change it on product z as well." There are obvious issues to address, such as ensuring that more valuable customers are given even faster and simpler experiences.

However, if you can identify "best customers" as they contact you, and get them a "best agent," you can often see significant new advantages for awesome service delivery. Best agents should be given more time with best customers and given the time to learn more from them, as we described in Chapter Seven. But you also need to understand the needs and preferences of best customers more than others and go that extra step to work with these preferences. One airline we know will not let its premium customers use its automated call services. This seems contrary to our core Best Service premises: shouldn't a best customer have more choice than one who delivers average revenue? Why does the airline assume that the Best Service for all valuable customers is staffed service?

In some industries it's hard to offer differentiated service. The revenue "range" for a residential utility is far smaller than the revenue range among a bank's customers; therefore, banks can more readily afford to segment service delivery and have higher-intensity service models for their high-net-worth private banking customers. However, even in industries with narrow margins, it's important to recognize the value of a customer and to understand the individual relationship. A customer with a gas account and an electricity account is still more valuable than one with just gas, and she should expect a "one-stop shop" in service interactions rather than to have to speak to separate gas and electricity contact centers. Similarly, in telecommunications, sorting out an issue for a customer who has a mobile phone, a fixed line, and broadband is more critical than solving an issue for a customer who has only a prepaid mobile phone. Therefore, understanding the value of customers and considering when and how they need to be treated differently are key parts of delivering awesome service.

DELIVER "VIRTUAL" NO SERVICE: EMBRACE ALL DELIVERY CHANNELS AND ASSOCIATED PARTNERS

In some companies, service extends beyond the corporation. At times this is a conscious decision to outsource parts of service, but in other industries, the structure of the business dictates collaboration. Amazon, for example, needed postal companies and shipping firms to deliver on time (a structural issue), but also chose to use an outsourced provider to handle some of its e-mails, in particular those arriving in the middle of the night in the United States, as the Web site was, and is, used by customers all over the world. Making these virtual service models work is very similar to getting other departments to collaborate and own the customer issues and contact codes. As we described in Chapter Six, a crucial mechanism for getting other companies to deliver for your customers is to align their economic interests with the service treatment you want for the customer.

Outsourcers will also want to use the client company's Value-Irritant Matrix, the Skyline report, and other core elements outlined in Chapter Two to help reduce CPX for unwanted contacts and to see a rise in CPX for wanted ones. This means that outsourcers might see less revenue over time in their contracts, unless the rate of growth in customers or subscribers is great, but bonuses can be used to offset that loss from the shorter AHT or fewer customer contacts, and their margins will be higher.

If you calculate the number of contacts needed to resolve a case, similar to snowballs, aim to get this ratio as close to 1.0 as possible (also called resolve in one or one and done); consider also using this as the pricing mechanism for outsourcing companies so that they also focus their energies toward challenging demand. It is also important to develop outcome measures, such as repeat ratios or resolution rates, as well as customer-defined quality measures, instead of internal quality measurements. All these measures need to have "bite": if 90 percent of a contract is based on quantity and only 10 percent on quality, you can be confident that an outsourcer will focus on productivity first. It was a great day in the history of Amazon service when the outsourced provider produced fewer repeat contacts (snowballs) than the in-house centers. Some in the company thought that would never happen, but the third-party provider had the incentives to deliver that outcome and succeeded.

Educate Managers and Customers

Much work needs to be done educating today's managers, tomorrow's managers, and the customers themselves to ensure that Best Service is applied and expanded consistently. Today's company employees, from the CEO to the agents themselves, need to be able to embrace the Lean–no defects approach for each and every contact that "slips through the cracks" of self-service or proactive alerts. This will require greater discipline to collect "why" and not "what" reasons behind customer contacts, accepting that criticisms are gifts, and finding ways to collect and apply voices from customers.

Tomorrow's managers need to learn about the realities of this challenging discipline in colleges and graduate schools, which do a decent job introducing the basics of marketing, operational theory, and staff management, but rarely, if ever, address customer support. Instead, customer support has been learned on the job, and like all on-the-job training, the process is fraught with the passing down of the lessons learned yesterday, including wrong metrics and coping with dumb contacts rather than challenging demand. We will work closely with tomorrow's business, marketing, and operations curricula to infuse Best Service alongside Lean manufacturing, double entry accounting, and the 5 Ps.

And last, customers need to be educated. As mentioned earlier, probably the best wall banner at Amazon's contact centers was "Have you educated a customer today?" The company spent extra time at the end of each call and each e-mail response to let customers know how they could obtain answers or make changes themselves, without resorting to calling or e-mail the next time. By doing this whenever customers did have to contact Amazon, and by making instructions very clear throughout the Web site, the company steadfastly and constantly educated the customer to know what to expect, when, and why.

Much work still needs to be done to counter years of customer abuse or benign neglect. Companies will have to reassure customers: "We want to make it really easy for you to contact us, but we will challenge the reasons why you needed to contact us so that we can provide engaging self-service with high success rates and useful proactive alerts and messaging; we will own the reasons why you needed to contact us, across the company and from our CEO down to each agent; we will listen to what you're saying and act on those learnings so that we can help you in the future.

Celebrate Success and Weed Out Old Practices

In March 2003, right after the ACSI announced its second annual Internet retail scores for U.S. customer satisfaction, Amazon's CEO Jeff Bezos devoted the home page of the Web site, the company's most valuable "real estate," to reinforce this educational message to all its customers and to Amazon management.

> Dear Customers,
>
> The American Customer Satisfaction Index is, by far, the most authoritative and widely followed survey of customer satisfaction . . .
>
> In ACSI's words:
>
> "Amazon.com continues to show remarkably high levels of customer satisfaction. With a score of 88 (up 5%), it is generating satisfaction at a level unheard of in the service industry . . . Can customer satisfaction for Amazon climb more? The latest ACSI data suggest that it is indeed possible. Both service and the value proposition offered by Amazon have increased at a steep rate."
>
> Thank you very much for being a customer, and we'll work even harder for you in the future . . .

Wouldn't it be refreshing to see all companies share with their customers how much more easily they have made it for their customers to do business with them? Let's see them publish how many customers are using self-service. Let's see more annual reports featuring CPX rates and showing their decline, and have companies confess to the dumb things and practices that they have eliminated. We can't wait to read those annual reports and press releases!

In Conclusion—Old Practices Must Go

It's time to move away from yesterday's speed metrics, which put customer support in the position of whipping boy or neglected department starved of attention and funding. Companies that will succeed in Best Service will use CPX and tailored metrics and embrace customer support's central role as the company's heartbeat. They will find customer service areas to be the best source of great new ideas from customers and from staff. By practicing the seven core Principles we have set out in Chapters Two through Eight that we collectively call the Best Service Is No Service, companies can raise the bar for supporting customers—and after all, each of us is a customer, so this will benefit everyone. Organizations can simultaneously improve the customer experience and customers' satisfaction, reduce operating costs, and increase staff satisfaction because everything works the way it is supposed to work, with "quality as version 1," not version 2 down the line. Every company can work to challenge demand for service, remove those dumb things done to customers, and strive to deliver the Best Service, which is, in essence, no service. Good luck!

APPENDIX A: BEST SERVICE SURVEY

At the end of Chapters Two through Seven, we asked you to take a short survey to determine the potential gap between your company's current level of service and Best Service Is No Service. We repeat the survey in full here. Please select the most appropriate response to each of the following twenty questions, arranged by chapter, and then consult the section "Scoring Your Answers" to see if your company is delivering Basic Service, Better Service, or Best Service.

Chapter Two: Eliminate Dumb Contacts (pages 29–66)
1. How many possible customer contact codes or reasons does your frontline contact center or customer service staff capture for each contact?
   a. We do not capture or track contact codes or reasons in the contact center.
   b. Fewer than twelve.
   c. Twenty to thirty or so.
   d. Hundreds or maybe thousands of possible combinations.
   e. I have no idea.
2. How do your other customer-facing employees and how does the Web site itself code customer interactions?
   a. Differently than the way we do it in our contact center.
   b. We do not collect reason codes outside the contact center.
   c. From our Web site we do capture and log which pages our customers view; they appear as "contacts" juxtaposed with agent-handled contacts.
   d. We capture Web logs, but they're buried in our data servers and are used to analyze Web page speeds.

3. What is the chief driver for your customer contacts?
   a. I don't know.
   b. Customer orders, necessary life events of the customer, critical things we need to know from customers, shipments, and other key issues.
   c. A bunch of reasons outside our control.
   d. Mistakes that the customer service department made in the first place.
   e. Customer complaints.
4. How widely do you share CPX (contacts per X, where X equals customers, accounts, orders, transactions, and so on)?
   a. We capture and know CPX, but do not share it inside the company.
   b. We do not know CPX or have never measured it.
   c. CPX is widely known across the company.
   d. We share CPX within the company and discuss CPX trends with our investors and shareholders.

Chapter Three: Create Engaging Self-Service (pages 67–100)
5. Our customers
   a. Love our self-service, and tell us why.
   b. Don't use our self-service as much as we would like or had anticipated.
   c. Are mostly unaware of the self-service we offer.
   d. Would never use self-service even if we offered them incentives.
   e. Self-service doesn't apply in our business.
6. Our sales and service staff
   a. Move our customers to self-service options if the customer prefers it that way.
   b. See the Web site or our IVR system as a source of problems.
   c. Understand what our self-service does and actively promote it.
   d. Know less about our self-service than our customers do.
   e. Have no self-service to promote.
7. Our company
   a. Tracks the extent to which customers are being successful in self-service channels and drives improvements from those data.

    b. Captures the take-up rates of our self-service channels.
    c. Asks customers periodically what they think of their self-service experience.
    d. Sees no benefit in self-service; for us, every interaction needs a human touch.
    e. Has self-service, but doesn't track its use in any detail.

Chapter Four: Be Proactive (pages 101–126)

8. What is the ratio of proactive communications and alerts to inbound customer-initiated contacts in your company?
    a. We do proactively contact our customers, but I do not know this ratio.
    b. We do not provide any sort of proactive alerts.
    c. Approximately 1:10.
    d. Close to 1:2 or 1:3.

9. How often do you set priorities for customer issues along some sort of impact-urgency matrix?
    a. Never.
    b. Some of the time.
    c. All of the time.
    d. Only for big issues.

10. In our company,
    a. Proactive contacts do not apply.
    b. We use proactive alerts in exceptional circumstances, such as for a product recall.
    c. We have a range of issues or reasons that trigger our reaching out to the customer.
    d. Rather than wait for our customers to contact us, we use proactive contacts wherever possible.

Chapter Five: Make It Really Easy to Contact Your Company (pages 127–166)

11. Our customers
    a. Have no choice in how they contact our company.
    b. Can decide how to contact us, but have few options.
    c. Are free to use any contact mechanism they wish.
    d. Are using contact channels that we would prefer they didn't use.

12. Our Web site
  a. Has a Contact Us section that allows customers to send a structured e-mail.
  b. Provides access to a phone number if customers look hard enough at the bottom of the Contact Us section.
  c. Gives our customers as much information about other contact mechanisms as possible, including a phone number on almost every page.
  d. Has a "click to call" function that links them to an agent in seconds.
  e. Hides our phone numbers, because we want customers to remain on the Web site.
13. Our organization's customer contact channel strategy is focused on
  a. Ensuring that our customers use the mechanisms that we want them to use.
  b. Maximizing the amount of information flowing from customers to us.
  c. Using the cheapest possible channels.
  d. Nothing—it is not really discussed very much in our company.

Chapter Six: Own the Actions Across the Organization (pages 167–204)
14. In our company, customer service is
  a. Solely the responsibility of the customer service department.
  b. Part and parcel of everyone's role, and a shared accountability across the whole company.
  c. Discussed at all levels, but managed solely by the customer service team.
  d. Part of marketing.
15. In our company, the CEO
  a. Reviews issues in service only when key targets aren't met.
  b. Treats customer service as a cost center.
  c. Sees customer service as one of our most important departments, critical to our decisions and strategy.
  d. Takes a continuous interest in service and ensures that all parts of the company contribute to service outcomes.
  e. Says that customer service is important, but really has no interest in customer service.

16. Our frontline customer-facing staff
    a. Are empowered to make decisions that help the customer.
    b. Perform their role within broad policy guidelines.
    c. Are measured and monitored on process and policy adherence.
    d. Cannot be trusted without tight process controls.

Chapter Seven: Listen and Act (pages 205–242)

17. In our company,
    a. Customers are surveyed monthly or quarterly by marketing for their satisfaction with our service delivery, using a limited sample.
    b. We follow a single index as the key measure of customer satisfaction.
    c. Customer satisfaction is gathered from multiple touch points and is used all over the organization.
    d. There is no mechanism to gather data on customer satisfaction.

18. In our company, the CEO
    a. Takes time at least once per month to listen to customers at the front line.
    b. Has never spent time listening to customers at the front line.
    c. Views marketing as the department to find out about what our customers want and need.
    d. Visits the front line briefly one or twice a year to meet the teams.
    e. Reads verbatim comments from customers that we capture.

19. In our company,
    a. Customer focus groups are convened periodically to gain insights about customers and to develop action programs.
    b. There is a clearly defined process to listen to customer suggestions through multiple listening posts in a closed loop.
    c. There is no process for gaining insight into what our customers are saying.
    d. Our frontline staff submit suggestions to improve our customers' experience, but rarely, if ever, hear what happened afterwards.
    e. Other departments ask our customer service team for information about our customers.

20. In our company,
    a. Customer-facing employees record notes about each customer interaction as an audit trail of what has been said.
    b. Our customer interaction system logs each interaction with the customer, but no one ever reads or uses the logs.
    c. The frontline staff see it as their role to capture key insights from customers and forward them for action.
    d. We use a contact recording system as an audit trail of customer contacts, often mining it for insights.

SCORING YOUR ANSWERS

Use the following grid to score your answers to the twenty questions in Chapters Two through Seven. Scoring is based on a three-point scale: 3 = Best Service; 2 = Better Service; 1 = Basic Service; and 0 = Ad Hoc, even less than Basic Service.

Chapter Number and Title	Question Number	A	B	C	D	E
Two: Eliminate Dumb Contacts	1	0	2	3	1	0
	2	1	0	3	2	
	3	0	3	0	1	2
	4	1	0	2	3	
Three: Create Engaging Self-Service	5	3	1	0	0	0
	6	2	0	3	0	0
	7	3	1	2	0	0
Four: Be Proactive	8	1	0	2	3	
	9	0	1	3	2	
	10	0	1	2	3	
Five: Make It Really Easy to Contact Your Company	11	0	2	3	1	

Chapter Number and Title	Question Number	A	B	C	D	E
	12	1	1	3	2	0
	13	1	3	2	0	
Six: Own the Actions Across the Organization	14	0	3	1	2	
	15	1	0	3	3	0
	16	3	2	1	0	
Seven: Listen and Act	17	1	2	3	0	
	18	3	0	0	1	2
	19	1	3	0	1	2
	20	1	0	3	2	

How Did You Do?

0–20 = Basic Service

You have a lot of work to do and many benefits to derive by applying the ideas in this book. If you really think they don't apply in your company and industry, you may be in trouble and don't know it yet, or are in denial. Have a look in particular at the areas where you scored 0 or 1, and compare the answers worth 2.

21–40 = Better Service

You are on the right track, and you implement some of the key customer service programs well. You need to look back over the areas where you scored a 1 or 2 and assess how you can score a 3 instead.

40–60 = Best Service

You are getting a lot right and may just have to apply selected areas from this book, but also make sure that you don't fall behind when customer demand heats up in the future. Look at any areas where you didn't get a 3 and determine what happened.

How You Scored by Chapter, and What Your Score Means

Chapter Two: Eliminate Dumb Contacts

What does it mean if my company got low scores (a total of 3 or less)?

You may not know enough about why contacts are occurring today. Low scores also suggest that you are not effective at capturing contact reasons, thinking through their causes, or understanding why customers are compelled to initiate contacts with your staffed channels.

What does my company need to do?

- Streamline the contact coding system with "why" reasons and owners.
- Apply the Value-Irritant Matrix to identify remedial actions per contact code.
- Examine the root causes and drivers of customer contacts.
- Assess the complexity of dealing with your company from the customer's point of view.
- Start to challenge demand.

Chapter Three: Create Engaging Self-Service

What does it mean if my company got low scores (a total of 3 or less)?

Your self-service is not effective, or you have not considered why it is not working well. You have not considered how much you need to promote and support self-service tools.

What does my company need to do?

- Measure the impact of your self-service programs to ensure a higher success rate.
- Apply usability techniques in design.
- Simplify the number of self-service options provided.
- Update your FAQs every week, if not faster, with hot topics.
- Get your staffed channels more involved and make it clear that part of their role is to promote self-service and educate the customers in how to use that channel.

Chapter Four: Be Proactive

What does it mean if my company got low scores (a total of 3 or less)?

You are waiting for customers to contact you even when you know that you have caused a problem that will produce a customer contact. You have not considered the areas in which proactive contact could save your company money and improve the customer experience.

What does my company need to do?

- Identify where you can avoid contacts through the use of proactive alerts.
- Assess the criticality of different contact reasons, again from the customer's position.
- Explore mechanisms that will make proactive contact cheap and effective.

Chapter Five: Make It Really Easy to Contact Your Company

What does it mean if my company got low scores (a total of 3 or less)?

Your company is trying to control how customers contact you, thereby limiting their choice. Or you might not be aware of how much pent-up demand there is for customers to tell you what they think about your products or service.

What does my company need to do?

- Find ways to give customers more options for how they contact you.
- Provide incentives and encouragement to use new contact channels.
- Respond quickly to e-mail.

Chapter Six: Own the Actions Across the Organization

What does it mean if my company got low scores (a total of 3 or less)?

You still treat customer service as the responsibility of the customer service department. You hamper your service staff with rules and regulations that are imposed on them by others, frustrating customers and your agents.

What does my company need to do?
- Assess who really drives service interactions and therefore needs to own the issues.
- Consider charging back costs to make ownership stick.
- Explore areas where you can give staff more freedom to serve customers rather than follow rules.

Chapter Seven: Listen and Act

What does it mean if my company got low scores (a total of 3 or less)?

You have not figured out that your customer service teams are talking to or e-mailing and chatting with thousands of customers every day. You are not exploiting the ability of frontline staff to act as your ears to the customer, and you probably have satisfaction tracking that is hard to influence or change.

What does my company need to do?
- Analyze how to tap into customer contacts as a gold mine of insights about customers and their issues.
- Explore satisfaction tracking mechanisms that focus on action rather than keeping score.
- Question the value you are getting from existing customer feedback or satisfaction mechanisms.

Appendix B: Glossary

Customer service, like many other functions and professions, uses too many abbreviations, acronyms, and arcane terms, some with multiple meanings. Here are the definitions for the terms used in Best Service:

ABA, abandonment rate The percentage of time that a customer does not complete the path he wants to take; used in reference to a customer's trying to call a phone number, trying to navigate an IVR system, or engaging in a lengthy chat session

ACW, after-call work The amount of time that it takes the customer service agent to produce notes, coding, and other details following the phone call, e-mail, or chat session

AHT, average handle time The time that it takes, on average across all customer service agents, to process the contact, plus all wrap-up time (see *ACW*)

ANI, automatic number identification See *CLI*

CLI, caller line identification Same as ANI in North America; identifies the number from which the customer is calling, often matched automatically in the contact center with customer data so that the agent does not have to ask for basic account data

CPH, contacts per hour The number of customer interactions per hour that each agent is expected to handle

CPX, contacts per X The number of customer-initiated, agent-handled contacts over time (for example, per week or per year) that are driven by X, with X being orders, transactions, new installations, and so on; Amazon's early CPX was CPO, contacts per order placed (for example: 2.50 = for every customer ("X"), there are 2.5 contacts. The lower the CPX, the simpler and more effective the processes.)

CRM, customer relationship management   Either (1) the process by which companies attempt to get closer to their customers by combining contact and purchase history with other details, or (2) the hardware and software systems that combine and present these data; we prefer (1), as (2) gets us too wrapped up in system integration language instead of VOC

Customer change management   The end-to-end process to figure out how to modify or redirect customer behavior, including thinking through whether customers will be *able* to use self-service and whether they will *want* to use self-service; often ties into carrots and sticks that companies extend to their customers

DIHT, dynamic individual handle time   Coined by coauthor Bill Price; different planned and tracked agent handle times, matching the customer's needs and the issue with agent skills; the opposite of the same AHT per issue or per agent

Dumb contacts   Coined by coauthor Bill Price; unnecessary or unwanted customer contacts caused by underlying mistakes, confusion, or defects that companies need to address instead of simply "coping with demand"

FAQ, frequently asked questions   Most recently expressed customer concerns or questions, together with simple explanations or answers; key with FAQ is to make sure that they are updated often, and that they use customer language and not company-speak

FCR, first contact resolution   Usually expressed as a percentage; customer contacts that are resolved without follow-up by the customer or by the agent to the customer, but including all the agents involved before the customer hangs up—for example, transfers to other agents through escalation or to seek a specialist to resolve the issue (see *FPR*)

FPR, first point resolution   Usually expressed as a percentage; customer contacts that are resolved without follow-up by the customer or by the agent to the customer, without resorting to internal transfers, escalations, or support by anyone other than that first agent

Golden thirty seconds   Coined by coauthor Bill Price; the opening of a call with the customer, when she is poised to tell the customer service agent what she attempted before picking up the phone, and to talk about other frustrations or insights, usually dismissed by the customer service agent trained to move quickly to the "solution space"; we advocate listening much more closely to this opening, and benefiting from what the customer is prepared to share

GoS, grade of service   The percentage of calls or e-mail answered within a defined time standard; for example, 80% percent of calls answered in 60 seconds (or, 80/60) or percent of e-mail responses within 24 hours

IBP, internal best practices   As developed by coauthor Bill Price, looking inside your own company to find procedures and approaches that can be cloned in others parts of the company, usually after observations "on the front line" with the agents; see also *OBP*

IVR, interactive voice response   Phone-based system that enables the customer to enter digits onto the touch-tone pad or speak plain or "natural" language in order to obtain automated information (such as account balance or order status) or provide information to the company

KPI, key performance indicator   Usually plural, and overplayed in most companies that forget that the *K* stands for *key;* supposed to profile the most important metrics or operational criteria that differentiate good service from poor service; can include speed metrics (such as AHT or CPH), quality scores measured internally or by the customer post-interaction, attendance, resolution rates (such as FCR or FPR), and other data routinely collected and reported

Last contact benchmarking   As developed by coauthor Bill Price, comparing your operations with the best experiences that your customers have had recently, not necessarily with your direct competitors; used in OBP

Lean   Term for process used most often in manufacturing, stemming from the Toyota Production System (TPS), to eliminate waste or defects; can readily be applied to customer service en route to Best Service by eliminating dumb contacts

MECE, mutually exclusive and collectively exhaustive   An old McKinsey & Company exhortation to ensure that all the evidence to support recommendations is effectively structured; used in Best Service to create customer contact coding that attaches to unique owners

Mystery contact   Coined by the coauthors; similar to popular "mystery shopping" where trained consultants or company executives use a checklist to ensure that customers are greeted and served properly, against company standards (here, consultants and/or company managers and executives experience their service operations as if they were a random customer)

OBP, outside best practice   As developed by coauthor Bill Price, profiling your operations versus the best practitioners in any industry, with scoring based on importance; see also *last contact benchmarking* and *IBP*

Owner   The unique senior executive in the company whose department causes a particular category of customer contacts

RACI, responsible or action or consulted or informed   Standardized approach to assigning roles and responsibilities for the company's managers and departments, often (as we use it in Chapter Four) to trace the customer journey to get an issue raised and resolved

Rule of 7 plus or minus 2   When confronted with random lists, most people can typically remember between five and nine items, or "7 plus or minus 2"; tells us that IVR menus and other customer support choices for customers should be limited

Skyline   Developed at Amazon to display the newly streamlined customer contact codes, and now a reporting system connected with WOCAS that includes contact codes, activity-based costing, owners, and target CPX

SMS, short message system   Also known as text messaging, another form of customer contact and access into the customer service operation; many younger consumers and non-U.S. customers are now actively using SMS to communicate with each other and, increasingly, with customer care operations

Snowballs   Repeat contacts, or 100 percent minus FCR or FPR; calculated using input-output ratios per team, center, and enterprise

Success rate   Usually follows "self-service" and expressed as a percentage; when customers do not need to contact an agent after attempting to obtain information or conduct a transaction through automated means

Take-up rate   Usually follows "self-service" and expressed as a percentage; when customers attempt to use an automated solution instead of contacting an agent

VOC, voice of the customer   The art and science of listening to what the customer is telling the company, either directly (for example, verbatim comments) or indirectly (for example, via customer service); see also *WOCAS*

WOCAS, what our customers are saying   Process of collecting VOC from frontline employees with whom the customers interact on a regular basis; now, a formal product that collects, codes, scores, routes, and reports VOC through the frontline employees

Appendix C: Bibliography

Accenture. "Poor Customer Service Drives Nearly Half of U.S. Customers to Take Their Business Elsewhere, Accenture Survey Finds." Aug. 7, 2006. Available at http://accenture.tekgroup.com/article_display .cfm?article_id=4394.

Accenture. "Switched onto Switching: Poor Customer Service Is Top Reason Customers Switch Service Providers." 2005.

Babcock, C. "Process by Design: Let Users Develop the Workflow." *InformationWeek*, Aug. 1, 2005, p. 59.

Bailor, C. "Listening with Interest." *CRM*, Feb. 2005, pp. 29–32.

Belchor, J. "Press '0' If You've Had Enough." Aug. 15, 2006. Available at www.emarketer.com/Articles/Print.aspx?1004108.

Bliss, J. *Chief Customer Officer: Getting Past Lip Service to Passionate Action.* San Francisco: Jossey-Bass, 2006.

Braff, A., and Leogue, S. "Mobile's Dissatisfied Customers." *McKinsey Quarterly*, 2004, no. 3, pp. 10–12.

Burt, J. "Dell Seeks Users' Inputs in Defining Strategy." *eWEEK*, Mar. 26, 2007, p. 27.

Canning, S. "Best Service Means Fewer Painful Calls." *The Australian*, Mar. 17, 2005.

Caulfield, B. "How to Win Customer Loyalty." *Business 2.0*, Mar. 2004, pp. 77–78.

Chao, L. "Bypassing Phone Trees." *Wall Street Journal*, Nov. 22, 2005, p. D1.

Chordas, L. "The Ultimate Niche." *Best's Review*, Nov. 1, 2002. Available at http://loyaltyeffect.com/loyaltyrules/Library_Articles_details .asp?ID=9956.

Conner, D. R. *Managing at the Speed of Change.* New York: Villard Books, 1993.

Cullum, Phillip. "The Stupid Company. How British Business Throw Money Away by Alienating Customers." The UK National Consumer Council, 2005.

Darlin, D. "Complaining Correctly Can Pay Off." *New York Times*, Dec. 6, 2006, pp. C1, C6.

"Dell to Add Linux as a PC Option." *Seattle Post-Intelligencer*, May 2, 2007.

Drink, S. "Care in Need of a Cure." *Los Angeles Times,* June 18, 2007. Available at www.latimes.com.

Duvall, M. "What's Driving Toyota?" *Baseline,* Sept. 2004, pp. 36–53.

Fishman, C. "Betrayed! The Biggest Lie in Business: The Customer Is in Charge." *Fast Company,* Apr. 2001, pp. 115–128.

Fong, M., Fowler, G. A., and Oster, S. "A Year Out, Beijing Games Test China's Rising Power." *Wall Street Journal,* Aug. 8, 2007, pp. A1, A9.

Gillis, C. "37 Fruitless Calls to Microsoft." *King County Business Journal,* Sept. 1, 2003, p. A8.

Glagowski, E. "Customer Champions." *1to1 Magazine,* Apr. 2007, pp. 36–37.

Godin, S. *Permission Marketing: Turning Strangers into Friends and Friends into Customers.* New York: Simon & Schuster, 1999.

Golub, H. "Improving Service Quality." McKinsey staff paper, Mar. 1981.

Grant, P. "1-800-USELESS." *Wall Street Journal,* July 26, 2004, p. R5.

Hammer, M., and Champy, J. *Reengineering the Corporation: A Manifesto for Business Revolution.* New York: HarperCollins, 1994.

Harmon, A. "Consumers Spurn the Human Touch." *Seattle Post-Intelligencer,* Nov. 17, 2003, pp. A1, A10.

Hirschman, A. O. *Exit, Voice, and Loyalty: Responses to Decline in Firms, Organizations, and States.* Harvard University Press.

Holtzman, C. "Nordstrom Shuts Service Dept." *Puget Sound Business Journal,* Mar. 10–16, 2006, p. 3.

Horovitz, B. "Whatever Happened to Customer Service?" *USA Today,* Sept. 26–28, 2003, pp. 1A-2A.

Jaffe, D. "Applying Usability to Self Service and Sales." Accenture white paper, 1999.

Jaffe, D. "Don't Improve Contacts, Eliminate Them." LimeBridge Australia, 2005.

Jaffe, D. "Learn from the Leaders: Listen and Act on the Voice of the Customer." LimeBridge Australia, 2006.

Jaffe, D. "Learn from the Leaders: The Best Service Is No Service." LimeBridge Australia, 2006.

Jaffe, D. "Five Myths of Contact Centre Performance Management." LimeBridge Australia, 2007.

Jaffe, D. "Learn from the Leaders: Managing Performance." LimeBridge Australia, 2007.

Jones, T. O., and Sasser, W., Jr. "Why Satisfied Customers Defect." *Harvard Business Review,* 1995, *73*(6), 88–102.

Keiningham, T. L., Perkins-Munn, T., and Evans, H. "The Impact of Customer Satisfaction on Share-of-Wallet in a Business-to-Business Environment." *Journal of Service Research,* 2003, *6*(1), 37–50.

Krug, S. *Don't Make Me Think: A Common Sense Approach to Web Usability.*
(*2nd ed.*) Berkeley, Calif.: New Riders Press, 2005.

Lawson, M. "Listen and You Will Be Prosperous." *Australian Financial Review,* Oct. 14, 2004, pp. 1–3.

Lee, J. "The Best Service Is None at All, Says ex-Amazon Boss." *Australasian Business Intelligence,* Mar. 2005. Available at http://findarticles.com/p/articles/mi_hb4692/is_200503/ai_n17631769y.

Levitan, B. "Improving Customer Loyalty Through Proactive Communications." *Customer Inter@ction Solutions,* Feb. 2004. Available at www.tmcnet.com/call-center/0204/0204crm1.htm.

Lundquist, E. "Let Customers Drive Innovation." *Innovations,* Summer 2006, p. 6.

Mandela, N. *Long Walk to Freedom.* New York: Little, Brown, 1994.

Mant, A. *Intelligent Leadership.* St. Leonards, Australia: Allen & Unwin, 1999.

Martin, J. "All You Can Bank On Is Poor Service." *Financial Times,* July 9–July 10, 2005, p. W2.

Massey, P. "How Do Customers Get Fast + Simple Experiences from Companies Like Amazon." Budd white paper, 2005.

Massey, P. "Making Your Business Fast + Simple for Your Customers." Budd white paper, 2005.

Massey, P. "100 Things You Can Learn from first direct." Budd white paper, 2005.

Massey, P. "Making It Easy When Customers Contact Cisco." Budd white paper, 2006.

Massey, P. "100 Things About 21st Century Demand Drivers and Metrics." Budd white paper, 2006.

Massey, P. "100 Things You Can Learn from eBay." Budd white paper, 2006.

Massey, P. "100 Things You Can Learn from Google." Budd white paper, 2007.

Mavin, D. "Keeping the Faith." *National Post,* Feb. 22, 2006, p. FP3.

McGregor, J. "Leading Listener Winner Trader Joe's." *Fast Company,* Oct. 2004, pp. 82–83.

Meyer, D. *Setting the Table: The Transforming Power of Hospitality in Business.* New York: HarperCollins, 2006.

Mintz, J. "PC Maker Dell Again Offers Windows XP." *Seattle Post-Intelligencer,* Apr. 20, 2007, p. D2.

Nielsen, J. *Designing Web Usability: The Practice of Simplicity.* Berkeley, Calif.: Peachpit Press, 1999.

Nocera, J. "Put Buyers First? What a Concept." *New York Times,* Jan. 5, 2008. pp. B1, B9.

Peppers, D., and Rogers, M. *The One to One Future.* New York: Currency/Doubleday, 1993.

Peters, T. *The Pursuit of Wow! Every Person's Guide to Topsy-Turvy Times.* New York: Vintage Books, 1994.

Peters, T. *Circle of Innovation.* New York: Vintage Books, 1999.

Peters, T., and Waterman, R. H., Jr. *In Search of Excellence: Lessons from America's Best-Run Companies.* New York: HarperCollins, 1982.

Pombriant, D. "Sales and Service: It's Time for a Merger." May 24, 2005. Available at www.customerthink.com/article/sales_and_service_its_time_for_a_merger.

Price, B. "AHT, Not." *CC News,* July 2000.

Price, B. "Are We Stuck?" Driva Solutions white paper, 2002.

Price, B. "The Best Service Is No Service." Driva Solutions white paper, 2002.

Price, B. "Getting Unstuck." Driva Solutions white paper, 2002.

Price, B. "Making CRM Come to Life." *E-Business Review,* 2002, pp. 25–31.

Price, B. "For a Driving-Force Metric, Consider CPX." Aug. 16, 2005. Available at www.customerthink.com/article/for_a_driving_force_metric_consider_cpx.

Price, B. "The Wonderful World of Wikis Is Changing the Face of CRM." Apr. 30, 2007. Available at www.customerthink.com/article/wonderful_world_of_wikis.

Price, B. "Connect Online for Better Customer Care." May 14, 2007. Available at www.customerthink.com/article/connect_online_better_customer_care.

Reddy, S. "Expanding Banks Bemoan Lack of Qualified Tellers." *Wall Street Journal,* July 17, 2007, p. B1.

Reichheld, F. "The One Number You Need to Grow." *Harvard Business Review,* Dec. 1, 2003.

Reichheld, F., and Teal, T. *The Loyalty Effect: The Hidden Force Behind Growth, Profits, and Lasting Value.* Cambridge: Harvard Business School Press, 2001.

Reppa, R., and Hirsh, E. "The Luxury Touch." Apr. 3, 2007. Available at www.strategy-business.com/press/enewsarticle/enews040307?tid=230&pg=all.

Seddon, J. *Freedom from Command and Control: Rethinking Management for Lean Service.* Oxford: Productivity Press, 2005.

ServiceXRG. "Service Resolution Optimization: The Power of Process and Knowledge." Wellesley, Mass.: ServiceXRG, 2004.

Shapiro, B. P., Rangan, V. K., and Sviokla, J. J. "Staple Yourself to an Order." *Harvard Business Review,* July-Aug. 2005, pp. 165–174.

"Southwest Airlines Blog Takes Off." *USA Today.* Available at www.usatoday.com/travel/flights/2006-04-27-southwest-blog_x.htm.

Spencer, J. "In Search of the Operator." *Wall Street Journal,* May 8, 2002, pp. D1-D2.

Spencer, J. "Cases of 'Customer Rage' Mount as Bad Service Prompts Venting." *Wall Street Journal,* Sept. 17, 2003, p. D4.

Stross, R. "Apple's Lesson for Sony's Stores: Just Connect." *New York Times,* May 27, 2007, p. C3.

Taylor, W. C. "Companies Find They Can't Buy Love with Bargains." *New York Times,* Aug. 8, 2004, p. C1.

Taylor, W. C. "To Charge Up Customers, Put Customers in Charge." *New York Times,* June 18, 2006, p. C5.

Thompson, B. "Customer Experience Management: The Value of 'Moments of Truth.'" White paper. 2006, p. 6.

Tilin, A. "The Smartest Company of the Year: And the Winner is . . . Toyota." *Business 2.0,* Jan./Feb. 2005, pp. 65–70.

"Tying Supply Chain to Customers." *IndustryWeek,* Dec. 16, 2005. Available at www.industryweek.com/ReadArticle.aspx?ArticleID=11124.

Virgin, B. "Businesses Should Fix, Not Hide, Problems." *Seattle Post-Intelligencer,* May 18, 2004. Available at http://seattlepi.nwsource.com/virgin/173721_virgin18.html.

Watson, B., editor. "By the Numbers: Customer Service Woes." June 5, 2007. Available at www.baselinemag.com/article2/0,1540,2141914,00.asp.

Weier, M. "Good Hands Aren't Enough." *InformationWeek,* Apr. 23, 2007, pp. 49–50.

Womack, J. P., and Jones, D. T. *Lean Solutions: How Companies and Customers Can Create Value and Wealth Together.* New York: Free Press, 2005.

Yuan, L., Dade, C., and Prada, P. "Texting When There's Trouble." *Wall Street Journal,* Apr. 18, 2007, pp. B1, B10.

Notes

Introduction
1. Jones and Sasser, 1995.
2. Survey of one thousand U.S. consumers, conducted by Accenture and ICR, 2006.
3. Study of seventy-seven hundred U.K. customers, conducted by UK Customer Care, 2005.

Chapter One
1. Switched onto switching, U.K. National Consumer Council, 2005.
2. Accenture consumer study cited in Dumb customer by U.K. National Consumer Council, 2005.
3. Spencer, 2003.
4. Reddy, 2007.
5. Keiningham, Perkins-Munn, and Evans, 2003.
6. Peters, 1994, p. 4.
7. http://redtape.msnbc.com/2007/05/ever_wonder_why.html, 2007.
8. Fishman, 2001.

Chapter Two
1. "The Customer Service Hall of Shame," www.moneycentral.msn .com, n.d.
2. www1.eere.energy.gov/femp/operations_maintenance/om_preventive_ main.html, n.d.
3. "Tying Supply Chain to Customers," 2005.
4. Drink, 2007.
5. www.druglibrary.org/schaffer/misc/driving/s14p5.htm.
6. "The Customer Service Hall of Shame," www.moneycentral.msn .com, n.d.
7. Amazon.com, shareholder letter, *Annual Report,* 2002, p. 1.

Chapter Four
1. Chordas, 2002.
2. http://gettingaroundgermany.home.att.net/autobahn.htm, n.d.

3. www.aquilar.co.uk/tracetek_performance.php, n.d.
4. Yuan, Dade, and Prada, 2007.
5. Pombriant, 2005.
6. Glagowski, 2007.

Chapter Five
1. Stross, 2007.
2. Bendigo Bank Web site and Roy Morgan Banks Satisfaction Ratings.

Chapter Six
1. Holtzman, 2006.
2. Conner, 1993.
3. Vita Palestrant, *The Age,* July 2005 (Money section).

Chapter Seven
1. Mandela, 1994, pp. 171–172.
2. www.amillionpenguins.com, n.d.
3. www.collectspace.com/archive/archive-0906.html, 2006.
4. Reichheld, 2003.
5. www.mymms.com/customprint, n.d.
6. McGregor, 2004.
7. "Southwest Airlines Blog Takes Off," 2006.

Chapter Eight
1. Fishman, 2001.
2. www.resellerratings.com/store/Zappos, n.d.
3. http://linkedin.com/answers, n.d.
4. www.ciao.co.uk/Egg_Review_5273088, n.d.
5. http://fiendishgleeclub.vox.com/library/post/customer-service-gone-shockingly-right.html, 2007.
6. www.airlinequality.com/Forum/kingfisher.htm, n.d.
7. Peppers and Rogers, 1993.

ACKNOWLEDGMENTS

We produced this book "virtually"—Bill Price from Bellevue, Washington, in the United States, David Jaffe from Ivanhoe, Victoria, in Australia; on airplanes to and from Chicago, Paris, Perth, and many other places; via frequent calls late Sunday U.S. time, midday in Melbourne; and together on several occasions, notably at Peter Massey's 1765-era home in Benenden, Kent, in England, after our tenth LimeBridge partner meeting. We should also thank Beatrice and Joe Guinane, David's in-laws, for hosting us when we started fleshing out many of the ideas.

We thank our LimeBridge colleagues across the world for their support, bad and good cases and stories, and active deployment of Best Service, particularly Peter Massey and David Naylor in the United Kingdom for their passion for Fast + Simple processes and coaching in how to set about writing a book; Osama Taniguchi in Japan for showing us the Japanese way to Best Service; Frederic Jurain, Philippe Tisserand, and Joseph Kort in France for inspiring us with French style and humor; Stephan Pucker in Germany for his passion for the WOCAS and Skyline ideas; M. D. Ramaswami in India for his tireless enthusiasm for new business ideas; Tony Bruno in Hong Kong for his willingness to take a different perspective; Toby Detter in Sweden for his strategic and marketing perspectives and unique Scandinavian approach; and Ian Northmore and Lynne Eccleston from Singapore for their perspectives on the people side of service.

David also thanks Paul Lewis, his business partner in Australia, for giving him the time to write the book and supporting it along the way; Regan, Stuart, Joan, Sara, Eve, and Mike in Australia for being rock-solid consultants while David was periodically distracted. David also learned from and thanks supportive clients and core Chief Customer Officer Forum members Tony Forster, Kate Christiansen, Richard Bowden, Ian Whitehead, Tim Hunt-Smith, Diana Eilert,

Phil Craig, Samantha Bartlett, Trish Campbell, Geoff Roberts, Sue Hayes, Vanessa Heaperman, Jim Mitchell, Brendan Bloore, Peter Bryant, Jenny Bailey, Andrew Taylor, Pam Rebecca, Damien Regan, Andrew Hume, Melinda Charlesworth, Vicki Shields, Helen Wells, Pat McCafferty, Marcus Judge, Dean Tillitson, Drew Unsworth, and Leanne Crocker. Jane Hemstritch, Terry Neill, Glenn Sedgwick, John Skerritt, and Derek Young have provided leadership, support, and guidance through David's career—thanks to all!

Bill thanks his U.S.-based colleagues past and present Alan Winters, Bob Racioppi, Cass Nevada, Chris Doran, David Morad, Doug Cassell, Earl Newell, Guido Haarmans, Jamie Erze, Jim Bartz, Jim Folk, Jon Mittmann, Linda Chidester, Pat Larson, Paul Davis, Wendy Taylor, Wes Pitman, and Zulma Pereira for their continued dedication with our clients, their editorial advice, and their loyalty to the relentless pursuit of Best Service. Bill learned from Best Service enthusiasts, too many to name, who have shared their stories with us, but in particular Dick Hunter, Harvey Trager, Jardon Bouska, Jeanne Toulouse, Steve Jarvis, Terri Capatosto, and Art Hall. Bill's early inspirations for Best Service over the course of his career include Ben Slivka, Bert Quintana, Bob Waterman, David Risher, Jane Slade, Jeff Bezos, Jeff Bussgang, Jeff Robison, John Egan, Ken Jones, Kevin Sharer, Sanjeev Aggarwal, Scott Ross, Tom Peters, and Warren Jenson—thanks, all, for showing how to do it.

We could not have brought our book to life without the incredible partnership with Amy Packard, Carolyn Miller Carlstroem, Karen Murphy, Mark Karmendy, Michele Jones, and Rob Brandt at Jossey-Bass, starting with Neil Maillet, who convinced his company to publish *The Best Service Is No Service.*

We thank Jon Kudelka for his fanciful cartoons and artistry; Michael, David's lawn-mower man, because David swapped lawn-mowing time for book time; Erika and Rachel and Rebecca and Patrick, for putting up with their dads' periodic absence and apparent preference for laptops and PCs over their children; and Sue and Trudi for their love, encouragement, and inspiration. Sue, David's wife, also gave us some crucial review comments, and Trudi, Bill's wife, provided lots of Best Service examples, so thanks again.

David needs to acknowledge Bill's amazing vision and ideas. His thinking had been instrumental to our business success for much of the last five years. He'd given up his time for many visits to Australia and thrown his intellect at many very grateful Australian companies. There was not a second's hesitation back in November 2004 when Bill asked if anyone wanted to help him write a book. I think my arm shot up so fast that I was in danger of dislocating my shoulder. I'm not sure that either of us knew quite what we were getting ourselves into, but it's been a very satisfying experience and a unique one. Bill's amazing array of practical ideas coupled with my framework-based editing and creative skills have, we hope, produced a book worth reading. Thanks for the opportunity, Bill, to achieve something special together.

Last, Bill Price needs to acknowledge that without David Jaffe's tireless pressure to produce a book to share his passion to challenge customer demand for service, his tireless restructuring and terrific stories, and his contagious excitement, *The Best Service Is No Service* never would have happened—good on you, mate!

ABOUT THE AUTHORS

Bill Price founded Driva Solutions, LLC, in September 2001, after serving as Amazon's first global VP of customer service. He cofounded the ten-country LimeBridge Global Alliance to help build clients' customer service strategies and improve operational performance, and chairs the thirty-four-organization Global Operations Council that he formed in early 2002 to share "best practices and worst experiences."

Price started his career with McKinsey & Company in its San Francisco and Stockholm offices, working on what turned into *In Search of Excellence.* He then became COO at an early IVR service bureau, ACP, which MCI acquired; he built MCI Call Center Services' automation, consulting, and agent outsourcing divisions, and was named one of the first Call Center Pioneers by *CRM* magazine's editors in 1997.

Price is a frequent keynote speaker, graduate school CRM instructor, and advisory board member. He graduated from Dartmouth College and the Stanford Graduate School of Business, and lives in Bellevue, Washington, where he maintains his weekly running regimen.

David Jaffe lives in Melbourne, Australia, and is the consulting director of LimeBridge Australia, the specialist customer experience business. He grew up in England and studied philosophy, politics, and economics at Oxford University before migrating to Australia.

Jaffe has been a consultant for twenty-two years in Britain, Ireland, and Australia. He has worked across many industries in customer-facing sales and service areas, such as branches, call centers, self-service, and administration. He began his career with Accenture, where he became a national partner with responsibility for the CRM practice for Asia-Pacific financial services. He then joined AT Kearney as a principal in their Financial Institutions Group. He left AT Kearney to help found LimeBridge Australia.

Within LimeBridge Australia Jaffe leads thought leadership development and is ultimately responsible for all client projects. He has spoken at numerous conferences in Australia, Asia, and North America. He created the Chief Customer Officer Forum in Australia and is a sought-after speaker at events across the world.

He is a keen chorale singer, runner, and after-dinner entertainer.

INDEX

1-Click Service, 17–18

A

Abandonment rate (ABA), 287
Accountability, 11, 16–17, 166–169; Amazon, 176–178, 190–191, 200; assigning to the right level, 195–201; bad cases, 171–176; the Berlin Wall, 170; contact center problems, 178–179; within customer service, 181–183; financial accountability, 192–195; Five Why's, 187–188; framework, 183–201; good cases, 176–183; island hopping in WWII, 170; lack of individual accountability, 197–201; lack of information, 184; making accountability stick, 189–195; matrix management, 174–175; McDonald's, 179–180; ministerial accountability, 169–170; Nordstrom, 180–181; ownership tests, 188–189; penal measurement system, 197; policy shields, 173, 175–176, 196–197; shooting the messenger, 171–172; sponsorship, 190–191; systems spaghetti, 173–174; targets, 191–192; tearing down the walls, 183–189
After-call work (ACW), 181–182; defined, 287
Airlines, proactive contact, 105
Alaska Airlines, 108
Amazon: accountability, 176–178, 190–191, 200; challenging demand, 43–45; easy contact, 142–143; great service experiences, 274–275; integrating channels to manage change, 94–95; listening to customers, 17–18, 221–222; multichannel integration, 79–81; proactive contact, 107–108
American Customer Satisfaction Index (ACSI), 5, 26, 27, 209–210
Annual reports, 245–246
AOL France, 111–112
Apple, 140
Appreciative customers, 246–247
Asleep at the wheel, 39–41
ATMs, 88–89
Australian Cancer Council, 104
Autobahn, 102–103
Automated feedback tools, 233–234
Automatic number identification (ANI). *See* caller line identification (CLI)
Average handle time (AHT), 14, 38–39; defined, 287

B

Bank of America, 142
Bendigo Bank, 161
Berlin Wall, 170
Best agents, 272
Best Service, 26–28, 242–245; roadblocks to, 247–251. *See also* great service experiences
Best Service Principles, 8–14; objections to, 19–21
Bezos, Jeff, 18, 43, 190–191, 221
Bills, 42–43
Blogs, 235–236
Bouska, Jardon, 47
Brand, impact of poor service on, 24–26

British Telecom, 15
"But our customers are happy" problem, 248, 250–251

C

Cable & Wireless (C&W), 217–218
Call chokers, 133
Call factories, 45–47
Caller line identification (CLI), 287
"Can't afford it" problem, 247, 250
"Can't fix it" problem, 247, 249
Capatosto, Terri, 179–180
Carlson, Jan, 32
Carpetbaggers, 41–42
Challenging demand, 32–33; bad cases, 38–43; driving safety, 37–38; establishing a closed-loop system, 53–57; framework, 49–63; good cases, 43–49; hardware manufacturing, 35–36; health care, 26–27; preventive equipment maintenance, 35; Toyota, Lean, and Deming, 33–35
A Change of Heart (Drink), 37
Channel prisons, 133–134
Charrette planning process, 130–131
CheckFree, 47–48
Command-and-control environments, 199
Company blogs, 235–236
Contact elimination, 47
Contacts: number required of customers, 6–8; understanding the reasons for, 50–53; unnecessary, 31; what to eliminate, automate, simplify, improve, or leverage, 57–61. *See also* dumb contacts; easy contact; proactive contact; repeat contacts
Contacts handled per hour (CPH), 38
Contacts per hour (CPH), 287
Contacts per order (CPO), 43–45, 191
Contacts per X (CPX), 54–55; defined, 287
Cost reallocation, 193–195
Costs, increased, 24, *25*

Critical reviewers, 245
Cross-sell theory, 20
Cross-selling, 41
Customer change management, 95; defined, 288
Customer notes, 213–215, 218–220
Customer relationship management (CRM): defined, 288; software, 50
Customer service: accountability for, 11; example of poor service, 3–4; number of contacts required, 6–8; speed vs. effectiveness, 14; speed vs. quality, 13–14; why it matters, 21–26; why it's broken, 3–8. *See also* best service; great service experiences; poor service; self-service
Customer XTC (customer ecstasy), 43
Customer-focused processes, 263–271

D

Danaher, 36
Deep support, 121
Dell, 35–36, 45–47, 227; Direct2Dell, 235–236
Deming, Edward, 33
Deming Prize, 33–34
Department warriors, 42
Designated owners, 54
Detractors, 22, *23*
Diabetes self-testing, 69
Don't Make Me Think (Krug), 92
Drink, Susan, 37
Driving safety, 37–38
Dumb contacts, 31; defined, 288; eliminating, 8–9, 15
Dynamic individual handle time (DIHT), 55, 260; defined, 288
Dyson U.K., 48–49

E

Easy contact, 10–11, 16, 126–129; allowing two-way control, 158–163; Amazon, 142–143; Apple, 140; bad cases, 131–138; Bank of America, 142; call chokers, 133; channel prisons, 133–134; Charrette planning process, 130–131; consciously incompetent companies, 132–134; encouraging contacts, 152–154; framework, 143–163; good cases, 139–143; hours of operation and customers' needs, 138, 156–157; how the contact will be handled, 145–147; human support, 159; i-select, 140–141; last contact benchmarking, 144; laying the foundation, 144–150; matching contact channels to needs, 154–155, 161–162; matching contact type to need, 160; maturity levels, 128; missing at the moment of need, 136–138; opening the floodgates, 150–158; overwhelming options, 134–135; policy shields, 135–136; providing choice, 155–156; removing cost and barriers of contact, 157–158; staying tuned to customers, 162–163; Teensurance, 131; unconsciously incompetent companies, 134–138; USAA Insurance, 139–140; Virgin Air, 141; what the contact will achieve, 149–150; when the contact will be handled, 147–149; Wikimania, 129–130

EBay, 15

Effectiveness of service, vs. speed, 14

E-mail, 146, 220–221

Enlightened hospitality, 18

Enterprise space shuttle, 207–208

Exchanges, 56

F

FAQ, 288

Fast + simple processes, 266–268

First contact resolution (FCR), 14, 61, 260; defined, 288

First direct bank, 78–79, 109–110

First point resolution (FPR), 61, 260; defined, 288

Forgetting who the customer is, 13

Frequently asked questions. See FAQ

G

Geographical separation, 5

Golden thirty seconds, defined, 288–289

Gorbachev, Mikhail, 170

Grade of service (GoS), defined, 289

Great service experiences, 13–14, 18–19, 242–245; Amazon, 274–275; awesome service delivery, 251–253; customer-focused processes, 263–271; matching service to the customer, 271–273; measuring what really matters, 253–262; "virtual" no service, 273–276. See also Best Service

Greene, Moya, 123

H

Halsey, William F. "Bull", 170

Hardware manufacturing, 35–36

Health care, 26–27, 104

Hewlett-Packard, 261

Hours of operation and customers' needs, 138, 156–157

Hunter, Dick, 35–36, 45–47

I

In Search of Excellence (Peters and Waterman), 174

Incompetence, 72–74

Information gap, 11–12

Information Technology Infrastructure Library (ITIL), 114–115

Interactive voice response (IVR), defined, 289

Internal best practices (IBP), 260; defined, 289

I-select, 140–141

J

Jenson, Warren, 192–193

JetBlue Airways, 25–26

Juran, J.M., 33

K

Key performance indicator (KPI), 289

Kingfisher Airlines, 270–271
Krug, Steve, 92

L

Laptop batteries, 105–106
Last contact benchmarking, 144, 260; defined, 289
Lean, 33–35, 36, 45–47; defined, 289
Listening to customers, 11–12, 17–18, 204–205; Amazon, 221–222; automated feedback tools, 233–234; bad cases, 208–215; Cable & Wireless (C&W), 217–218; chained to the office, 211–212; company blogs, 235–236; customer notes, 213–215, 218–220; dangers of denial, 209–210; declining reputation for service, 210–211; Enterprise space shuttle, 207–208; framework, 222–238; good cases, 215–222; learning to act, 236–238; learning to listen, 223–230; listening for free, 225–227; listening posts, 224–225, 231; listening to systemic pain, 227–229; listening to the front line, 229–230; local partnerships vs. global management, 208–209; Mars Company, 215–216; Nelson Mandela and the NAC, 206; Net-Bank, 220–221; readers writing books, 207; smart ways to listen, 230–236; text and speech analysis, 231–233; Trader Joe's, 222
Lost revenue, 22–24

M

M&M candies, 215–216
Mallya, Vijay, 270–271
Mandela, Nelson, 206
Mars Company, 215–216
Massey, Peter, 266
McCafferty, Pat, 17
McDonald's, 179–180
MCI, 261
McLeod, Fiona, 17

Meadows, Ivy, 114
Measurements, 253–254; customer-centric measures, 255–257; measurement mayhem, 254–255; new metrics, 260–261; outsourcer measures, 261–262; things to get right, 259; wacky behaviors, 257–259
MECE, 51, 52
Medibank Private, 110–111
Meter-reading, automatic, 70
Meyer, Danny, 18
A Million Penguins, 207
Mind-set of the organization, 158
Ministerial accountability, 169–170
Mobile phone technology, 146
Motorola Razr, 106–107
Mutually exclusive and collectively exhaustive (MECE), defined, 289
Mystery contact, 289–290

N

National Action Council (NAC), 206
Nationwide Building Society, 81–83
NetBank, 220–221
New York State Department of Motor Vehicles, 83–85, 96
Nimitz, Chester, 170
Nordstrom, 180–181
Novadental Clinic, 15–16

O

Orienteering, 69–70
Outside best practice (OBP), 260; defined, 290
Overwhelming options, 134–135
Owner, 290
Owning actions. *See* accountability

P

Penal measurement system, 197
Penguin, 207
Personal safety, 104
Peters, Tom, 23
Policy shields, 135–136, 173, 175–176, 196–197
Pombriant, Denis, 121

Poor service, 21–22; impact on brand and reputation, 24–26; increased costs, 24, *25*; lost revenue, 22–24

Preventive equipment maintenance, 35

Principles of Best Service, 8–14; objections to, 19–21

Proactive contact, 10, 15–16, 100–102; airlines, 105; Alaska Airlines, 108; Amazon, 107–108; AOL France, 111–112; Autobahn, 102–103; bad cases, 105–107; capabilities, 112–116; closing the loop, 122–123; designing into long-running processes, 118–122; first direct bank, 109–110; framework, 112–123; good cases, 107–112; health care and personal safety, 104; laptop batteries, 105–106; Medibank Private, 110–111; Motorola Razr, 106–107; priority matrix and service levels, 115; Puget Sound Energy (PSE), 108–109; stay home messages, 104–105; TraceTek, 103–104; triggers for, 116–118; XM radio, 109

Process mapping, 47–48

Promoters, 22, *23*

Puget Sound Energy (PSE), 108–109

Q

Quality of service, vs. speed, 13–14

R

RACI framework, 120–121

Reagan, Ronald, 170

Recovery theory, 19

Reliability, Dyson U.K., 48–49

Repeat contacts, 31; eliminating, 61–63

Reporting, 53–54

Reputation, impact of poor service on, 24–26

Responsible or action or consulted or informed (RACI), defined, 290

Revenue lost, 22–24

Rewards, and consequences, 57

Right Care, 47

Rodda, Emily, 207

Rowan of Rin, 207

Rule of 7 plus or minus 2, 290

S

Self-service, 66–67; bad cases, 71–78; channel wars, 75–76; creating engaging self-service, 9–10, 15; customer-controlled, 86–87; deadly sins preventing, 67–68; design by committee, 74–75; engaging the customer, 81–83; E-Z Visit, 83–85; framework, 85–96; giving the customer control, 78–79; good cases, 78–85; incompetent, 72–74; integrating channels to manage change, 93–96; multichannel integration, 79–81, *82*; neglectors, 71–72; nonsensical, 74; outside customer service, 69–70; restrictors, 71; sales prevention, 76–78; usable designs, 87–93; wasting the customer's time, 76

Short message system (SMS), 290

SHOUT, 48

Skyline, 54, 192; defined, 290

Snowballs, 61–63; defined, 290

"Someone else's problem" problem, 247, 248–249

Speech analysis, 231–233

Speed of service: bad cases, 38–39; vs. effectiveness, 14; vs. quality, 13–14; when the contact will be handled, 147–149

Sponsorship, 190–191

Stay home messages, 104–105

Success rate, 290

Survey, 64, 98, 124, 164, 201, 238–239, 277–286

Switching levels, 4

T

Take-up rate, 290

Targets, 54–56, 191–192

Teensurance, 131
Telstra, 81, *82*
Text analysis, 231–233
Toyota, 33–35
TraceTek, 103–104
Trader Joe's, 222
Trager, Harvey, 36

U

Union Square Cafe, 18–19
Unnecessary contacts, types of, 31
Up-selling, 41
U.S. Internal Revenue Service Employee Resource Center, 255
U.S. Navy, 35
USAA Insurance, 16, 139–140

V

Value-Irritant Matrix, 59–60, 271
Virgin Air, 141
Voice of the customer (VOC), 291

W

Wacky behaviors, 257–259
Warm body theory, 20–21
What our customers are saying. *See* WOCAS
"What problem?" problem, 247, 248
Wikipedia, 129–130
WOCAS, 17, 229–230, 249; defined, 291

X

XM, 109

Y

Yarra Valley Water, 16–17, 226

Z

Zero-based approach to contacts, 51–52
Zuboff, Shoshana, 121